Advance Praise fo~

Conflict Radicalize.
Revised and Exp~

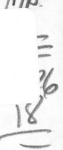

"In this timely update, McCauley and Mos~ ~~~ and the role of emotion in radicalization for the first time, offering a working theory on the emotional state of individuals who choose to act without the more well-understood forces of group dynamics spurring them on. In addition, they describe one of the great challenges facing the analytical community when it comes to radicalization—the disconnect between the relatively large number of people who hold radical opinions and the relatively small number of people who act out on those opinions. Their 'Two-Pyramids Model', as they refer to it, will undoubtedly serve as a cornerstone of future counterterrorism policy and programmatic decisions, as well as a framing device for robust academic debate. One cannot grapple with the challenge of radicalization, or participate in a meaningful conversation on the topic, without having read this book."

—William Braniff, Executive Director, National Consortium for the Study of Terrorism and Responses to Terrorism (START), University of Maryland, College Park

"The new, updated version of this book comes at a most appropriate time. What drives some individuals to engage in deadly terrorist attacks, often at the cost of their own lives? Avoiding easy stereotyping, this work compares quite different versions of murderous terrorism, from Russian revolutionaries who were trying to overthrow repressive Czarism, to contemporary American anti-abortion fanatics, to the most recent Muslim terrorists who seek martyrdom by massacring innocents. Using vast amounts of historical and comparative research and profound psychological insights, McCauley and Moskalenko show that there is no simple answer, and no single ideology that is at fault. Nevertheless the authors demonstrate that a combination of situational and personal circumstances that lead individuals to such actions can explain what motivates them. Predicting all attacks may be impossible, but the better understanding the book offers and the solutions it proposes can help us limit the damage and avoid making the situation worse."

—Daniel Chirot, Herbert Ellison Professor of Russian and Eurasian Studies, University of Washington, and co-author of *The Shape of the New: Four Big Ideas and How They Made the Modern World*

"In the first edition of *Friction*, McCauley and Moskalenko produced one of the most important and comprehensive studies of radicalization available. In this updated edition, coverage is expanded to address the challenge of radicalization with 'lone-wolf' terrorists, along with their two-pyramid model that delineates a critical distinction between radical opinion and radical action. Superbly written with rich detail and example, it represents a significant advancement of the field."

—Anthony F. Lemieux, Director of the Global Studies Institute, Georgia State University

"Following terrorist attacks in Paris, San Bernardino, and Orlando, government officials and publics are urgently seeking to identify and thwart the next mass casualty killer. In this extremely accessible and well-documented study, Moskalenko and McCauley build on their previous research to assess recent attacks, with particular emphasis on the "lone-wolf" and "family pair" varieties. The authors do not shy away from potential controversy. For example, in emphasizing the importance of means and opportunity, they suggest that, rather than scanning Facebook pages or surveilling mosques, it might be more useful for authorities to concentrate on shooting ranges and gun clubs. Overall, this is a very compelling, well-researched and timely book that should be on the bookshelf of every scholar or practitioner interested in the complex subject of terrorism and political violence."

—Paul J. Smith, Professor, Naval War College, and author of
The Terrorism Ahead: Confronting Transnational Violence in the 21st Century

"Deftly applying insights from the psychology lab and knowledge distilled from analyzing recurrent paths to political violence, both past and present, McCauley and Moskalenko explain how mentally sound people can end up committing terrible acts. Readers learn why love is more relevant than brainwashing in the development of a terrorist, how a group of army recruits resembles a terrorist cell, why people without radical beliefs may join radical groups, and why only a tiny minority of those with radical beliefs take the step to violent action. With the concept of jujitsu politics, the authors make the case that terrorists, despite that designation, are often at least as intent on provoking anger in their targets as on instilling fear—reaction, no less than action, is essential to the dynamics of terrorism."

—Joel Wallman, Program Officer, The H.F. Guggenheim Foundation for Violence Research

Praise for *Friction: How Radicalization Happens to Them and Us*

"So much has been written about radicalization that is generic or apocryphal that the field needs desperately to find a contribution that is systematic, research-based, clear, and persuasive. And that is the task that McCauley and Moskalenko have taken on, and triumphantly achieved. The book works analytically; it works because it tells the tales of the violent and radicalized comprehensively, and it works because it does not just focus on 'them', but on 'us', and on the inter-relationship. In short, it is the most important book written on this complex and politicized subject to date."

—**Stuart Croft, Professor of International Security, Warwick University, UK, and author of *Culture, Crisis and America's War on Terror***

"What do militants of the old Russian terrorist group, People's Will, and current-day Al Qaeda have in common? Going beyond stereotypes of terrorists' pathological personalities, this book presents compelling evidence of a complex set of causal mechanisms working at the individual and group levels. In many and diverse contexts, this book shows the importance of identification and politicization processes in transforming grievances into action in underground violent organizations."

—**Donatella Della Porta, Professor of Sociology, European University Institute, and author of *Social Movements, Political Violence, and the State: A Comparative Analysis of Italy and Germany***

"In this brilliant book, McCauley and Moskalenko exploit our interest in true crime stories to help us overcome our inability to think objectively about the Islamic terrorism we are now battling. They tell us stories about the first modern terrorist group, fighting the Czar in the late 19th century, and then show us the same patterns at work in American homegrown terrorists and Islamic terrorists. This is social psychology at its best dramatic stories exemplifying accessible theories, backed up by clever experiments and set into multiple historical contexts. You'll understand terrorists for the first time, and you'll see how we can best thwart their goals by refusing to play their game."

—**Jonathan Haidt, Professor of Psychology, University of Virginia, and author of *The Happiness Hypothesis: Finding Modern Truth in Ancient Wisdom***

"People commonly react to horrendous acts of violence such as the 9/11 attacks by searching for explanations that focus on the culprits. In strong contrast, McCauley and Moskalenko argue that terrorism is fueled by the friction between radical extremists and the individuals and ideas they oppose. This thoughtful, yet readable, book shows that horrendous or not, terrorists cannot escape basic principles of social psychology—but then, neither can the rest of us."

—Gary LaFree, Director, National Consortium for the Study of
Terrorism and Responses to Terrorism (START), and author
of *Losing Legitimacy: Street Crime and the Decline
of Social Institutions in America*

"Anyone concerned with predicting or intervening against intergroup violence should read this book. The authors engagingly present a wide range of case studies to show how individuals, groups, and mass publics are mobilized for political conflict."

—Todd Leventhal, Director of Interagency Strategic
Communication Network, U.S. Department of State

"This book introduces twelve mechanisms that underlie political radicalization and lead to violence and terrorism. In their highly systematic yet readable account, the authors identify mechanisms that can be found at work in every terrorist group, whatever its ideology. The authors provide new and effective tools for understanding political events, and for recognizing and controlling the extent to which radicalization affects all of us. Cases of modern and 19th century terrorists are interwoven to offer vividness and historical depth."

—Ifat Maoz, Director, Smart Communications Institute,
Hebrew University of Israel

"Both long-term students of political violence and a more general readership will find this book fascinating. It will not only be used in the classroom, but (at least in my personal case) be kept on the shelf as a reference book on key social psychological mechanisms of political radicalization. In my opinion, no other work so smoothly integrates a sophisticated treatment of social psychology into the important, and poorly understood, subject of political violence and terrorism."

—Roger Petersen, former Arthur and Ruth Sloan Chair of Political
Science, Massachusetts Institute of Technology, and author of
*Understanding Ethnic Violence: Fear, Hatred, Resentment
in Twentieth Century Eastern Europe*

"McCauley and Moskalenko markedly advance and order our understanding of how individuals are radicalized and why the process often yields terrorists. The authors impart needed discipline and common sense to a field where abstract theory unconnected to reality often dominates. Most important, the authors describe and analyze the very personal, dramatic, disorienting, and frequently searing experiences that put men and women on radicalization's path."

—Michael Scheuer, former senior officer, Central Intelligence Agency; Adjunct Professor, Security Studies Program, Georgetown University; and author of *Imperial Hubris and Osama bin Laden*

"In this excellent book, the authors describe the personal experiences and psychology of individuals, as well as the dynamics of groups, which lead to radicalization. Mechanisms of radicalization- including personal and political grievances, ideals, inducement by friends, the attractions of risk-taking and status, and the interdependence of people in groups-are highlighted through stories of terrorists in earlier times and today. This is a compelling, highly readable book that offers impressive understanding of terrorist individuals and groups."

—Ervin Staub, Founding Director, Psychology of Peace and Violence Program, University of Massachusetts at Amherst, and author of *The Roots of Goodness and Resistance to Evil: Inclusive Caring, Moral Courage, Altruism Born of Suffering, Active Bystandership, and Heroism*

"McCauley (*Why Not Kill Them All?*), co-director of the Solomon Asch Center for the Study or Ethnopolitical Conflict, and Moskalenko, a research fellow at the National Consortium for the Study of Terrorism and Responses to Terrorism, seek a more complex discussion of terrorism, and methodically examine radicalization. A better understanding of the mechanisms under which terrorism thrives can lead to more efficacious counter-terrorism policies. A valuable contribution to the ongoing dialogue."

—*Publishers Weekly*

"This book may be of value for students in various introductory, and even some advanced, university courses. Instructors in criminal justice, sociology, political science, and psychology may want to consider this volume for their classes' reading lists."

— Frederick J. Frese, PsycCRITIQUES

"The beauty of *Friction* is in the organization and writing. McCauley and Moskalenko discuss twelve radicalization mechanisms distinguished at three levels: individual, group, and mass radicalization. To illustrate these mechanisms, the authors liberally sprinkle a wide range of cases throughout the book that take the reader back and forth from the nineteenth century to the present and across many political contexts and cultures.... *Friction* is an excellent book to introduce a wide range of students to research on radicalism and can also serve as a springboard to new research that fills gaps they highlight in existing explanations of radical politics."

—**Robert Futrell, University of Nevada, Las Vegas,**
Journal Mobilization

"Written for the lay reader, with recommended reading lists after each chapter, *Friction* takes a well-integrated and thoughtful approach to the many drivers of unrest and upheaval. It offers valuable insights to students of history, politics, psychology, and war."

— **Elissa Malcohn, review in Psych Central**

"*Friction* takes a refreshingly newer look at radicalization, and it should be on the list of every reader who is interested in studying and understanding radicalization. Everyone who is fighting against radicalized individuals should read this book so they have a baseline understanding of what they are up against and how individuals who are radicalized can take a perceived wrongdoing from an event in their childhood or early adulthood and use that event as a foundation for radicalization later in life. On a positive note, if one wants to radicalize others for the good of humanity, reading this book will help him or her understand what is involved in motivating others to join a cause and find passion for that cause."

—**Robin L. Thompson, NASA Counterintelligence Office,**
review in *Journal of Strategic Security*

FRICTION

CLARK McCAULEY AND SOPHIA MOSKALENKO

FRICTION

How Conflict Radicalizes Them and Us

REVISED AND EXPANDED EDITION

OXFORD
UNIVERSITY PRESS

OXFORD
UNIVERSITY PRESS

Oxford University Press is a department of the University of Oxford. It furthers
the University's objective of excellence in research, scholarship, and education
by publishing worldwide. Oxford is a registered trade mark of Oxford University
Press in the UK and certain other countries.

Published in the United States of America by Oxford University Press
198 Madison Avenue, New York, NY 10016, United States of America.

Library of Congress Cataloging-in-Publication Data
Names: McCauley, Clark R., author. | Moskalenko, Sophia, author.
Title: Friction : how conflict radicalizes them and us / Clark McCauley, PhD,
Sophia Moskalenko, PhD.
Description: Revised and expanded edition. | Oxford ; New York : Oxford
University Press, [2017]
Identifiers: LCCN 2016012695 | ISBN 9780190624927 (pbk. : alk. paper)
Subjects: LCSH: Radicalism—Psychological aspects. | Political
violence—Psychological aspects. | Terrorism—Psychological aspects.
Classification: LCC HN49.R33 M43 2017 | DDC 303.48/4—dc23 LC record available
at https://lccn.loc.gov/2016012695

1 3 5 7 9 8 6 4 2
Printed by Webcom, Inc., Canada

Contents

Section 4: Wrapping Up

Acknowledgments

W E HAVE PILED UP large debts in writing this book. We owe thanks to Bryn Mawr College for supporting the Solomon Asch Center for Study of Ethnopolitical Conflict, which has been the occasion of our continued collaboration. We owe thanks to the Department of Homeland Security (DHS) for support of our research through the National Consortium for the Study of Terrorism and Responses to Terrorism (START), although of course our opinions should not be attributed to START or the DHS. We owe special thanks to three scholars whose work has shaped our understanding of radicalization and terrorism—Martha Crenshaw, Donatella Della Porta, and Michael Scheuer—and to our Oxford editors Lori Handelman and Abby Gross for their faith in the project. Clark owes thanks to the Harry Frank Guggenheim Foundation and its program officer Karen Colvard for opportunities to learn about terrorism in the 1980s and to Petter Nesser for permission to quote from his case study of Muhammad Bouyeri. Sophia owes thanks to Roman Kamenetsky for permission to use documents from his website collection of materials relating to People's Will (www.narovol.narod.ru). And of course we owe thanks to our families for putting up with our focus on matters that are not always good dinner table conversation.

CHAPTER ONE

Introduction

I N THE FILM *Good Will Hunting* psychiatrist Sean McGuire (played by Robin Williams) gets into an argument with his old college roommate, a renowned MIT professor, Gerry Lambeau (Stellan Skarsgård). Sitting in an almost empty bar, the two men discuss the future of Will Hunting, a brilliant but troubled and unmotivated young man. Lambeau demands that McGuire push Will to apply himself and fulfill his promise. Lambeau compares Will to another math prodigy and says he is convinced that Will can be the future of mathematics. McGuire responds:

MCGUIRE: Hey, Gerry, in the 1960s there was a young man that graduated from the University of Michigan. Did some brilliant work in mathematics. Specifically bounded harmonic functions. Then he went on to Berkeley. He was assistant professor. Showed amazing potential. Then he moved to Montana and blew the competition away.

LAMBEAU: Yeah, so who was he?

MCGUIRE: Ted Kaczynski.

LAMBEAU: Haven't heard of him.

MCGUIRE: (Yelling to the bartender)
Hey, Timmy!

TIMMY: Yo.

MCGUIRE: Who's Ted Kaczynski?
TIMMY: Unabomber.[1]

Robin Williams does a great job with this scene, and the triumph of his parable goes beyond the point his character is trying to make. With Lambeau, we are shocked at the unexpected turn in the career of Ted Kaczynski, whose early promise gives no hint of the murderous and unrepentant terrorist who killed three and injured dozens in a series of sixteen bomb attacks carried out between 1978 and 1995.

They Must Be Crazy

How are we to understand Kaczynski's transformation? Easiest is an appeal to psychopathology. "That Unabomber, he's crazy," we think, recalling the photos of an unshaven, disheveled man with a heavy, detached gaze. This interpretation dilutes our surprise and anxiety and leaves us with a comforting picture of the familiar world where normal people do not do crazy things.

How realistic is this picture? Consider another young man, the son of a wealthy businessman.

His father's business was among the leading enterprises in the country. But instead of growing up arrogant and spoiled, the son was rather shy and developed a serious interest in religion. Unlike his friends, who in their late teens were chasing after girls, he kept his eyes on work and prayer. He married early and fathered several children. He left his university and became first a rising star in the family business, then the organizer of an NGO, then a war hero, then a prominent voice for political change in his home country. Through all these successes, the young man kept a simple lifestyle, raising his children in discipline and relative austerity.

It is a good bet that most bar patrons around the world would know his name: Osama bin Laden. Although it may be comforting to imagine that Osama bin Laden is mentally ill, that would be wishful thinking. To build an international organization such as al Qaeda, to plan and commission attack missions around the world, to draw individuals to sacrifice their lives for his cause—these are the accomplishments of a strong and calculating mind.

---

1. Bender, L. (Producer), & Van Sant, G. (Director). (1998). *Good Will Hunting* [Motion picture]. United States: Miramax.

They Must Be Evil

If we admit that bin Laden is not crazy, we might yet want to explain his aberrant behavior by declaring him evil. The appeal of this interpretation is its simplicity. Evil is incomprehensible, but it is also rare. How many truly evil people have we met? We mostly interact with fallible human beings like ourselves. A rare individual, whether crazy or evil, does not require a revision of our worldview. And it is easier to think of someone as evil who is as different from us as Bin Laden, with his religious fanaticism, wagging finger, robes, and bearded foreign features. But what if evil came closer to home?

A new generation of students entered their country's best universities. An era of political reforms enabled many of them to be the first in their family to attend college. Many came from underprivileged backgrounds, supported by newly instituted government loans and scholarships. They saw themselves and were seen by others as the best and the brightest of their generation. Their talent, good fortune, and the promise of a bright future filled them with excitement: they were going to be the generation of change; they were going to make the future of their country as bright and promising as their own future; they were going to stand up for those least able to help themselves. Discussion groups led to student organizations, and organizations led to political action. Students wrote, protested, marched, and demonstrated. When they had no effect, they escalated to illegal actions, including sit-ins, break-ins, and destruction of property. A small fraction of the student movement went underground as a terrorist organization dedicated to bringing down the corrupt government that ignored them.

In the United States in the 1960s and 1970s these student terrorists called themselves the Weather Underground. But the same story, word for word, describes another group of students, one that caused far more death and destruction than the Weather Underground. In the Russian Empire of the 1870s idealistic students with high hopes for their own future and empathy for the plight of Russia's downtrodden peasants turned from protest to violence. The People's Will, a terrorist organization, was responsible for hundreds of bombings and assassinations, including the murder of Czar Alexander II.

It is troubling to think that student idealism could lead to similarly vicious terrorist groups in different places, at different times, and under different banners. The hundreds of students who joined the Weather Underground and the People's Will could not all be crazy or evil.

They're Not Like Us

How do apparently normal people end up as radicals who commit violent acts? Our final refuge may be in the thought that we are immune to that kind of transformation. Students are notably unformed characters, unstable and susceptible to all kinds of influences. Normal people—people like us—are not so easily moved to political violence. Except . . .

A Western democracy, proud of its tradition of personal freedoms and human rights, has a history of international interventions to restore peace and stop atrocities. One day ethnic fanatics attack the country's largest city, killing or injuring thousands. Shock and disbelief evolve into grief and outrage. Hundreds of ethnic immigrants are rounded up on suspicion of being related to the attack and are detained without access to the legal system. To get information from individuals suspected of militant activities, the government issues a secret mandate to torture them. The government's violations of internationally recognized standards of human rights are exposed by the media. Nevertheless, the government is reelected by a majority of its citizens.

This transition took place in the United States after the terrorist attacks of 9/11. Americans embraced the unthinkable in search of retribution and security. We were radicalized: our feelings, beliefs, and behaviors all moved toward increased support for violence against perceived enemies, including sometimes Arab and Muslim Americans. We idealized American values, gave increased power to American leaders, and became more ready to punish anyone seen as challenging patriotic norms.

More generally, radicalization is the development of beliefs, feelings, and actions in support of any group or cause in conflict. Radicalization in response to threat is so reliable that terrorists can count on it as a strategy. It can move a talented mathematician, a rich man's son, a group of idealistic students, or a whole nation toward political violence. Radicalization is not something that happens only to others—the mentally ill person or the evil character. It is a psychological trajectory that, given the right circumstances, can happen to any person, group, or nation. The trajectory is not right or wrong: it is amoral in the sense that radicalization can occur for causes both good and bad.

At least occasionally, however, we might wish to limit or control political radicalization and the violence that can emerge from radicalization. If we cannot understand why normal people turn to violence, we cannot hope to stop that violence, to reduce it, or to immunize against it. If we cannot understand radicalization, we will have to live with its effects—including the extremes of terrorism.

At the gateway to understanding radicalization there is a tollbooth. Those who enter must leave behind the orderly and comfortable world in which normal people do not do terrible things. Full admission requires examining how we are ourselves susceptible to radicalizing influences. Once inside the gate, however, there are new tools for interpreting political events and new power to recognize and control the extent to which radicalization affects us.

Beyond Ideology

The mechanisms of radicalization introduced in this book are more specific than the radical ideology often seen as the source or "driver" of political radicalization. A common view of jihadist terrorism, for instance, is that it is the product of a strand of Islamic extremism associated with Wahhabism and Salafism. This is both too simple and too general to be useful for understanding radicalization.

The first difficulty is that most Wahhabists and Salafists do not support terrorism. The stronghold of Wahhabists is Saudi Arabia, where the government has not retreated from Wahhabist Islam even as it attacks jihadists within the kingdom. *Salafi* Muslims are fundamentalists who strive to live an Islam of the seventh century; most aim to withdraw from the spiritual contaminations of the modern world and are not interested in political change, with or without violence.

A second difficulty with making bad ideology the explanation of terrorism is that ideas are not the same as action. Polls in Muslim countries indicate that millions sympathize with jihadist goals or justify terrorist attacks. But Muslim terrorists number only in the thousands. The challenge is to explain how only one in a thousand with radical beliefs is involved in radical action.

Still another difficulty with the bad ideology account of terrorism is that it is not easily generalized from one kind of terrorism to another. Terrorism as a tactic of political conflict is thousands of years old. The United States has seen anarchist terrorism, Ku Klux Klan terrorism, Puerto Rican nationalist terrorism, Weather Underground terrorism, and, in Oklahoma City, right-wing terrorism. Terrorism is a tactic available to desperate groups in every country, in every century. Our goal is to identify mechanisms of political radicalization that work for every terrorist group, whatever its ideology.

Examples Old and New

Friction juxtaposes case studies of modern terrorists with profiles of some of the members of People's Will, the first modern terrorist group, who operated in imperial Russia in the late nineteenth century and succeeded in assassinating Czar Alexander II. The young men and women who comprised People's Will could not be more different from modern Islamic terrorists in terms of their goals and grievances. People's Will members were atheists. They did not oppose foreign dominion or a hostile culture. Instead, they claimed to fight for the rights of the Russian peasants against the Russian monarchy. They did not have the Internet, AK-47s, or cell phones, and it is fair to assume none of them ever saw a madrassa. Yet, as we will show, the ways they became radicalized were eerily similar to the paths of notable members of al Qaeda. The parallels between atheists and religious fanatics, between Russians and Arabs, between the nineteenth century and the early twenty-first century, between terror against one's own government and terror against foreigners—these parallels are evidence of the broad usefulness of the mechanisms identified. The same mechanisms can be seen at work in very different times and places.

Cases drawn from anti-czarist terrorism are helpful in another way. The United States and its allies, especially the United Kingdom and Spain, have suffered major jihadist attacks on and after September 11, 2001. Terrorism and radicalization have overwhelming personal meaning for those who are targeted. A few of us know someone who was a victim of these attacks; many know someone who served in Afghanistan and Iraq. Probably most of us can recall the fear, anger, and helplessness we experienced in response to images of crashing planes, burning buildings, blackened rail cars, fleeing victims, and dead bodies. As a result, names such as bin Laden, al-Zawahiri, and al-Zarqawi come with emotional associations that can make it difficult for us to find motive or reason in their stories. But Zhelyabov, Perovskaya, and Michailov are complete strangers to us—they evoke no emotional reaction. Their crimes, horrible as they were, took place far away and long ago, making it easier to scrutinize, analyze, and perhaps even empathize with them.

For each mechanism of radicalization, we first introduce a character or episode from the history of People's Will. After identifying the relevant mechanism and linking it with relevant social science theory and research, we draw a parallel to one or more modern examples of terrorism where the same mechanism is at work. In order to set the stage for our examples from anti-czarist terrorism, we conclude this opening chapter with a brief introduction to the Russia in which People's Will developed.

Coming of Age: Russia in the Mid-1800s

In the middle of the nineteenth century Russia was an enormous undeveloped agrarian state. The czar, Nicholas I, was an autocratic ruler who had ascended to the throne amidst a revolt of the noble class and the Royal Guard. Having brutally suppressed the revolt and hanged its instigators, Nicholas quickly gained a firm grip on every lever of power in the country. Dissent of any form was not tolerated. Even a titled aristocrat faced humiliating physical punishment, imprisonment, and a one-way trip to Siberia for speaking in unflattering terms about the czar or the social order in Russia. For poor folk, any talk or action perceived as causing trouble for the ruling class carried a sentence of death by beating with sticks. An atmosphere of distrust, fear, betrayal (writing to the authorities about someone's antigovernment remark was a good way to get rid of the person), and unrelenting suspicion was characteristic of Nicholas' rule.

Life was most difficult for the serfs, who were the majority of the Russian population. Serfs were treated as property and conveyed by inheritance; owners could trade, sell, torture, or kill them as if they were cattle. Families were routinely broken apart as masters lost some of their serfs in games of cards or simply transferred them from one estate to another. Male serfs risked being sent to the army for a term no less than twenty-five years, a service from which few returned: disease and severe physical punishment killed more surely than the enemy. Serfs were not allowed to own land or, indeed, much of anything.

With the beginning of industrialization, many serfs were sent to work in factories in the city. They were housed in barracks in inhumane conditions. Instead of money, they were paid with coupons that they could only redeem at the factory store for bare necessities, making it impossible for them to leave. The minuscule barter payment the workers received was unrelated to hours worked or productivity; most of their earnings were collected by their owner. Industrial accidents, as well as malnutrition and infectious diseases, made working in city factories a hell no less than laboring on a nobleman's estate.

A Campaign of Change

This was the Russia that Alexander II inherited from his father. He was an impressionable young man, despite his father's attempts to turn him into a "real man" by military training. With his teacher Zhukovsky, a romantic Russian poet, Alexander traveled across Russia for several months. Perhaps as a result of his observations during the trip, Alexander decided early in his rule that Russia needed fundamental reforms.

First, he decided to build a railroad system across the vast territory of Russia. This phenomenally grand project was successful, enabling quick communication between previously isolated parts of the Russian Empire. Its effects are easily underestimated by a Westerner unfamiliar with the harsh Russian climate and the state of the roads. For close to six months of the year the roads were either muddy or covered with snow, making long-distance travel available only to the very rich or very desperate. With the wide-reaching railroad, a trip from Moscow to Crimea that used to take weeks now took only two days.

Next, Alexander II loosened press censorship, formerly so tight that the most generous outcome for an ironic writer was to be declared mentally ill and put under house arrest. Alexander's liberalization led to the publication of numerous journals and books that openly criticized the social order in Russia and called on the Russian youth to change it by a variety of means, from self-sacrificial dedication to work and public welfare to outright revolt against the czar's rule. Some of these publications were quickly closed down or heavily censored, but often too late to prevent their proliferation through copying and illegal import from abroad.

Alexander II also allowed foreign travel, and in unprecedented numbers young people went to foreign universities to study. Abroad they experienced firsthand a society without slavery that enjoyed a free press and a parliamentary government.

Education, formerly a privilege available only to the richest and noblest of the Russian elites, was made available to many from the middle and lower classes (as well as to minority ethnic groups) through stipends and scholarships. Inevitably, conflicts emerged between students and university officials, sometimes resulting in mass student demonstrations that were crushed by arrests and expulsions from university "without right of return." From the ranks of the expelled came a curious category of perpetual students who maintained a distinctive image: worn clothes, disheveled long hair, and an argumentative style. Having left the lands and occupations of their fathers and no longer willing or able to join the ranks of city workers or peasants, perpetual students survived by living in communes with meager incomes from tutoring and occasional short-term teaching contracts.

The most ambitious and most controversial reform that Alexander cherished in his heart for years was to free the serfs. His wife, a liberal German princess, fully supported his ideas, as did his younger brother, Prince Konstantine. From everyone else, Alexander encountered only opposition. The ruling elite did not want to give up the lifestyle that depended on the unpaid labor of serfs; nor did they want to give up their monopoly of higher education. Already threatened by earlier reforms, the richest Russian families expressed their strong disagreement with the czar's reforms. Keeping in mind that some of his ancestors were murdered in their own royal palaces by discontented noblemen, Alexander tried to compromise.

Perhaps the most troublesome compromise was the reform that canceled serfdom but endowed the serfs with barely enough land to feed their families. Adding to the burden, they had to pay a high mortgage to the previous owner for the land they were "granted." Many were forced to keep working for the same master as before, with minimal pay, the same working conditions, and a grudge against the government. Those who worked in factories at the time of reform were not dealt any land at all, leaving them homeless and at the mercy of factory owners. Ensuing peasant revolts were brutally suppressed by the army with hundreds of unarmed people shot. This, in turn, led to unrest among the university students, who took the side of the oppressed.

By 1866 Alexander II had reigned for eleven years. He had antagonized the nobility in his efforts to modernize the underdeveloped slave nation that his father had left him. However, many of his reforms were partial and did not earn him new sources of support. He liberated the serfs, but failed to give them enough land to survive independently of their former masters. He gave new educational opportunities to many, but after a few years excluded dissidents from the universities and left thousands of young people without a trade or degree but with thrilling experiences of antigovernment activism and radical ideas. He loosened the government's grip on the press, but then closed the most popular political magazines and imprisoned some of the best political minds of the day. The result was a surge of underground publications. After eleven years of Alexander's rule, the horrors of his father's regime were forgotten, and a new generation who never knew the fear of pitiless tyranny had risen to question their role in the future of their country.

Looking Further

De Graaf, B. (2010). The nexus between Salafism and Jihadism in the Netherlands. *CTC Sentinel* 3(3): 17–22. Available at https://www.ctc.usma.edu/posts/the-nexus-between-salafism-and-jihadism-in-the-netherlands. Accessed April 26, 2016.

Pipes, R. (2003). *The Degaev affair: Terror and treason in tsarist Russia*. New Haven: Yale University Press.

Tessendorf, K. S. (1986). *Kill the tsar!* New York: Atheneum.

Радзинский, Э. С. (2007). *Александр II: жизнь и смерть*. Москва: АСТ. [Radzinskij, E. (2007). *Alexander II: Life and death*. Moscow: АСТ.]

SECTION 1

Individual Radicalization

Westerners tend to think in individualistic terms and see history through significant historical figures: American independence was largely the Founding Fathers' prophetic vision; freedom for slaves was one of Lincoln's greatest accomplishments; World War II was the result of Hitler's evil genius. The Judeo–Christian tradition places responsibility for deeds, both good and bad, on the one who will be held accountable in the eyes of one God. Western judicial systems place criminal responsibility (given the accused is of age and sound mind) with the individual. If a sheriff stops a citizen for speeding, the fact that others were speeding right next to the car that was stopped does not excuse the driver. "My friends were doing it, so I did it too" is not a valid defense in a court of law, any more than Adam was excused because Eve took the first bite of the apple. Only recently have U.S. conspiracy laws and antiterrorism laws attempted to punish certain kinds of group membership.

In this individualist tradition, the personality psychology pioneered by Freud, in which individual motivation was given great attention, often with little attention to environmental and social influences, took root and flourished. Similarly, common-sense psychology of Westerners tends to emphasize individual disposition over situational circumstances when explaining the causes of human behavior. The great exception to this tendency is when we are explaining our own bad behavior, when we are likely to blame those very circumstances we ignore when explaining others' bad behavior.

This tendency—to see the individual as primarily responsible for his or her actions, no matter how strong the situational constraints—came

Me, the situation; others, their dispositions.

to be known as the *fundamental attribution error* in social psychology. For example, one experiment asked participants to read an essay about Fidel Castro and guess the writer's true attitude toward the Cuban leader. Some participants were told that the essay was written as part of a debate team preparation and that a coin toss had assigned the writer to write a positive essay. Participants largely ignored the situational influence (debate assignment) and judged that the writer was personally favorable toward Castro—little different from participants who read the essay without hearing it was a debate assignment.

In short, Western culture and Western psychology make it easy to read behavior as a reflection of the beliefs, feelings, and preferences of the actor. The first section of our book is thereby made easy: we identify six mechanisms of political radicalization that are consistent with the Western default of individual attribution. Two of these mechanisms are familiar in popular accounts of terrorist motivation: personal and group grievance. Others are less familiar: slippery slope, thrill seeking, love, and unfreezing. One common account of radicalization is missing: nowhere do we suggest that radicalization is explained by abnormality or psychopathology. Rather we aim to show how normal people can be moved toward criminal and violent behavior by normal psychology.

Looking Further

Jones, E. E., & Harris, V. A. (1967). The attribution of attitudes. *Journal of Experimental and Social Psychology* 3: 1–24.

Sabini, J. (1995). *Social psychology* (2nd ed.). New York: Norton. Chapter 8, The self in cultural perspective.

CHAPTER TWO

Personal Grievance

Harm to self or loved ones can move individuals to hostility and violence toward perpetrators.

A Wounded Ego

In the history of Russian terrorism, individual trajectories to terrorism varied greatly. Andrei Zhelyabov's is unusual because it seemed to have started very early, when he was still a child.

Zhelyabov was born in 1851 in the provincial Nikolaevka in the south of the Russian Empire and spent the first ten years of his life as a serf. Stubborn and rebellious, Andrei was a constant liability for his father, who was concerned with jeopardizing the master's favor. As a result, Andrei was sent to spend most of his time with his maternal grandfather, where his attitudes and ambitions were more accepted. His grandfather was a member of the Unreformed Russian Orthodox Church—a rare opposition to the omnipresent Russian Orthodox Church. Under the previous Czar Nicholas I "the Unreformed" had been severely persecuted, tortured, killed, or exiled; but under the more liberal administration of Alexander II, they were merely ostracized. Andrei's grandmother was a free woman before she met Andrei's grandfather and, after much grieving, gave up her freedom to marry a serf. In this household of unorthodoxy Andrei's rebellious temperament found empathy and support.

An unusually intelligent boy, Andrei realized he had been dealt an unfortunate fate. At most he could aspire to be an *upravlyauschij*—a serf coordinator like his father and subject to the same treatment at his master's whim as any other serf. When Andrei was nine years old, his favorite aunt was raped by their master. Because the family all lived in a small house together, Andrei was acutely aware of the event. Despite tradition Andrei's grandfather attempted to seek justice and pressed charges against the rapist. Nothing ever came of the matter: the courts were presided over by local noblemen who were free to issue judgment without a trial. They ruled, as they usually did, in favor of a fellow nobleman. The family humiliation, more pronounced because of Andrei's grandfather's defiant attempt to seek justice where it could not be found, cast a further shadow over the already grim life of Andrei and his loved ones. In Andrei this humiliation festered into a palpable anger and bitterness against the nobility. In his autobiography he recalled a vow he gave himself at ten years of age to murder the rapist when he grew up, and the intense anger he felt for over two years after the event took place.

Everything changed for Andrei with the 1861 emancipation reform that liberated serfs. In theory at least he now had the same freedom, the same opportunities as the sons of nobility. He took entrance tests at a prestigious gymnasium in the nearby town of Kertch and scored high enough to qualify for a full scholarship, including room and board.

In addition to his intelligence, Andrei had other advantages. He was exceptionally good-looking: tall, tanned from working outside in the summer, with a mane of dark hair and attentive, sharp eyes. Memoirs paint a picture of a charismatic, magnetic individual. At the same time, he was only a peasant boy, always indigent, in drab and poorly fitting clothes. No doubt the contrast of the riches hidden within the apparent poverty was only starker for proud Andrei. A classmate recalled that some teachers used a familiar *ty* to refer to students instead of the more formal and respectful *Vy*, every time making Andrei blush crimson with anger and embarrassment.

It appeared early on that he had a taste for making trouble, and he was implicated in many student misdeeds. One other notable character trait came through in a letter he submitted to the admission committee of the Novorossiysk University in Odessa. The letter requested, indeed almost demanded, that he be granted admission *and* a stipend based on his outstanding ability as well as on his financial hardship. On this occasion, the admissions committee held a special meeting where the chair expressed his outrage at the nerve of this young man. The resolution was that Andrei was to take an entrance exam to qualify—an unusual practice. He passed, however, and was granted both admission and the stipend he had requested. He had overcome extreme odds, humble origins, and poverty to gain recognition that he was as good as—possibly better than—those rich children of noblemen!

Early reports thus depict Andrei Zhelyabov as an exceptionally intelligent and charismatic young man, aggrieved by his family's humble background, with an attitude of entitlement and disdain for the powerful. From the day Andrei was granted a pass to the university his trajectory to radicalism became unmistakable.

At the university he participated in student communes, largely because they provided cheap room and board, but not least because he enjoyed the intellectual influence he had over other students. He liked the center stage, the forum for his strong personality and ideas. He took part in a number of student protests, including one that finally got him kicked out of the university without the right to reapply. The protest was to support a student who got into a verbal argument with a professor. Characteristically, Andrei did not personally know either the student or the professor, and he had not witnessed the episode. Nevertheless, a university investigation report found that Andrei Zhelyabov was one of the main instigators and organizers of the student protests on this occasion. All the progress he had made by entering the university was lost. The resentments and grievances he had harbored since the rape of his aunt, calling on him to challenge authority at every opportunity, proved stronger than the appeal of a good life.

As a result, without the support of his stipend, this natural leader and intellectual had to work as a tutor to the children of landowners, much like the one who had so humiliated his family. He became a perpetual "former student"—an ever-growing population category that emerged from the government's harsh reactions to student protests. Stuck between two worlds—his peasant origins to which he saw no possible return and the professional career that was closed to him by the government's sanctions—Zhelyabov was hardened in his initial grievance.

He found the student communes the only outlet for his ambitions. Here, he could give speeches and participate in debates, very quickly coming to extreme views on the necessity of relentless terror to change the political system that he felt was corrupt and unyielding. Here, he enjoyed admiration and respect not only for his abilities as a speaker, but also for his daring views. Here, he enjoyed a special status for his peasant origins and brute physique.

The main concern of student activists at the time—helping the peasants—was a personal issue for Andrei. His exclusion from the normal career path facilitated his involvement in the radical movement, leading to new arrests, new grievances, new loyalties, and new goals. The initial childhood grievance and rebelliousness ascended onto an ideological platform; the initial weak ties with the civil society were irreparably broken; the connections to the underground life and people grew stronger.

As if the grudges he already held against the government were not bad enough, Andrei was arrested for passing a comforting note to an imprisoned comrade. A simple note of concern and support landed him in prison, where, as a peasant, he was kept in the worst possible conditions. Released, he participated in the "going into the people" movement, was again arrested, and was sent to St. Petersburg for the famous Trial of 193, where he was acquitted. With little effort, he was becoming a decorated veteran in the activists' war with the government. When the most radical members of the activist group Land and Freedom assembled in Lipetsk to discuss transitioning to terrorism, Zhelyabov, not yet a member, was invited. He became the ideologue and enforcer of the terrorist group that was founded in Lipetsk: People's Will.

Zhelyabov evolved, with the help of government repressions, from a gifted troublemaker into a serious radical. He was only thirty years old when he was executed for terrorism, already an accomplished member of a terrorist organization that he had helped to build, with a history of political imprisonments and participation in a number of terrorist acts, including the successful assassination of Czar Alexander II.

The Psychology of Personal Grievance

Radicalization as a result of personal grievance is a popular idea, much cited in explanations of suicide terrorism. Chechen "Black Widows" are frequently described as seeking revenge against Russians for their own experiences of rape or for the deaths of husbands, brothers, or sons at Russian hands. Tamil Tigers of the suicide brigades called the Black Tigers are often said to be survivors of Sinhalese atrocities. Many accounts of Palestinian suicide terrorists point to attacks by Israeli Defense Forces against neighbors or loved ones as motives for self-sacrifice.

Radicalization by personal grievance seems familiar because it fits our own experience. When someone wrongs us, we want justice; often we want revenge. The difference is subtle but important. Justice means that the one who mistreats us should be punished. Revenge means that we should be the ones who do the punishing. The targets for both justice and revenge—the perceived perpetrators—can be either individuals or whole categories of persons. This IRS official treated me unfairly *or* the IRS treated me unfairly; nineteen Arab Muslims attacked the United States on 9/11 *or* Muslims attacked the United States on 9/11.

Zhelyabov wanted revenge against the landowner who had raped his aunt; later, when local landowners blocked the case against the rapist, he wanted revenge against landowners as a class. His life as a terrorist can be understood as motivated by a powerful confluence of personal revenge with abstract ideas of justice for serfs that were held by many university students.

Anger and Aggression

The emotion underlying justice and revenge is anger. Perceived injustice from a specific perpetrator results in anger against this individual. More abstract perceptions of injustice—landowners oppressing serfs, whites oppressing blacks, Russians oppressing Chechens—result in anger or outrage against a whole class or category of perpetrators. In the heat of anger people can do rash and dangerous things, and anger is often invoked to explain acts of terrorism that carry high costs to the perpetrator. Can anger be the underlying cause of radicalization through grievance?

Research in the psychology of emotions offers two theories of anger. The first, originating with Aristotle, contends that perception of slight or insult leads to anger and desire for revenge. Aristotle's theory points to the importance of social norms about what constitutes slight or insult—disrespect—because these norms can be quite different in different societies and over different times in history. In this theory, insult evokes anger and a desire to retaliate.

The second theory, originating in twentieth-century animal learning psychology, was first called *frustration-aggression theory* and later expanded to become *pain-aggression theory*. It contends that any punishing experience leads to anger and an increased propensity for aggression. Punishing experiences include not just frustration (being blocked from a desired goal) but any kind of discomfort, even the unpleasantness of excessive heat or painful cold. Animals shocked by electricity, for instance, will try to bite anything in reach. Similarly, people made to experience pain or frustration may show increased and indiscriminant aggression. Pain-aggression theory, unlike Aristotle's theory, is reflexive and less specific about the target of aggression: punishment makes us irritable.

By either of these two theories, Zhelyabov should have been angry when his aunt was raped and further angered when local landowners blocked justice against the rapist. Aristotle's insult-anger theory would say that Zhelyabov perceived his aunt's rape and the further injustice of the landowners as a personal insult for which he sought revenge against both rapist and landowners. Pain-aggression theory would say that Andrei felt the pain of his aunt's rape and frustration from justice denied, leading him to hostility and aggression toward the perpetrators.

Fadela Amara—Activist, Radical, Minister

Fadela Amara was appointed in 2007 as France's secretary of state for urban policy, responsible for bringing new services and new jobs to the 5 million poor immigrants packed into some of France's least attractive suburbs. Amara is a Muslim and a left-wing feminist who believes in liberty, equality, fraternity—and secular socialism. She became a high-ranking government official without having graduated from one of the selective *grandes écoles* that are the usual path to status and influence in France. She emerged instead from the "Lost Territories" of French Muslims for whom she is now responsible.

> In 1978, when she was 14, in the housing project near Clermont-Ferrand where she was born, she saw her brother, Malik, 5, killed by a drunk driver. She saw the police side with the driver and, "most important, I saw the police use racist remarks toward my parents, particularly my mom," she said. "It was a very violent seizure of conscience," like an electrical shock, she has said. Ever since, she said, "I'm angry, and I don't accept that in my country there are injustices."[1]

---

1. Erlanger, S. (2008). A daughter of France's "Lost Territories" fights for them. *New York Times*, June 14. Available at http://www.nytimes.com/2008/06/14/world/14amara.html.

Radicalized at an early age, she became a fierce campaigner against racism and for women's rights—including within her own Arab Muslim community, where young women had strict rules of behavior and dress and where punishment for violation of these rules was often vicious. Offended by cases of gang rape and immolation for perceived immoral behavior, Amara organized a rally for women's rights in 2003 that concluded with some 30,000 people participating in an illegal march on Paris.

This case offers two remarkable aspects. The first is that Fadela Amara traces her radicalization to a single defining moment of anger in response to racist disrespect for her mother. Her first efforts to do something about the injustice she perceived led her to interpret her personal grievance in terms of a more general group grievance: injustice toward immigrant Muslim women. Compared with the initial individual grievance, the group grievance was larger in two ways: she moved from seeing her mother as victim to seeing Muslim women as victims, and she moved from seeing anti-immigrant Frenchmen as perpetrators to seeing fellow immigrants as also victimizing Muslim women.

The second noteworthy aspect of Amara's history is that radicalization does not always escalate all the way to violence. Waging fierce battle against injustice brought Amara to lead an illegal march on Paris, but the march was not violent; she moved on to trying to advance her radical ideas within the French government. She described herself as a militant, but she worked for the same President Nicholas Sarkozy who, as interior minister during the 2005 immigrant riots, famously referred to the rioters as "rabble" and "scum." In her trajectory to radicalism Amara became passionate, militant, and a lawbreaker; but she stopped short of violence and tried to work within the system she had been fighting.

Radicals such as Fadela Amara present a particular challenge for government policies relating to police and security. Their ideas are extreme, their vision is conflictual and militant, they break the law—but they aren't violent. Sometimes radicals of this kind can be the wave of the future, as freedom riders were in the U.S. civil rights movement. But sometimes they progress to violence, including terrorism, and sometimes their example may encourage others to violence.

For the government, the challenge is to determine whether and how to suppress those with militant ideas. The danger, however, is that suppression can transform nonviolent individuals and groups—those who survive government suppression—into hardened terrorists.

From Personal to Political Grievance

There seems to be an easy path from personal grievance to anger to aggression toward the perpetrator. Our own experience of anger makes this path plausible. But the cases considered here raise two complications about this path.

The first complication is the transition from revenge against a particular perpetrator to justice against a particular class or category of people. Zhelyabov could have given his life to attack the man who raped his aunt. He could have attacked one or more of the landowners who refused to bring charges against the rapist. Instead he developed a sense of outrage against landowners as a class and a strong identification with the plight of peasants as a class. In short, his outrage moved from personal to political.

Similarly Amara could have tried to identify and attack the particular policemen who treated her mother with racist disdain or perhaps attack the police force of Clermont-Ferrand. Instead she developed a sense of outrage against racism and disrespect for Muslim women, whether the disrespect came from non-Muslims or from Muslim men. And she came to identify with the plight of all Muslim immigrant women in France. Like Zhelyabov, her outrage moved from personal to political.

In contrast, there are occasions in which a personal grievance stays personal, and the victim acts for revenge against a particular perpetrator. In February 2010, Joseph Stack, a fifty-three-year-old software engineer, flew his Piper Cherokee into an IRS office building in Austin, Texas. He left behind a manifesto detailing his anger against the IRS for squashing his business and taking his retirement savings. The manifesto also expressed anger against a government that would bail out bankers while crushing individuals like himself, introducing an element of larger political motivation even in this case. But the focus of Stack's anger was the IRS, and his target was the IRS. There was no obvious positive identification with a group of similar victims, and the personal did not become political as it had for Zhelyabov and Amara.

The complication of the path between personal grievance and political violence is then the psychology of attribution in which both victims and perpetrators are raised to the level of classes or categories. We need a theory that can describe when and how individual events are interpreted in terms of conflict between groups. After the attacks of September 11, 2001, for instance, why was it easy for many Americans to react to the actions of nineteen Arab Muslims with hostility toward all Arabs and Muslims? Psychology does not currently offer the kind of attribution theory required.

The second complication of the path from personal grievance to political violence is that the experience of anger is relatively brief. Psychologists studying emotion, whether anger or any other emotion, try to measure the emotion or its effects only in the minutes immediately after instigating the emotion. How can an emotional experience that lasts only minutes explain political violence that is planned and carried out over periods of months and years?

Like the distinction between the personal and the political, the mismatch between brief emotion and long-term political action points to the human capacity to care about abstract categories of people. The next chapter focuses on this capacity as it is expressed in identification with one group and grievance against another group.

Looking Further

Sabini, J. (1995). *Social psychology* (2nd ed.). New York: Norton. Chapter 13, Aggression.

Wiesenthal, J. (2010). The insane manifesto of Austin crash pilot Joseph Andrew Stack. Available at http://www.businessinsider.com/joseph-andrew-stacks-insane-manifesto-2010-2.

Прокофьев, В. А. (1965). *Желябов. Жизнь замечательных людей*. Москва: Молодая гвардия [Prokof'ev, V. A. (1965). *Zhelyabov. Life of extraordinary people*. Moscow: Molodaya Gvardia].

CHAPTER THREE

Group Grievance

Threat or harm to a group or cause the individual cares about can move the individual to hostility and violence toward perpetrators.

Vera Zazulich: "Another's Grievance Is My Grievance"

Born in imperial Russia in 1849, Vera Zazulich grew up amid broad political reforms and social unrest. She came from an impoverished noble family, but she received a good education in private boarding schools and earned a teaching degree. Working as a secretary and a bookbinder in St. Petersburg, Vera made a decent living but gravitated toward student discussion circles and radical rhetoric. She was arrested for her activism in 1869 and exiled to a remote village, but she returned to the capital only to become involved with a new activist circle. Vera's dedication to her fellow student activists dictated her extreme reaction to an event about which she learned from newspapers.

In July 1877, as was often the case, a peaceful student demonstration ended with arrest and imprisonment of participants. Among them was a student, Bogolubov. One day the prison where he was held was visited by General-Governor Trepov, a textbook autocrat and egomaniac. Trepov crossed the courtyard twice. On the first crossing Bogolubov took his hat off to the governor, but on the second he failed to do so. The governor screamed for Bogolubov to take his hat off and, in a fit of rage, ordered that the prisoner be publically flogged. This caused a revolt by the other prisoners. The newspapers circulated rumors about the incident, as well as about other cruelties perpetrated by the governor.

Vera Zazulich, who had never met the student in question, was outraged by the unfairness of the governor—but even more so by the absolute lack of repercussions for such arbitrary despotism. Her deep sympathy was not motivated by fear of suffering the same fate as Bogolubov: in Alexander II's Russia, a noble-born woman such as Vera was in no danger of being subjected to corporal punishment. Nor was her outrage limited to Trepov. She planned, with her friend Maria Kolenkina, to assassinate two governmental officials infamous for offenses against student activists. The young women drew lots as to who would kill whom, and Zazulich's target was Trepov.

She had inquired through her activist connections whether any group, including the terrorist People's Will, was planning to do anything about the incident and had received no positive answer. After some soul searching, Zazulich decided to take justice into her own hands even if it meant sacrificing her own life. Vera went to see the governor during his weekly hours for public audience. When she was allowed into his study, Vera pulled a gun out of her clothing and shot Trepov in the stomach. She did not attempt to flee the scene and was arrested. The governor later recovered from his wound.

Vera's criminal trial was widely publicized. The best defense lawyers, products of the educational reforms of the new regime, offered to represent her pro bono. The prosecution, on the other hand, had trouble recruiting attorneys, settling finally on a personal friend of the judge. The courtroom was overflowing, and crowds gathered outside. Notable public figures, including Dostoyevsky, came to see the trial.

On the witness stand Vera was stoic, calmly explaining her motivation and readiness for the consequences of her actions. She knew she had to do something, she said; she had to act on her conscience. The eighteen jurors selected by the defense lawyer (the prosecution declined to participate in juror selection) acquitted the defendant of all charges. The crowd cheered. As the judge recalled, even the VIP gallery behind him, reserved for governmental officials, was cheering, clapping, and stomping in support. As soon as Vera Zazulich walked out of the court building, unknown benefactors whisked her away to a conspirator's apartment where she was supplied with fake documents, money, and tickets enabling her to take refuge in Switzerland. She left

Russia just in time; the outraged czar had issued an executive order for her immediate arrest despite the court's ruling.

And so, with the help of unknown friends, with the blessing of the media, and at the pleasure of society, Vera's act of terrorism was not only unpunished but glamorized. People's Will and other radical circles published pamphlets and newspapers praising Vera's act. Ivan Turgenev, a prominent Russian writer and nobleman, dedicated a poem to her. In the poem a young girl is about to throw her life away for the good of others, although she knows full well how painful it may be. The poem ends with two voices calling after the girl. "Fool!" says the first voice. "Saint . . ." whispers the second.

Why such an uproar about what Zazulich had done? Was it the fact that she was acquitted—a miracle, as though higher justice had been served for someone who would not tolerate injustice? Was the public moved by this apparent act of destiny? But public reaction was precisely the reason she was acquitted—the jury and the lawyers, after all, were members of the public. It could not have hurt that she was a young, attractive, well-bred woman, the kind of woman people in that day and age were more inclined to forgive. But the support she received went far beyond forgiveness.

Vera's subsequent political career proved unorthodox. Unlike most other radicals of the time, Vera publically denounced terrorism after her act and remained unwavering in her nonviolent stance to the end of her life. In fact her later friendship with Lenin was spoiled by her literary opinion pieces criticizing Bolsheviks for their violence and cruelty, including the murders of Nicholas II and his family. Although she was allied with Plechanov (leader of the activist movement Land and Freedom) after her emigration to Switzerland, she later distanced herself from him. She came to believe that he was too theoretical and disconnected from the real problems of the Russian folk.

Zazulich's rich life became involved with the most prominent political figures of her generation. She served as a credible courier for Sergei Nechaev (radical theorist and murderer; see chapter 11), first delivering a letter from his fake imprisonment to People's Will members, then, years later, helping him plot his escape from prison. She was friendly with the highest-ranking members of the executive committee of People's Will, including Zhelyabov, Perovskaya, and Michailov. She corresponded with both Karl Marx and Friedrich Engels. She helped Lenin publish his revolutionary newspaper *Iskra* (*The Spark*), in which her own writing appeared. She met and debated Leon Trotsky. These key political players were all interested in Vera Zazulich, whose only credit was an unsuccessful assassination of a minor official. They gravitated to her, even though she pledged no allegiance and denounced their methods. What was so compelling about this provincial girl?

She was not oppositional, stubborn, or ideological. Politically, she was not loyal to methods, people, or ideas. It was the voice of her conscience that she listened to. Perhaps there is something inherently appealing about a person so true to her own moral standards, even if they are not shared by everybody. Vera Zazulich was not avenging her own pain; she was not seeking status or power; she was not trying to win public favor. She was completely altruistic in doing what her conscience told her to do, no matter what the consequences. Giving your life for someone you never met, out of conviction, is admirable. Placing others' well-being above your own conveys humility and heroism that most people can appreciate, although few can muster (see chapter 13).

Zazulich wanted justice and made herself, as she saw it, the instrument of that justice. She herself was not wronged and did not feel that she alone could be the one to bring justice against the governor (she drew lots with Kolenkina to determine their targets). The governor did not insult or punish Zazulich or anyone close to her. Rather, she felt that her act was the last and only chance for justice.

Psychology of Group Grievance

Sometimes an individual is moved to individual radical action in response to political trends or events. The motivating grievance can be that of another individual or group or cause, even though this victimization does not include any direct harm to the one radicalized. Zazulich was one such individual, but there are others. Theodore Kaczynski, the Unabomber, is another example.

Kaczynski gave up a position as assistant professor of mathematics at the University of California Berkeley to live in a remote area of Montana. There he felt he could escape the threat of technological progress that he had come to fear and detest. Such progress is made, he believed, only by denying human nature—especially the need for meaningful work—and by crushing individual freedom. He emerged occasionally from his wilderness cabin to hand-carry or mail bombs to people he saw as leaders of the industrial-technological progress he feared. His bombs killed three persons and wounded twenty-three.

John Allen Muhammad was similarly motivated by a political grievance. With his young protégé Lee Boyd Malvo, Muhammad killed ten people and wounded two in forty-seven days of sniper attacks carried out in and around Washington, DC, in 2002. Muhammad was a veteran of seven years in the Louisiana National Guard and nine years in the U.S. Army; he was discharged after the Gulf War as sergeant. He became a convert to Islam and black separatism and, according to Malvo, hoped to extort several million dollars from the U.S. government and use the money to found a pure black community in Canada. Muhammad was not forthcoming about the origins of this plan, but it appears that he reacted to what he saw as the victimization of black people in the United States.

A very different example of an individual radicalized by political grievance is Clayton Waagner. Beginning in the 1970s Waagner was convicted of various acts of theft, burglary, and attempted robbery. In September 1999 he was driving with his wife and children in a Winnebago that broke down. Police found firearms (illegal for a convicted felon) in the stolen vehicle, and Waagner admitted that he was planning to use the weapons to kill abortion providers. Convicted and sentenced for theft and firearms violations, he escaped from prison in February 2001. While on the run he posted an Internet threat to kill those who worked for abortion doctors and claimed to have target information on forty-two such employees. He kept moving with auto thefts and bank robberies, but in his spare time he managed to organize a massive anthrax hoax.

In October 2001 he sent out 285 letters to abortion clinics across the United States; the letters, with the return address of the U.S. Marshall Service that was chasing him, contained white powder and an anthrax threat. Coming soon after the still-unsolved anthrax attacks that followed the 9/11 attacks, these letters were taken seriously—and seriously disrupted clinic operations. In November, still on the run, he sent out 269 more letters to abortion clinics. Anticipating doubts and accelerated testing after the first hoax, he included in the white powder traces of a substance known to test positive in the most common test for anthrax. Again he succeeded in shutting down many clinics. Captured in December 2001, Waagner is serving a thirty-year jail sentence in the U.S. Penitentiary, Lewisburg, PA. His book, *Fighting the Great American Holocaust*, offers an unusual look into the mind of one highly intelligent "lone-wolf" terrorist.

Waagner's impact is the more remarkable because he threatened violence but never actually killed or injured anyone. He worked alone, leaving his family members to fend for themselves. His book suggests that, on the run, he knew how to find antiabortion sympathizers but was careful not to implicate any of them in his crimes. He mentions a granddaughter born dead as the event that precipitated his turn to terrorism, but his grievance is not in doubt. Clayton Waagner may have begun as a petty criminal, but he ended with what he saw as a God-given mission to make war on those "who make war on the unborn."

Individual radicalization to political violence is relatively rare. Still, as these examples demonstrate, Zazulich is far from unique in her solo trajectory to political violence. None of these trajectories can be explained in terms of personal grievance—unless a teaching position at Berkeley (Kaczynski), a bitter divorce and child-custody battle (Muhammad), or a wife and nine children (Waagner) can count as grievances.

Even in these examples, however, the individual has some connection to a larger political movement. Kaczynski's ideas drew on critics of the twentieth century's *Brave New World*; Muhammad participated for a period in the Nation of Islam; and Waagner used the web sites of antiabortion groups such as the Army of God. The lone-wolf terrorist depends on others for ideas if not for action (see introduction of section 3).

More than for other mechanisms of radicalization, there is a probability of some degree of psychopathology for those moved to act alone against group grievances. Psychiatric testimony at Kaczynski's trial indicated that he suffered from paranoid schizophrenia. Although groups of radicals are unlikely to tolerate the unreliability that goes with psychopathology, individualist radicals can be responding, at least in part, to their private demons.

But this is not always the case. Zazulich's history shows no trace of psychopathology. John Allen Muhammad had no history of mental disorder, was found competent to stand trial, and received a death sentence. Waagner was convicted for crimes that showed planfulness bordering on genius. How is it possible for a normal individual to move to radical political action without the goad of personal grievance yet without group support? For explanation we turn to the psychology of altruism and the psychology of identification.

Altruism and Strong Reciprocity

Readiness to sacrifice for friends and family is so common that it is often seen as natural and no more in need of explanation than having two eyes. But sacrifices for non-kin present more of a puzzle. Why would Zazulich, Muhammad, and Waagner make sacrifices in the interest of non-kin?

One answer is called *strong reciprocity*. Among animals that live in groups, including humans, there are advantages to cooperation. A hunter who gets lucky today will benefit from sharing meat with the rest of the group—if he or she can expect to receive a share in the group's food supply on a less successful day. Sadly, the advantages of reciprocity can be reaped by cheaters—those who defect from cooperation, contributing no resources yet profiting by those who do. Over time, pure altruists in the group will lose out as more and more and more members take the easy route of doing less and getting more.

Both animals and humans can solve this problem by punishing cheaters. A group can reap the benefits of altruism if it has members willing to carry out justice at a price to themselves. Altruism can succeed if there are enough individuals who respond in kind—tit-for-tat—to both cooperation and cheating. Strong reciprocity describes this combination of two tendencies, to cooperate and to punish. The combination can be successful where the tendency to cooperate, taken alone, would disappear under the costs of cheaters.

Research in cooperation often uses economic games. In such games, each participant makes choices in a situation where the consequences of these choices depend on choices made by others. In a prisoner's dilemma (PD) game, participants face a choice between cooperating and defecting, where defecting means putting self-interest ahead of cooperation. Defection is always rewarded. Cooperating is rewarded if the other chooses to cooperate, but punished if the other chooses to defect.

These contingencies are designed to imitate the consequences of real-life cooperation and defection. Imagine meeting someone for the first time: you can act nice or act mean. You have no idea what the other person is likely to do. Extending a hand and smiling at someone who then spits on you leaves you looking—and feeling—stupid. On the other hand, extending a hand and smiling at someone who does the same might be the beginning of a beautiful friendship.

In some PD games, participants are offered a chance to use some of their own winnings in order to "punish" defectors—paying to reduce the payment to those who do not reciprocate cooperation. To continue the real-life metaphor, imagine being offered an opportunity to punish the jerk who would spit on you—or on someone else—in response to a smile and an extended hand. Would you pay for such a chance?

Results of PD games show that most individuals begin by trying to cooperate and that most individuals are ready to pay extra to punish those who do not cooperate. Importantly, it is not just those who suffer the defection who are ready to pay to punish the defector. A third party is often willing to pay to punish a defector despite the fact that the one punishing did not suffer personally any loss to the defector. Not only will we pay to punish those who spit on us in response to our kindness, we will even pay to punish those who spit on others.

Even in these simple games, then, individuals are willing to pay personal costs to punish bad behavior that does not affect them personally. Punishing bad people—carrying out justice—in this perspective becomes an expression of altruism no less than helping good people. There is reassuring news about this kind of altruism. Research in many cultures indicates that between 40 percent and 60 percent of game participants are willing to pay to punish defectors!

To this extent Zazulich's example in shooting the governor becomes a little less mysterious. She carried out justice for her group, at a personal cost. If we are ready to generalize from bad individuals to bad groups—a projection not yet studied in the game theory literature—then Muhammad and Waagner can also be seen as extreme examples of individuals incurring personal costs to punish perceived malefactors. We assume that this generalization is easy when the price is right. How many individuals would pay ten dollars to see a million dollar fine levied on every Wall Street employee who made more than a million dollars in 2009? Presumably the extreme personal cost of radicalization to violent action is the barrier that stops many individuals who otherwise would act to punish individuals and groups perceived as oppressors.

Another way of understanding third-party punishment begins, not from the problem of cheaters prospering, but with everyday experience. Human beings care about others, to the extent that we can sometimes put others' well-being above our own.

Group Identification

The psychology of identification is both wide and deep in human affairs. Identification with another means caring about the other person's welfare. Positive identification means we feel good when the other is safe, prospering, or growing, but we feel bad when the other is in danger, failing, or diminished. Negative identification is an inverse concern for the welfare of another: negative identification means we feel good when the other is in trouble, and we feel bad when the other is safe and prospering.

The capacity for positive identification extends far beyond those near and similar to ourselves. We can come to care about the welfare of groups that we are not part of (Tibetans), about individuals we do not know personally (Britney Spears), about groups we do not know personally (Dallas Cowboys football team), about fictional characters (Tiny Tim), and about companion animals (Hero the dog and Shoesy the cat). In all of these cases, our concern for the welfare of the other goes beyond any economic value to the self. That is, our own material welfare is not significantly improved by raising the welfare of Tibetans, Britney Spears, the Dallas Cowboys, Tiny Tim, Hero, or Shoesy. Nevertheless we invest real money, real time, real anxiety, real tears, real pride, and real joy in the ups and downs of others whom we care about. And when what we care about is threatened, conflict is likely to ensue.

Here is the key point: the foundation of large-scale intergroup conflict is the human capacity for group identification. We can care about large and abstract groups so much that the welfare of the group can compete with our personal welfare. When we give money or time toward helping a victim group, or a religious, ethnic, or national group, we put group interest above self-interest to the extent that the same money and time could have been enjoyed more selfishly.

Of course identification is cheap, and action is expensive. Many who identify with a group or cause extend only sympathy. Few extend resources, and even fewer are ready to accept the personal risks of illegal, let alone violent, action in support of the group. Out of all who sympathized with the student flogged for failing to doff his hat to the governor, what explains why only Zazulich and her friend took it on themselves to shoot the governor? Of all who sympathize with the problems of African Americans, what explains how only John Muhammad was ready to take up random violence against white Americans? Of all who see abortion as murder, why was Waagner among the few ready to threaten violence against abortion providers?

There is no easy answer to this question. Our three examples of normal individuals radicalized by group grievance—Zazulich, Muhammad, Waagner—do not have much in common. A tender-hearted secretary, a macho ex-soldier, and a criminal turned crusader—these examples do not suggest a common personality type. Each had an enormous emotional commitment to the cause for which he or she turned to violence, but this commitment was likely more a result of the radicalizing trajectory than a cause or explanation of this trajectory. Chapter 15 examines in more detail the puzzle of lone-wolf terrorism and a possibility of profiling lone-wolf terrorists.

We turn now to try the relevance of our analysis on a modern example of radicalization by political grievance.

Ayman al-Zawahiri—From Intellectual to Terrorist

Young Ayman had learned his grievance against the Egyptian government before he got out of short pants. His family had opposition politics on one side and science and religion on the other.

Ayman's father, Dr. Mohammed Rabie al-Zawahiri, was a professor of pharmacology at Ain Shams University in Cairo. Ayman's uncle was a dermatologist, and more than two dozen members of Rabie's extended family were physicians, chemists, or pharmacists. In Ayman's generation, counting relations both by descent and by marriage, the number of physicians in the Zawahiri clan totaled more than forty. Despite this tradition of success in medicine, the family was perhaps more famous for its religious scholars, one of whom was rector of Al-Azhar University, arguably the most prestigious post in the most prestigious center of Islamic learning in the world.

Ayman's mother, Umayma Azzam, also came from a notable family. Her great-uncle had married the daughter of a Libyan resistance leader who had fought against the Italians; later he became the first secretary-general of the Arab League and was given the title of *pasha* by the Egyptian government. Her father had studied in London and became dean of the School of Literature at Cairo University; later he served as ambassador to both Saudi Arabia and Pakistan and became the first administrator of Riyadh University in Saudi Arabia.

If the Zawahiris were more scholarly, the Azzams were richer and more political. Particularly influential for Ayman was his maternal uncle, Mahfouz Azzam, an attorney living in Maadi, a small suburb of Cairo where Ayman was brought up.

In 1936, Mahfouz was in third grade; the man teaching him Arabic was Sayyid Qutb. Mahfouz became devoted to his teacher, and their bond persevered over many years. Both spent time in jail for antigovernment activities, and it was after one such sojourn in jail that Qutb published his book *Milestones*, which remains today an inspiration for those Muslims who would replace secular government with an Islamic state. The government responded to *Milestones* by arresting Qutb again and condemning him to death.

Mahfouz Azzam had become Qutb's lawyer and was able to visit him just before the execution. On that visit Qutb inscribed his personal copy of the Koran and gave it to Mahfouz—a martyr's parting gift.

From Qutb to Mahfouz and from Mahfouz to Ayman came a radical critique of the Egyptian government as hopelessly corrupt and a radical alternative in the purity of government by Sharia. Along with the radical vision came a radicalizing personal experience of suffering at the hands of the government. The government had twice jailed Ayman's uncle and had jailed, tortured, and finally executed his uncle's dearest friend and mentor.

Ayman was not naturally inclined to action; as a child he is described as religious, bookish, a lover of poetry, and uninterested in sports. He was fifteen years old when Qutb was executed in 1966. That same year Ayman helped form an underground cell to forward Qutb's ideas. It was not long before his experience of grievance became even more personal.

In the 1970s Ayman's cell joined with several others to form Jamaat al-Jihad. The jihad group was like the Muslim Brotherhood in seeking to make Egypt an Islamic state, but, unlike the Muslim Brotherhood, al-Jihad despised compromise and gradualism. After completing medical school in 1974, Ayman served three years as a surgeon in the Egyptian army. On return from the military service he opened a clinic in the same building in Maadi that he lived in with his parents. He married in 1978, and in 1980 he spent four months in Pakistan working for the Red Crescent Society and treating Afghan refugees, many wounded by Russian bombs and land mines. He went again to Pakistan for two months in 1981.

Ayman returned to an Egypt in turmoil. The Islamic revolution in Iran in 1979 had provided a model of the kind of Islamic state that Islamic radicals had been seeking in Egypt. In response to this new challenge Anwar Sadat reversed his policy of accommodation with Islamic groups and organizations and jailed those he saw as troublemakers. A military cell within al-Jihad set in motion a hasty plan to kill Sadat. When the plot succeeded, the new government of Hosni Mubarak rounded up thousands of suspected conspirators. Ayman was arrested before he could leave on another trip to Pakistan.

The common fate of suspected conspirators in Egyptian prisons was humiliation and torture. By several accounts Ayman broke under torture and cooperated with security forces in a trap set for Essam al-Qamari, a charismatic army officer who had planned with Ayman to bring down the government with a bomb attack on Sadat's funeral. In his memoir, *Knights under the Banner of the Prophet*, Ayman was probably referring to his own experience in this passage: "The toughest thing about captivity is forcing the mujahid, under the force of torture, to confess about his colleagues, to destroy his movement with his own hands, and offer his and his colleagues' secrets to the enemy."[1]

After a trial that dragged on nearly three years, Ayman was convicted of weapons offenses, sentenced to three years, and released for time served. Whether from his own suffering in prison or from shame in having betrayed a friend, he left prison a hardened extremist for whom death was not horror but release. He looked back on the early days of al-Jihad as a kind of amateur hour with mistakes that should never be repeated. To his earlier grievance of hurt to loved ones—his uncle and his uncle's mentor Qutb—was now added personal grievance for hurt and humiliation he had experienced directly and personally. Ayman al-Zawahiri left prison with these personal grievances framed as part of a larger victimization of devout Muslims, that is, with a sense of grievance that integrated revenge with jihad.

The special power of this framing—the combination of personal and political motives—requires special attention.

Synergism of Personal and Group Grievance

In looking back over our examples of individual radicalization by grievance, it becomes clear that personal and group grievance are seldom far apart. There are examples in which personal grievance comes first and examples in which political grievance comes first, but in all cases the personal and the political are soon joined.

Our clearest examples of personal grievance are Zhelyabov and Amara. Zhelyabov reacts first to the rape of his aunt; but soon the target of his hostility is expanded to landowners in general, and his identification with the victim is expanded from his aunt to serfs in general. Amara reacts first to victimization of her mother; but soon the target of her hostility is expanded from racist policemen to anyone— including immigrant men—who disrespects immigrant women, and

---

1. Wright, L. (2006). *The looming tower*. New York: Knopf. p. 53.

her identification with her mother is expanded to identification with the welfare of all Muslim immigrant women.

Our clearest examples of group grievance untainted by mental disorder are Zazulich and Waagner. Zazulich's identification with students led her to attack the governor who victimized a student, but she had had the prior experience of being arrested for connection with student activist circles and expelled for a time from St. Petersburg. That is, she had some experience of personal grievance against the government and its prisons. Similarly Waagner's early history of arrest and conviction for theft, burglary, and robbery may have given him some personal grievance against the criminal and justice system he experienced.

The blending of personal and political is most pronounced in the case of al-Zawahiri. He hears first about the suffering of his uncle and his uncle's mentor Qutb at the hands of the Egyptian government, but from the very beginning their experience is interpreted for him as the suffering of devout Muslims trying to replace secular injustice with Sharia justice. After Qutb is hanged, Zawahiri's antigovernment activity brings him up close and personal experience of the victimization of Islamists in Egyptian prisons. He leaves prison a hardened terrorist, as ready to accept death as to mete out death to the enemy.

In short, particular cases of individual radicalization indicate that personal and political grievances tend to be found together. The distinction between personal and political grievance is important for understanding the potential range of cases of individual radicalization, but we believe that the great majority of cases will show, as Zawahiri's case shows, a near-seamless blend of personal and political grievance.

A useful aspect of this analysis is that it can help resolve the mismatch between the day of anger and the day of revenge in response to grievance. As noted earlier, personal and political grievances are usually understood to move individuals by eliciting strong emotion: anger or outrage. This explanation amounts to claiming a kind of temporary insanity in which even self-interest is lost in the blaze of anger and its impulse for revenge or justice. In psychological research on emotions, however, strong emotion is understood as temporary, something experienced or studied over periods of minutes. The brevity of strong emotion raises problems for accounts of revenge or justice that depend on anger, especially in cases where revenge or justice is sought over days, weeks, or even years.

To the extent that grievance depends on identification, however, it can be steadier than the vagaries of strong emotion. Individual radicalization usually occurs with a blending of personal and group grievance, a blending in which personal grievance means hostility or negative identification with a group seen as perpetrators of injustice, and group grievance means positive identification with a group seen as the victims of this injustice. These reciprocal positive and negative identifications provide stable incentives for intergroup conflict, as successes of the positive-identification group are rewarding and successes of the negative-identification group are punishing. The stability of group identifications can explain the stability of intergroup conflict, revenge, and justice-seeking despite the brevity of emotions of anger and outrage.

It follows that the mental life of individuals radicalized by grievance will not be marked by continuous or even continual strong emotion or by the physiological arousal that accompanies strong emotion. Rather, individuals radicalized by grievance can be steady, planning, and workmanlike—as indeed most of our examples seem to have been.

Still, if there is a predictor of the transition from group grievance to action, it may be in the domain of sympathy and empathy. Of the many who sympathize with a group or cause, perhaps those who feel the most are most likely to sacrifice themselves for others. Indeed, studies of altruism have shown the importance of sympathy and empathy in predicting help for a stranger in distress. Although altruism research has not yet examined the relation between empathy and aggression toward the perpetrator of a stranger's distress, the importance of individual differences in empathy for understanding political radicalization may be worth pursuing.

But individual differences in empathy cannot be the whole story. There are many possible targets for sympathy and empathy: sadly, the world offers many kinds and categories of victims. Women are abused by men, children are abused by parents, poor people are abused by the rich, workers are abused by employers. Something must happen to make the political personal. Lone-wolf terrorism requires the combination of strong capacity for sympathy with an experience that moves sympathy to personal moral obligation to act. For Zazulich it was seeing General-Governor Trepov getting away with flogging a student. For Waagner it was the death of his granddaughter. For Muhammad the tipping point, if any, is unknown. If both personality and personal experience are necessary for lone-wolf terrorism, then attempts to profile this combination must face considerable complexity. Although it offers no easy answers for security services concerned with lone-wolf terrorism, our perspective is consistent with a well-established finding in psychological research: individual behavior depends, not separately on person or situation, but on their interaction.

Looking Further

Batson, C. D., O'Quinn, K., Fultz, J., Vanderplas, M., & Isen, A. M. (1983). Influence of self-reported distress and empathy on egoistic versus altruistic motivation to help. *Journal of Personality and Social Psychology* 45: 706–718.

Cialdini, R. B., Schaller, M., Houlihan, D., Arps, K., Fultz, J., & Beaman, A. L. (1987). Empathy-based helping: Is it selflessly or selfishly motivated? *Journal of Personality and Social Psychology* 52: 749–758.

Cornes, R., & Sandler, T. (1986). *The theory of externalities, public goods and club good*. New York: Cambridge University Press.

Fehr, E., & Fishbacher, U. (2003). Third-party punishment and social norms. *Evolution and Human Behavior* 25: 63–87.

Fehr, E., Fishbacher, U., & Gaechter, S. (2002). Strong reciprocity, human cooperation and the enforcement of social norms. *Human Nature* 13: 1–25.

McCauley, C. (2006). The psychology of group identification and the power of ethnic nationalism. In D. Chirot & M. Seligman (Eds.), *Ethnopolitical warfare: Causes, consequences, and possible solutions*. Washington, DC: APA Books, pp. 343–362.

Moore, W. H. (1995). Rational rebels: Overcoming the free-rider problem. *Political Research Quarterly* 48: 417–454.

Moskalenko, S., McCauley, C., & Rozin, P. (2006). Group identification under conditions of threat: College students' attachment to country, family, ethnicity, religion, and university before and after September 11, 2001. *Political Psychology* 27: 77–97.

Olson, M., Jr. (1965). *The logic of collective action*. Cambridge, MA: Harvard University Press.

Simpson, B., & Willer, R. (2008). Altruism and indirect reciprocity: The interaction of person and situation in prosocial behavior. *Social Psychology Quarterly* 71: 37–52.

Waagner, C. L. (2003). *Fighting the great American Holocaust*. Kearney, NE: Morris Publishing.

Zillmann, D. (1988). Cognition–excitation interdependencies in aggressive behavior. *Aggressive Behavior* 14: 51–64.

Добровольский, Е. Н. (1978). *Чужая боль: Повесмь о Вере Засулич*. Москва: Политиздат. [Dobrovolsky, E. N. (1978). *Another's pain: A novel about Vera Zasulich*. Moscow: Politizdat.]

Засулич, В. И. (1931). *Воспоминания*. Москва: Политиздат. [Zazulich, V. (1931). *Memoirs*. Moscow: Politizdat.]

Кони, А. Ф. (1933). *Воспоминания о деле Веры Засулич* / Под ред. М. Ф. теодорови ча; Предисл. м. Ф. Теодоровича. Москва: Academia. [Koni, A. F. (1933). *Memoirs about the case of Vera Zazulich*. M. F. Teodorovich (Ed.), Moscow: Academia. Foreword by M. F. Teodorovich.]

Носов, Ю. (2006). Еще раз о деле Засулич и либеральном обществе. Как благословили терроризм. *Наука и Жизнь* 12. [Nosov, J. (2006). One more time about the case of Zazulich and the liberal society. How terrorism was blessed. *Nauka I Zhizn'* 12.] Available at http://www.nkj.ru/archive/articles/8334/. Accessed December 8, 2008.

CHAPTER FOUR

Slippery Slope

*Small involvements in political conflict can create new forces moving
an individual toward radicalization.*

Adrian Michailov—Reluctant Revolutionary

Among the wildly different stories of Russian terrorists of the nineteenth century, Adrian Michailov's stands out. His contemporaries from the radical movement often mention his name, indicating that he was at the center of plans and activities for a period of two to three years between 1875 and 1878. However, they rarely discuss his contribution to the movement or his personal qualities. From these accounts we learn only that he was at a certain meeting or that he authored a certain document. Vera Figner, a member of the Executive Committee of People's Will who emigrated to escape government sanctions, revealed in her detailed memoirs the reason for the coldness of others: Adrian Michailov became a traitor. Captured on suspicion of having connections with radical circles, Michailov admitted to having participated in terrorist acts, including the assassination of General Mezentsev. He also named his accomplices, in particular, Barannikov, who was captured as a result. Adrian Michailov survived his prison term and returned from his Siberian exile to European Russia in 1907.

Some time after his return from Siberia, Adrian wrote an autobiography for a Soviet encyclopedia. Here Adrian shows neither a pejorative tone toward the former ruling class nor any enthusiasm for his former comrades. At the beginning he writes emotionally about his experiences in the countryside, where he was sent to pose as a peasant and to carry out radicalizing efforts through personal contacts. Describing the time when he was called on by his comrades to return to the city, his narrative becomes dryer, his sentences lose colorful detail, and the personality of the author becomes obscured behind a formal chronology of events. The narrative is surprisingly passionless, for example, in talking about the author's participation in the assassination of General Mezentsev. Likewise, it is objective and detached in describing cooperation with the authorities—the betrayal of People's Will—upon his arrest. Unlike many of his fellow People's Will comrades, Adrian Michailov was not emotionally or intellectually invested in the idea of political terror. What, then, brought him into the forefront of the terrorist movement?

Adrian had the fortune of being born into a loving and enlightened family. His mother died when he was four, leaving him with only a vague memory of her. His father, an army supply officer, was an honorable and outspoken person—traits not welcomed in his profession. As a result, the family was shuffled from one base to another, until they ended up in the village of Georgievsk. This swampy locale was known for its deadly climate; government employees who caused trouble were stationed there, usually quite briefly, until they succumbed to malaria or some other malady.

When Adrian was ten years old his father died, leaving him in the care of his older sister. Luckily, Adrian's academic talent brought a scholarship to a boarding school in Stavropol, a southern Russian provincial town. In school Adrian, an avid reader, found a friend who had access to the attic of the local library where the forbidden literature was kept. Together they devoured progressive Russian and European writers of the time. It was in that library attic that Adrian became interested in social change. He was not personally familiar with the hardships of peasants, but the works of writers such as Chernyshevsky and Dobrolubov gripped his heart. Their call for a new Russia became his calling.

Upon graduation, Adrian's talent was again recognized as he, a provincial orphan, won admission and scholarship to the prestigious Moscow University. Here, he found a proliferation of student circles and communes offering a daily menu of discussions on a wide variety of topics. A number of prominent political figures from the radical movement emerging in St. Petersburg visited the groups that Adrian frequented in Moscow. By the end of his sophomore year, a strategic consensus evolved in these discussion groups: to go into the people, to become one of them, and to radicalize peasants from within.

"Going into the People"

Adrian's commune resolved to start a farm, and Adrian, one of three appointed founders, traveled to the remote village where he helped to buy land, a horse, a plow, and a pair of oxen. Officially the farm had an owner, a manager, and one paid worker (Adrian). In practice, farming the land required more workers. They hired a peasant who had four oxen, but no money or land, and started work.

Because of the press of farm work, Adrian's only radicalizing efforts were directed toward the hired peasant. In their long daily discussions they came to agree on many important political and philosophical issues. However, when it came to blaming the czar for the peasants' misfortunes, Adrian's representative of the proletariat remained obstinate: the czar could not be anything other than good and kind. Unsuccessful in this radicalizing attempt and prevented from working the land by the arrival of winter, Adrian left the farm and returned to Moscow.

Here, Adrian immediately tried to find another occupation to bring him closer to the land and working people. He finally succeeded in securing an apprenticeship with a blacksmith. Among the blacksmith's other apprentices were several who were also preparing to go into the people. These and other young activists lived in a commune near the workshop. Adrian became close with some of the activists; he discussed his thoughts and ideas with them, including his understanding of Marx's *Das Kapital*. Impressed, they recommended him to comrades in St. Petersburg as an expert who could help develop a political and economic platform for activists.

By the end of the summer the blacksmith's workshop was graduating many apprentices, and many activists were leaving to go into the people. Adrian seems to have been among the most successful in learning a new occupation. He had become a master blacksmith, in addition to which he learned to repair peasants' tools. In addition to a gifted mind, he had good hands.

Before leaving the political scene to work once more in the country, Adrian decided to take up the invitation of his activist comrades to visit St. Petersburg's circle of *narodniki*. He was to present Marx's economic theory and defend it during the discussion. A few days after his presentation, he was accepted as one of the members of what soon became "Land and Freedom," the first of several incarnations of the party that eventually produced "People's Will." (In Russian, the word for "freedom," *volya*, is also the word for "will.") When Adrian joined the circle, its program stressed integration with the peasants as the ultimate method of mass radicalization, with the goal of changing the form of government and bettering the peasants' lot. There was no mention of terrorism.

As Adrian wrote in his autobiography (here and in two quotations below), "At another time and under other circumstances I would have stayed here for a long time to personally get to know this family, yes, family, of prominent workers of revolution—charming people with colorful personalities. But a stronger force pulled me away—into the people. . . ."[1]

And so Adrian ventured again to another remote Russian village, along the Volga River, where an abandoned blacksmith's workshop offered him a chance to reconnect with his passion for hard labor among simple, apolitical people. Immediately overwhelmed with requests for service that he did not have the heart to refuse, Adrian worked sunrise to sunset, seven days a week. Within a few months illness and exhaustion confined him to bed. Unable to labor further, Adrian returned to Moscow hoping to make himself useful in political action. Here the narrative of Adrian Michailov's autobiography changes. Many words become abbreviated or shortened; clarifications appear in parentheses for quicker pace. There are fewer descriptions and reflections, more recitations of facts.

Idealism Fading

At this time the "going into the people" or *narodniki* movement was slowly dying out. The radicalizing efforts of the students were failing for many reasons. Some, like Adrian, found the peasants immovable in their belief in the czar's incorruptible goodness. Russian Orthodox religion maintained that the czar was personally blessed by God.

---

1. А. Ф. Михайлов. (1926). *Аβтобиография*. Ростов-на-Дону [Michailov, A. (1926). *Autobiography. Rostov-na-Donu.*] Available at http://narovol.ru/Person/michailovaf. htm. Accessed May 10, 2016. (All translations from Russian sources by S. M.)

Others simply could not get through the peasants' suspiciousness even to engage them in a discussion. It did not help that *narodniki* presented themselves as peasants while most had trouble looking, talking, or acting like one. Unfamiliar with the customs, *narodniki* would arrive at a tavern for dinner dressed in dirty working clothes, whereas the peasants would take care to wash and change before going out to eat. In speech, activists betrayed themselves by using complex vocabulary with "foreign" accents and incorrect dialect.

Finally, most *narodniki* discovered that, all politics aside, they could not stand to eat the rough food, wear the drab clothes, or live in cold barns the way peasants did. Above all, they could not work like peasants. They did not have the skills, the strength, or the stamina.

By the time Adrian returned to Moscow, the radical movement had started on a new project. Having failed to achieve peasant radicalization from within, young revolutionaries began plotting to achieve it top-down. Disappointed in the peasants' motivation and abilities to contest the status quo, they decided to work without the peasants. The idea was to "behead" the regime, thereby forcing the peasants to wake up and participate in creating a governing system that would be better than the old one.

In this ferment, Adrian seems to have felt not only exhausted but lost. He wanted to contribute to social change and to help peasants. But, unlike his comrades, he found joy in peasant work. Unlike his comrades, he felt he could achieve the ideals of Chernyshevsky's *What's to Be Done?* without resorting to violence. Nevertheless, as a loyal member of the *narodniki* movement, he looked to it for guidance.

First Assignment

Back in Moscow, Adrian was immediately filled in on recent events, one of which was the arrest of Petro, a beloved and trusted member of Land and Freedom. The group decided to free Petro during one of his routine walks to the bathhouse. Adrian was assigned a part in the plan: he was to be the coachman. This role apparently suited Adrian, as he was given the same assignment on several other occasions. His ability to act like a peasant and his skill with Barbarian, the horse that the radicals used in their operations at the time, were notably successful. Not so the plan to free Petro. The elaborate plot, involving over twenty people, failed because Petro was sick with typhus and could not make the leap from the pavement to the coach.

After the failed operation, Adrian traveled to St. Petersburg, the headquarters of Land and Freedom, to seek permission to return to the countryside and continue work there. "The very first day I started talking about it. The comrades categorically objected: events are storming, there is so much work and so few who can help—from here, the headquarters—not a single person could be spared." Instead Adrian was to bring Barbarian to St. Petersburg and once again play the role of coachman in the planned assassination of Governor Trepov. But before this plan was attempted, Trepov's assassination was attempted by Vera Zazulich, an individual not associated with a radical organization (see chapter 3).

Second Assignment

The next assignment again called for a coachman in an ambitious plan to free a number of political prisoners who were being moved from their trial in St. Petersburg to prisons in remote towns. This plan also failed—most prisoners' carriages took a different route than expected, and efforts to free the one prisoner who came down the expected road were unsuccessful.

On return to St. Petersburg, Adrian once again raised the question of going back to the country with one of the leaders of the movement. The response was again negative.

> "What's to be done?" said he. "There are so few of us; recently we started counting—how many real members of the organization are there—and could not even count to two hundred. What's to be done? Lack of people should be substituted with the speed of their rotation. The question with [General] Mezentsev is a question of honor. When we are finished with him, we will return to our main work, and there will be many of us." There was nothing left but to agree, my position left me no choice.

Third Assignment

Adrian's role in Mezentsev's assassination was, once again, serving as the getaway coachman. The story of the assassination is told in chapter 6. This daring murder of a major official on a popular street remained unsolved for several years. In the immediate aftermath of the operation, Land and Freedom decided to remove all participants from

St. Petersburg for safety, thereby solving Adrian's dilemma and allowing him to return to the country as he wished.

However, several months later Adrian was again called back to St. Petersburg. His writing talent was needed for Land and Freedom's newly instituted newspaper. The first issue of the newspaper was about to come out when news of several arrests caused Adrian, among others, to leave the printing press to go warn other comrades of danger. That same day he was arrested at an apartment of one of the comrades he was trying to warn. The arrest, as Adrian describes it, ended his "professional participation in the Russian revolutionary movement."

His connection to the earlier assassination was established through his horse. The owner of the hotel where Barbarian was stabled recognized Adrian as the coachman. According to Vera Figner, Adrian was confronted by the minister of internal affairs himself, admitted to his participation in the assassination, and gave as well the names of his two associates in the event. One of these associates, Kravchinsky, had by then long emigrated, as Adrian knew. The other was Barannikov. Although Adrian knew Barannikov's real name, he gave the authorities one of Barannikov's aliases. It took a while, but the secret police eventually connected the person with the name, and Barannikov was arrested.

In the Russian revolutionary movement there are courageous stories, outrageous stories, and tragic stories. Adrian Michailov's story is tragic. It is a story of a man with a good heart, a good mind, and good hands, who wanted nothing more than to do good. Like many other students, he became infatuated with the idea of working the land and helping the peasants. Unlike others, he succeeded in this aspiration. But because his idealism was wrapped in his relationship with the larger student movement, he felt obliged to follow its lead, even when this contradicted his own wishes and intuitions. Time after time he asked for the group's permission to disengage from the radical terrorist activity in favor of what he felt was a more fruitful path of activism and integration with the peasants. Time and again, he was given reasons why this was not possible or not timely. His ideological commitment to Land and Freedom did not progress past the stage where it was still an activist movement. In his autobiography he describes with pride several documents that he wrote or co-authored, all of which denounced terrorism as a tactic of social change.

Adrian Michailov did not try to take a heroic stand against cooperation with the authorities upon capture, as many of his comrades did. But the names he gave to the authorities were of one man, known to be beyond the government's reach, and an alias of another, whose real name he kept to himself. Perhaps this act reflects his ambivalence about his relationship with the movement. He shared goals with them, but not values; they were close to him in one respect but very distant in another. Most poignantly, they made him do something he did not really want to do.

Psychology of the Slippery Slope

Doing something one does not want to do? Can this really be an explanation for terrorism, especially if we are talking about an intelligent, educated, capable person? Surely getting involved in violence cannot be blamed on anything but the perpetrator's bad choices. From the legal perspective, this is definitely the case. But we are interested in the psychological perspective: can one be led to violent action by another person or group, without feeling hostility toward the target? That was the question that Stanley Milgram asked himself when he embarked on a series of now famous experiments in the 1960s.

Like many social scientists of his generation, and Jewish himself, Milgram wanted to understand the atrocities of World War II, the Holocaust, and the Nazi concentration camps. How could so many German citizens engage in violence against their peaceful Jewish neighbors? The Nuremberg trial of Adolf Eichmann, a mastermind of the Holocaust, began in 1961. Journalist Hannah Arendt attended the trial and reported her findings in a series of articles in *The New Yorker* magazine, later published as a book, *Eichmann in Jerusalem: A Report on the Banality of Evil*.

Arendt's major discovery was that Eichmann was not a monster or a maniac; in fact, he was not extraordinary in any respect. His testimony lacked passion or ideology and instead repeatedly pointed to the fact—obvious to the defendant, but incredible to most others—that he had just been following orders. The more he was pressed by the prosecution to admit to more hostile motivations, the more incredulous Eichmann became that "following orders" was not deemed an acceptable explanation. Three months after the beginning of the trial, Milgram began to test Eichmann's claim that normal individuals will engage in violence against an innocent target simply because they are told to do so.

Milgram's Experiment

In Milgram's obedience studies, participants were normal individuals, both men and women, varying widely in age, education, and socio-economic levels. They had responded to an advertisement soliciting participation in an experiment for a small monetary reward ($4.50). In a rigged drawing, participants drew the role of teacher in a "learning experiment" in which "Mr. Wallace," a middle-aged, heavy-set, friendly-looking man (in reality, the experimenter's accomplice), drew the role of learner.

The experimenter explained that the teacher would ask questions and give an electric shock for each wrong answer and then increase the shock level for each successive wrong answer. Mr. Wallace proved a very bad learner and made many mistakes. The surprising result of this experiment was that most teachers increased the shock, step by step, from 15 volts up to 30 volts to 45 volts, and so on up to 450 volts, a level that on the (fake) console carried a posted warning "Danger, Strong Shock, XXX."

In other words, most people put in the position of using shock to try to teach a slow learner (the actor playing Mr. Wallace) were willing to apply increasing shocks at each wrong answer, even when the learner started to scream with (simulated) pain and even after the learner mentioned a heart condition, fell silent, and stopped responding. Approximately the same results were obtained with female as with male "teachers" and with Australians, Japanese, Italians, and Germans, as well as Americans.

Why do two-thirds of all teacher-participants go all the way, raising the shock level past the point where the learner's silence suggests injury or even death? (It should be noted that this was one of the psychological experiments that so distressed professional psychologists that rules were instituted in all universities and research labs that now prohibit placing this much pressure on uninformed subjects.)

Most discussions of Milgram's research emphasize the authority of the experimenter, who wears the uniform of a responsible scientist—a white lab coat—and responds to any attempt to stop the shocks by saying that "the experiment requires that you go on" and "you have no choice, you must go on." The usual interpretation of Milgram's results is that participants defer to the experimenter's authority and expertise, suspending their own judgment and agency. But there is a variation of the experiment that points in another direction.

No-Authority Condition

In this less-known variation it is not the experimenter who comes up with the idea of raising the shock level with each mistake. Rather, in the "no-authority" variation, a "co-teacher" (another accomplice of the experimenter) asks and grades the questions, while the naive participant is the teacher who gives the shocks. The experimenter, summoned away for a "phone call," is no longer in the room when the co-teacher comes up with the idea of raising the shock level with each mistake.

Despite the absence of the experimenter and his authority, 20 percent of teachers go all the way to administering 450 volts. One-fifth is considerably less than two-thirds, and the difference is a reflection of how much authority the lab-coated "scientist" conducting the experiment actually carries. But a 20 percent compliance rate nevertheless represents a surprising level of inhumanity toward the supposed learner, especially when the co-teacher insisting on dangerous shock levels is perceived to be just another paid participant, no different from the participant delivering the shocks.

One way to explain this result is in terms of rationalization. According to dissonance theory, humans are likely to change their opinions to fit their behavior. Especially if we have done something stupid or dishonest, we are likely to come up with reasons that will justify or excuse us.

The dissonance interpretation of why 20 percent of participants will administer 450 volts in the absence of authority goes as follows. The finely graded levels of shock are a slippery slope, in which the best reason to give the next higher level of shock is that a slightly lesser shock has just been given. If the next level of shock is wrong, there must be something wrong with the previous level of shock already delivered. But if there is nothing wrong with giving the immediately preceding level of shock, the next level, only 15 volts higher, cannot be wrong either. If 300 volts was OK, how can 315 volts be wrong? But if 315 volts is wrong, how could 300 volts have been right? Having already given a number of shocks, participants feel a need to justify themselves and to preserve their self-image as decent people. The justification of the previous shock then rationalizes the next level of shock.

It is important to note that in Milgram's studies the dependent variable is radicalization in behavior, not in thoughts or feelings. The latter were not measured, and there is no way of knowing whether increasing shock levels were associated with changes in perception of and attitude toward the victim. Postexperimental interviews with participants found many of them in considerable distress, anxious about the victim's condition (yet apparently unable to translate that anxiety into opposing the experimenter or checking on the victim). Far from being hostile toward the person they might have killed, they are relieved to greet the actor warmly as the experimenter reveals the plot. In this study at least, escalating harm was unrelated to prejudice.

What had started as innocuous grew little by little into dangerous and extreme, but when and how this radicalization happened was obscured from the "teachers." Each increment in action was an easy step from the previous action. Having found a way to rationalize their last action, the teachers faced a choice of either condemning both their previous action and themselves or finding justification for an act hardly different from the last. Most kept going.

It is easy for observers to feel indignation at such apparent self-delusion and lack of moral compass. In fact, when Milgram asked psychologists, psychiatrists, and psychology graduate students what percentage of people they thought would proceed to the highest level of shock under the conditions of his experiment, these experts in human psychology judged on average that less than 1 percent would do so—only a few disturbed and deviant individuals. The difference between the expert assessment (1 percent) and the reality of two out of every three people (62 percent) is evidence that situations can have power that is not obvious to observers.

Like Adrian Michailov, Milgram's participants were free from hostility toward those whom they attacked. Like Michailov, they were unhappy about having to do as they were told. But like Michailov, they nevertheless proceeded to commit progressively more violent acts because a person of authority told them to do so and because the slippery slope of closely graded violent behaviors made it hard to find a place to stop.

Terrorist groups count on the power of the slippery slope in bringing new members to violence gradually. Testing recruits for obedience, testing to find undercover government agents, and desensitization to violence—these are accomplished together in slow escalation of assignments to newcomers. Here is Della Porta's description of a slippery slope.

> Once having joined an underground group, the activists would be required to participate at increasingly demanding levels of activity, whether in terms of the risk or the time involved. They usually began their careers in the underground by distributing leaflets or renting an apartment for

the group. The longer they remained underground, the more likely they were to end up participating in robberies and assassinations.[2]

The power of the slippery slope is that it can move individuals to opinions and actions that are in no way anticipated at the first step. This power necessarily limits any attempt to understand radicalization in terms of rational choice: there are terrorists who, looking back, cannot find any point at which they decided to become a terrorist. One thing led to another in a way that seems, in retrospect, inevitable. Michailov could not see the end of the road when he took his first steps into political thought and action, and neither could the young American jihadist we now turn to.

Slippery Slope to Jihad: Omar Hammami

His name came to public awareness in a blaze of headlines: "Jihadist Next Door"; "Alabama Boy Turned Shabab Leader in Somalia"; "Americans Assassinating Americans"; "A Converted American Who Joined al Qaeda." His face, his European features, and his American English became recognizable from YouTube and news videos in which he attacked U.S. policies and glorified Muslim fighters in Somalia. His path from Alabama to al Shabab was a slow progression in radicalization.

Omar's father was a Syrian immigrant to the United States who married a Christian woman in Alabama. Omar was baptized a Christian, but in high school (1999) he visited his father's family in Syria and became enchanted with the culture and the people. Back home he began to attend his father's mosque and became a Muslim, losing both his blond girlfriend and some of the status that had made him president of his sophomore class. In 2000, before the 9/11 attacks, he defended Osama bin Laden to high school classmates as a freedom fighter.

Scoring in the ninety-third percentile on the ACT as a junior, Omar skipped his senior year to enter the University of Southern Alabama. After the 9/11 attacks he faced new questions about Islam and began to study his religion more seriously. On campus he encountered the fundamentalist Salafi Islam that aims for a lifestyle in imitation of the prophet Mohammed. From the Salafi perspective, politics is a worldly distraction from Islamic practice, and killing civilians—as al Qaeda did

---

2. Della Porta, D. (1995). *Social movements, political violence, and the state: A comparative analysis of Italy and Germany*. Cambridge, UK: Cambridge University Press, p. 179.

on 9/11—is forbidden by the Koran. (As noted in chapter 1, Osama bin Laden's militant version of Islam engages only a minority of Salafis.)

In December 2002 Omar dropped out of college, complaining about the campus mixing of men and women that is forbidden in Salafi Islam. This was a significant step away from the secular American dream of self-advancement through education. Soon he took another step away from home by following a high school friend and fellow convert to Islam, Bernie Culveyhouse, to Toronto. They found Toronto Muslims more opposed to the U.S. war in Iraq than U.S. Muslims. In 2004 Omar was visiting an Islamic bookstore when someone asked him to "pray for the people of Fallujah," where U.S. troops were occupying the city for a second time.

This request initiated a political awakening that led Omar to abandon his Salafi distancing from political events. After the battle of Fallujah, he became consumed with events in Iraq and Afghanistan. Later, in a 2009 e-mail interview, he explained his sudden political interest as follows: "I was finding it difficult to reconcile between having Americans attacking my brothers, at home and abroad, while I was supposed to remain completely neutral, without getting involved."[3]

Omar began scouring the Internet for more information about events in the Muslim world. He was particularly impressed with a video documentary of Amir Khattab, a legendary jihadist who fought against the Russians in Chechnya. Khattab died a martyr, killed by Russian security forces with a poisoned letter. At this time Omar still disapproved of how al Qaeda attacked civilians and found the insurgency in Iraq too secular. He saw the answer to Muslim problems in a purer lifestyle, a personal jihad that would make the world better from the ground up.

In 2005 Omar married a Somali refugee, the sister of Culveyhouse's new wife. He and Culveyhouse moved their families to Egypt with the hope of studying Islam at Al-Azhar University. They found a place to live in Alexandria, but this Muslim metropolis seemed to them disappointingly secular. When their applications to Al-Azhar failed, Culveyhouse and his family left Alexandria to return to the United States. Omar felt betrayed and deserted by his friend—a loss of connection with implications that are the focus of chapter 7.

From Egypt Omar closely followed the news of a growing conflict for control of his wife's country, Somalia. In April 2006 he met another

3. Elliott, A. (2010). The jihadist next door. *New York Times*, January 27. Available at http://www.nytimes.com/2010/01/31/magazine/31Jihadist-t.html.

U.S. convert to Islam, Daniel Maldonado; together they began attending underground mosques and listening to radical imams. In June 2006 the Islamic Courts Union took control of Mogadishu, but by July Ethiopian (Christian) troops supported by the United States began moving into Somalia. By August 2006 Omar and Maldonado were using the Internet to write passionate calls for action against "the infidel invasion" of Muslim Somalia. In his 2009 e-mail interview, Omar looked back to say that he felt at this time that "*jihad* had become an obligation upon me."

On November 6, 2006, he told his mother, who was visiting him in Egypt, that he was going to look for a job in Dubai. Instead, he went to Somalia. He called his wife and said he was in Somalia to visit her family; later, he told his wife and parents that he was stuck in Somalia because someone had stolen his passport. In December 2006 Ethiopian troops took Mogadishu, and Omar joined al Shabab, an Islamic and nationalist militant group that aimed to force the Ethiopians out of Somalia.

By 2007 Omar had become a leader in al Shabab. As Abu Mansoor al-Amriki, he appeared in an al Jazeera interview with a scarf over his lower face to hide his identity. In March 2008, he appeared in a new video, leading al Shabab attacks in the field. In this video he appears and talks to the camera with his face uncovered: "It makes more of a statement if my face is uncovered."

This brief history of "The Jihadist Next Door"[4] shows how a slippery slope of gradual increases in commitment can produce a trajectory of radicalization. Omar enjoyed visiting Syria, converted to Islam, moved to a university environment and a Salafi form of Islam that discourages politics and attacks on civilians, dropped out of his university, moved from Alabama to Toronto, adopted an anti-war sentiment that identified with Muslims dying in Iraq and Afghanistan, moved to Egypt, lost his connection with Culveyhouse, joined Maldonado in urging action against invasion of Somalia, and finally moved to Somalia and became himself a militant and finally a leader within al Shabab. With every move to a new place, Omar moved on to new friends and more extreme opinions. Salafi religiosity kept him away from politics and violence for a while, but seeing U.S. troops in Muslim countries brought increased sympathy for Muslims he saw as victims of the war on terrorism (see chapter 2). Increased identification with Muslim victims broke

---

4. Ibid.

through his Salafi inhibitions and moved him to a more political and radicalized Islam.

It is important to notice that he reached the peak of opinion radicalization with his Internet postings urging action against the infidel invasion of Somalia, but these postings left him still far short of full commitment to radical action. He kept open a door to disengagement with the stories he told to his wife and parents, first about visiting his wife's family, then about a lost passport. Even after joining al Shabab, he masked his face for his first video, preserving some chance of exit. Finally, with the unmasked interview, he reached the peak of final and public commitment to al Shabab and its violence.

For Omar Hammami, radicalization occurred slowly with moves to new places and new comrades, but even after reaching the most extreme opinion—arguing openly for jihad on the Internet—his radicalization in action had barely begun. Even after going to Somalia, his steps toward radical action were slow and halting, with exit possibilities maintained until the unmasked interview. From a dissonance-theory perspective, the more public the commitment is, the greater is the need for justifying this commitment with new and increased commitments. The maximum of Omar's opinion commitment was Internet posting; the maximum of his action commitment was the unmasked interview. Both opinion and action show the incremental radicalization we have described as a slippery slope.

Groups, and perhaps mass publics as well, can show slippery-slope progression to radicalization. Trajectories of radicalization at these levels are described in later chapters.

Looking Further

Arendt, H. (1965). *Eichmann in Jerusalem: A report on the banality of evil.* New York: Viking Press.

Elliott, A. (2010). The jihadist next door. *New York Times Magazine*, January 27. Available at http://www.nytimes.com/2010/01/31/magazine/31Jihadist-t.html. Accessed March 5, 2010.

Milgram, S. (1974). *Obedience to authority: An experimental view.* New York: Harper & Row.

Sabini, J. (1995). *Social psychology* (2nd ed.). New York: Norton. Chapter 2, Social influence; Chapter 16, Attitudes and attitude change.

CHAPTER FIVE

Love

Love for someone already radicalized can move an individual toward radicalization.

Sophia Perovskaya—From Love to Violence

Unlike Andrei Zhelyabov, Sophia (Sonia) Perovskaya was born into the highest ranks of Russian nobility. Her father, Lev Perovskij, was governor of St. Petersburg, and among her relatives were Count Razumovski, the husband of Czarina Elizabeth II, and Vassili Perovskij, the governor of Orenburg. From a young age she had been trained by foreign tutors in European languages, sciences, and the arts and read classic literature extensively. Despite noble roots and her father's high position, the family lived relatively modestly: Lev Perovskij liked to gamble, and he kept a mistress.

Neither Sonia nor her mother Varvara saw much value in material wealth. Sonia preferred simple, dark dresses and disliked formal occasions for which fancy clothes, hairstyles, and manners had to be put on. When Sonia was fourteen years old, Czar Alexander II suffered an assassination attempt in St. Petersburg. He escaped unharmed because a peasant pushed the shooter's hand, causing him to miss his target. As governor, Lev Perovskij was immediately demoted for having inadequately organized city security and police services. His credits were stopped, and his new salary was a fraction of the original. The family could no longer afford their apartment in the city, and Varvara with the children moved to their Crimean estate in Kilburun, while Lev Perovskij stayed with relatives in St. Petersburg.

In Crimea Sonia was away from her father's keen eyes. Here she could read political literature procured by her older brother Vassilij, who came to visit with the family during a two-month suspension from his university studies for participating in student protests. Sonia and her siblings enjoyed life in the south, but Lev Perovskij's lavish lifestyle resulted in ever-larger debts and a threat of bankruptcy. The Crimean estate in Kilburun had to be sold to cover the debts. The Perovskij family reunited in St. Petersburg after more than a year—but in a much smaller apartment than the one they had during Lev's tenure as governor.

That fall, sixteen-year-old Sonia started Alarchin women's school, specializing in sciences and nursing. Here she met many women whose political views had already taken a nationalistic, democratic direction. These young women dreamed of contributing to the welfare of the peasants by becoming teachers and doctors and working in remote villages for little pay. They shared their illegal books with Sonia and took her to political and literary discussions. Sonia's early lack of interest in the vain pursuits of beauty and romantic attachments became even more pronounced as she started to wear men's clothing to avoid attention on the streets when she returned after late study sessions.

Lev Perovskij, rarely attentive to his children and their interests, nevertheless noticed the marked change in Sonia's appearance and her focus on political issues and demanded that she withdraw from the school and stop all contact with her new friends. Instead, Sonia left home, at age sixteen, after only a brief conversation with her mother and with nothing except the clothes she was wearing. There is no indication she ever saw her father again. She moved in with friends from school, who hid her from the police that her father's powerful contacts sent to look for her.

At this young age Sonia, highly intelligent and determined, saw no place for herself in the traditional role of a wife and a mother and thus saw no need to put up with the traditional despotism of her father. Her mother, on the other hand, suffered from Sonia's disappearance, became physically ill, and went to the homes of Sonia's friends to beg them to connect her with her missing daughter. Sonia's friends offered only polite refusals. On the grand path to alleviating suffering in Russia, one mother's suffering was apparently not worth alleviating. Her mother was perhaps the first victim of Sonia's political activity.

Homeless and penniless, Sonia lived in student communes where Spartan conditions and minimal food (mostly vegetarian, with lots of black tea) accompanied heavy political discussion deep into the night. The money came from group members, some with help from their parents, some with jobs as tutors, and a few with government stipends. As members of the commune were arrested, new ones joined the group; and as some communes closed, new ones formed.

Sonia was arrested as part of a group suspected of antigovernment action; charges against the group were later dropped, and they were released. However, because of the arrest, she was denied a diploma upon graduation from Alarchin. As a member of the famous Tchaikovsky (no relation to the composer) activist circle, Sonia became heavily involved in distribution of propagandistic literature published abroad. She was responsible for interaction with the contrabandists and for communication with the "target audiences."

Small and unassuming, wearing plain clothes, with her hair pulled neatly back into a braid, Sonia had a gift for relating easily with people of any background. This ability later became invaluable in her terrorist career, when her underground work required her to act quickly and believably to avoid capture. In 1872, a nineteen-year-old Sonia, armed with her nursing and teaching training, headed "into the people" with other students, attempting to carry democratic ideas to the peasants. Walking from one village to another she stayed in the homes of those who extended hospitality in exchange for her nursing services or tutoring, all the while attempting through conversation or literature to convince people of the ideas she so believed in.

Like many others who ventured "into the people," Sonia did not have much success in mobilizing the peasants. Instead, it appears from her letters at that time that she became more and more involved in the mission of making peasants' lives better, having seen the horrible conditions in which they lived. In 1873 she received a teacher's diploma in a provincial town where she did not have a criminal record and returned to St. Petersburg—back to her political activities as a part of the Tchaikovsky circle.

In 1874 she was again arrested for political activity and put in the Petropavlovsky Tower (Peter and Paul's Fortress). Her father, through his connections, had her removed and placed instead under house arrest on her mother's family property in Primorskoe, Crimea. Not wasting any time while under house arrest in Crimea, Sonia worked as a doctor's assistant and studied medicine, later assisting with the wounded in the Russo-Turkish War.

In 1877 a St. Petersburg judicial order brought her back for trial. This was the famous Trial of 193 in which 193 individuals were charged with political activity aiming to undermine the government. The trial lasted four months. The best lawyers, educated in the age of Czar Alexander II's generous educational reforms, defended the prisoners pro bono.

Most of the prisoners, including Sonia, were acquitted. In the course of the trial, press coverage demonstrated, in florid detail, the inadequacies of the judicial system, while the defendants' stories colorfully depicted the unfairness and cruelty of police and prisons. The defendants, who until then had often acted alone or as part of a small independent group, had an opportunity to meet new people and bond with them over a common grievance.

It was at this trial that Sonia met Andrei Zhelyabov (see chapter 2). Her activism in the following years became more effective and her ideology more focused. The Tchaikovsky circle, having failed to inspire peasant revolt, had dissolved. But Sonya was now a part of a much more structured and goal-oriented organization: Land and Freedom (*Zemlya I Volya*).

The Move toward Violence

The lack of political will among the peasants and their fear of persecution inspired Zhelyabov along with some members of Land and Freedom to propose political terrorism as the only way to help the peasants. They believed that, if the czar and his family were eliminated, peasants would join with the students in demanding democracy and adequate land endowment from the government.

Zhelyabov advocated "relentless, unending political terror" as the only way to crack the monolith of the monarchy and open a possibility of social change. His stance began instead to cause a rift in his own party. A sizable proportion of Land and Freedom, represented by Plechanov, refused to consider using violence to advance their goals. Among those opposing violence was Sonia Perovskaya.

Realizing that a confrontation between the two factions was inevitable, Zhelyabov and a dozen other notable advocates of terrorism met in secret in the small town of Lipetsk to prepare their presentation to the larger Land and Freedom party where they hoped to sway still undecided members to their side. They prepared arguments and speeches.

They made their case to the general assembly in Voronezh some days later. Plechanov argued against violence, and Sonia vocally sided with him. However, she could not help being in awe of Zhelyabov, with his great presence, imposing physique, and charismatic speeches.

At the Voronezh meeting he began to spend a lot of time alone with her, taking her on boat rides and walks in the woods. Realizing her importance to the group, her moral authority and leadership, he tried to convince her that violence was absolutely necessary to finish the important work that they had started together, that without violence all the suffering of comrades imprisoned and tortured would have been in vain. Nevertheless, Sonia's public stand was that "revolutionaries must not consider themselves above the laws of humanity. Our exceptional position should not cloud our heads. First and foremost we are humans."[1]

It was rare for Zhelyabov to find himself unable to convince someone despite his best efforts. He had always enjoyed particular success with female audiences, his charm and good looks aiding his arguments. Sonia's resistance must have intrigued him and made him want to figure out this plain, petite, blue-eyed comrade.

She, who always despised men, was in turn taken by Andrei's charisma and by the physical strength that he readily demonstrated to his friends. Once, he bent a metal rod with his bare hands; another time, he lifted a carriage with passengers off the ground, causing the horse to stop, by lifting the hind bar. Both Sonia and Andrei kept journals, but they avoided discussing personal details in writing. Their personal relationship that began in Voronezh can only be traced through memoirs of others who witnessed it. It seems these two individuals—independent, intelligent, and decisive—recognized one another as kindred spirits.

Meanwhile, at the meeting, the competing arguments were becoming redundant, and it was increasingly clear that no consensus would be reached at Voronezh. Sonia pleaded for the group to stay together in the name of the great work they had accomplished until now. But the split was inevitable. The terrorists organized into People's Will, while the nonviolent activists formed Black Repartition—the name emphasizing their goal of a fair distribution of black (fertile) land.

---

1. Available at http://socialist.memo.ru/firstpub/y06/insarov.htm. Accessed April 27, 2016.

At first Sonia worked with both groups. But soon she found out that a plan for a lethal attack on the czar and his family was under way, and Zhelyabov was among those at the heart of the plan. Her growing interest in Zhelyabov required that she became involved in any activity that he was a part of.

She had spent her youth denying herself all things she deemed vain and extravagant, instead pursuing intellectual and political goals. Zhelyabov, embodying the ideal she had cherished in her mind—an educated, intelligent, ambitious, liberated peasant—entered her heart. Shortly after she had publicly denounced violence in pursuit of nationalist goals, she became a critical part of a complex plan designed to blow up the train carrying the czar from his Crimean vacation back to St. Petersburg.

From this point until they stood side by side on the gallows, Zhelyabov and Perovskaya became masterminds and executives of People's Will's terrorism. Their romantic relationship became deeper as time went by. In their last year of life, they rented a flat together and lived as husband and wife. Uncompromising even with her sick and pleading mother, Sonia stepped over her convictions to be next to Andrei on the dangerous and ultimately lethal path that he chose.

Radicalization for Love

The prevalence of friends, lovers, and relatives among those recruited to terrorism has made personal relationships an important part of recent theorizing about terrorism, perhaps because it recovers the "known associates" approach to criminal investigation. As with criminal gangs, individuals are recruited to a terrorist group via personal connections with existing members. No terrorist wants to try to recruit someone who might betray the terrorists to the authorities. In practice, this means recruiting from the network of friends, lovers, and family. Trust may determine the network within which radicals and terrorists recruit, but love often determines who will join.

The pull of romantic and comradely love can be as strong as politics in moving individuals into an underground group. When Della Porta asked about his motivations for going underground, a member of the Italian Red Brigades made this reply: "There are many things I cannot explain by analyzing the political situation . . . as far as I am concerned it was up to emotional feelings, of passions for the people I shared my life with."[2]

German militants of the Red Army Faction were also drawn into the underground by devotion to friends. "There is widespread agreement among researchers that 'most terrorists . . . ultimately became members of [German] terrorist organizations through personal connections with people or relatives associated with appropriate political initiatives, communes, self-supporting organizations, or committees—the number of couples and brothers and sisters was astonishingly high."[3]

Devotion to comrades can lead a clique of friends to join a terrorist group together. According to Della Porta, "block recruitment" occurred for both the Red Brigades and the Red Army Faction. A small political group would hold a meeting, and if the vote favored joining the underground, all would join together.

After an individual joins a radical group, love for friends and comrades in the group is likely to increase further as common goals and common threats increase group cohesion. Interviews with thirty long-term members of Sinn Fein led Robert White to conclude that group solidarity, along with hope of making a difference for the group and its cause, were the two strongest forces holding militants together in the face of arrests and Loyalist attacks. Thus devotion to comrades is not only a force for joining a radical group; it is equally a barrier to leaving the group.

White quotes one Republican as follows: "There's times I've said to myself, 'Why? You're mad in the head, like'. But . . . I just can't turn my back on it. . . . there's too many of my friends in jail, there's too many of my mates given their lives, and I've walked behind—I've walked behind too many funerals to turn my back on it now."[4]

"The Smiling Terrorist"

Amrozi bin Nurhasyim was born in 1962 in Java, an island of 130 million people that is the heart of the island-chain nation of Indonesia. He

---

2. Della Porta, D. (1995). *Social movements, political violence, and the state: A comparative analysis of Italy and Germany*. Cambridge, UK: Cambridge University Press, p. 68.
3. Ibid., p.168, translating Wasmund, 1986, p. 204.
4. White, R. W. (1988). Commitment, efficacy, and personal sacrifice among Irish republicans. *Journal of Political and Military Sociology* 16: 77–90.

was the fifth of thirteen children born to Nur Hasyim in Tenggulun, a village of about 2000 people.

Nur Hasyim was a strict disciplinarian and followed a Wahhabist version of Islam more stringent than the Islam of many of his neighbors. As a youth he had paid his own way through a religious high school. He had fought in the struggle for independence, in which his brother was killed by Dutch soldiers. He was for many years a leader of his village, and he tried to raise his children to be champions of Islam.

Amrozi was a spectacular failure of his father's efforts. His mother's favorite as a boy, with a boyish grin that made others' smiles seem half-hearted, Amrozi was not interested in either schoolwork or the Koran. He was interested instead in motorbikes, the more powerful the better, and in flirting with local girls. He stole from his family objects he could sell for cash. He played pranks on schoolmates and teachers alike. His only redeeming value was that he could fix anything from a cell phone to a motorcycle. He was a fun-loving disgrace to his whole family.

After dropping out of high school, Amrozi headed off to Malaysia in search of work. He got a construction job, using explosives to blast away hillsides to make roads. After six months, he returned to his village and appeared ready to settle down. Now twenty-three years old, he married a local girl and returned to high school. The marriage produced a daughter but lasted only two years; Amrozi dropped out of school a second time and resumed his scapegrace ways. Perhaps the only thing he took from his father's religiosity was the idea that Javanese traditions of decorating and venerating graves are a kind of Islamic heresy. When bored, Amrozi would dig up graves, burn grave decorations, and even defecate on the grave cloths.

After a brief stint in jail for vandalizing graves, he tried again to settle down. He married a second time, but again the marriage lasted only two years. His second wife complained that he was like a child, always out running around. A police report years later described Amrozi as below average in intelligence, impulsive, adventurous—an immature personality easily influenced by others. The *other* with the influence to make this self-centered young man a terrorist was his brother, Ali Gufron, also known as Muklas.

Two years older than Amrozi, Muklas was a star student and a devout Muslim. He had persuaded his father to send him 125 miles away to the Ngruki boarding school, a magnet for young Indonesians opposed to the nationalist version of Islam promulgated by the Indonesian government. The Ngruki directors, Abu Bakar Bashir and Abdullah Sungkar, preached that laws made by men were illegitimate: Muslims should live by Islamic law alone. Muklas spent six years at Ngruki, two years as student and four more years as instructor. When the directors evaded prison by moving to Malaysia, Muklas followed them.

From Malaysia, Sungkar and Bashir decided to send some of their disciples to join in the war against the Soviets in Afghanistan. Muklas was among the first to volunteer, and his small contingent in 1985 was the beginning of a stream of about 250 Indonesians who would share the harsh life, rigorous training, and combat experience of Afghanistan. Muklas participated in at least one engagement led by Osama bin Laden, whose al Qaeda organization began as a base of support for Muslims from many countries who came to Afghanistan to wage jihad against the Soviets.

After the Russian defeat, the Indonesian "Afghans" returned home with new skills, new networks of trust, and new confidence in the power of jihad. They aimed to replace the authoritarian government of Indonesia with a pure Islamic state, and they turned to a campaign of terrorism to make this happen. Their most deadly attack was in the tourist district of the Indonesian island of Bali, on October 12, 2002. Three bombs killed 202 people, including 38 Indonesians and 152 foreign nationals (including 88 Australians).

Muklas directed the Bali attack. After his years in Pakistan and Afghanistan, Muklas had returned to Malaysia and, at the request of Sungkar and Bashir, organized a new Islamic boarding school (madrassa). Luqmanul Hakiem was to be a new Ngruki, for Indonesians living in Malaysia. While he was building Luqmanul Hakiem, Muklas received a visit from Amrozi. Possibly for security reasons, Muklas sent his brother away, and Amrozi again found work in construction in Malaysia. Two years later, Amrozi returned—and this time Muklas let him stay at the school, where Amrozi made himself useful helping the children and building whatever was needed.

Amrozi did not adopt a radical version of Islam because he was intellectually persuaded, and did not join in violence against infidels and apostates because he had suffered himself from those targeted. He joined in the life and work of the brother he admired in order to be with his brother, and he basked in brotherly approval when he later joined Muklas and their youngest brother, Ali Imron, in the campaign of terrorism that produced the Bali attacks.

Here is Sally Neighbour's summary of Amrozi's path to terrorism:

"It was Mas [brother] Muklas who raised my awareness to fight the injustice toward Islam." The effort that went into Amrozi's transformation would prompt Muklas to boast with a chuckle: "Thank God, with endless patience, bit by bit, to this day, he's also in the league of praiseworthy terrorists."[5]

Captured soon after the Bali bombs exploded (he bought the van for the bomb from a seller who knew him!), Amrozi proudly confessed his role in the plot. Talking and joking with the police, he soon earned headlines as "The Smiling Terrorist."

Amrozi and his brother Muklas were executed by firing squad on November 9, 2008.

Looking Further

Della Porta, D. (1995). *Social movements, political violence, and the state: A comparative analysis of Italy and Germany*. Cambridge, UK: Cambridge University Press.

Neighbour, S. (2005). *In the shadow of swords: On the trail of terrorism from Afghanistan to Australia*. New York: Harper Collins.

Ressa, M. A. (2003). *Seeds of terror: An eyewitness account of al-Qaeda's newest center of operations in Southeast Asia*. New York: Free Press.

Долгий В. Г. (1974). *Порог: Повесть о Софье Перовской*. Москва: Молодая гвардия. [Dolgij, V. G. (1974). *The threshold: A novel about Sophia Perovskaya*. Moscow: Molodaya Gvardia.]

---

5. Elegant, S. (2002). The family behind the bombings. *Time*, November 25.
    Available at http://content.time.com/time/world/article/0,8599,2047641,00.html.

CHAPTER SIX

Risk and Status

The attractions of risk taking and status can move individuals,
especially young males, to radical political action.

In Search of Adventure

Alexander Barannikov made a striking appearance: athletic, tall, grace-ful, with a dark complexion that he inherited from his Persian mother. His childhood friend was Michailov, the organizer of the Executive Committee of People's Will and a mastermind behind their most daring terrorist acts. During their summer breaks from school (they attended schools in different towns), they spent time together. Michailov introduced Barannikov to a world of underground literature and student circles, and Barannikov embraced it with a passion. His passion was not for the ideas he found in the literature or for the selfless goals of the student circles. Barannikov was not particularly taken with peasants' problems or with the socialist agenda. Instead, he was attracted to the danger of participating in activities that were forbidden, that could result in arrest. As his comrade Tyrkov recalls him,

> Barannikov was a person of a special kind . . . . he loved life, but only such life that would give him powerful experiences. When proclamations or some other underground literature would turn up in his

pocket, he tried to get rid of them as soon as possible and asked others to distribute them. This activity seemed to him too boring. But he was ready to be everywhere there was danger. His feelings about danger were simple, as if it were an ordinary thing, and he did not draw attention to his disregard for it. Bravery and courage comprised his inborn character.[1]

Barannikov attended a military academy at the insistence of his family. His father and older brother were military men, and he was to continue the tradition. However, he found the academy, with its endless drills, extremely routine and boring. A future in the military looked similarly bleak to a young man without connections. He would likely be sent to a remote town with no possibility to distinguish himself. In contrast, Michailov painted to him pictures of revolutionary life that included all that Barannikov wanted: danger, thrill, unpredictability, a chance to make history. Barannikov decided to leave the military and become a revolutionary.

To sever his ties with the military academy Barannikov faked suicide: he left his clothes with a suicide note on the riverbank. Not by accident, this manner of faked suicide closely resembles that of a main character of Chernyshevsky's *What's to Be Done?*—an inspirational novel for many students. Starting a new life as a radical, Barannikov followed in the footsteps of a radical character, pretending that he killed himself in order to be reborn.

Although Barannikov's close ties to Michailov kept him inside radical politics and the People's Will, his activities depended little on the movement's ideology. Like most young radicals, he went "into the people": working menial jobs, walking from village to village, sleeping on the side of the road, and eating "what God sent." For the *narodniki*, those students who went "into the people," this life was the means to an end: to spread propaganda and to radicalize the peasants by teaching them the fundamentals of socialist ideas. But Barannikov did not like to talk. Propaganda, discussions, and speeches were difficult and boring for him. That was not what he left his old life for! He yearned

---

1. Тырков, А. В. (n.d.). *К событию 1 марта 1881 года «Народная воля» и «Черный передел»: Воспоминания участников революционного движения в Петербурге в 1879–1882 гг.* [Tyrkov, A. V. (n.d.). *About the events of March 1, 1881 in People's Will and Black Repartition: Memoirs of participants in the revolutionary movement in Petersburg in 1879–1882,* p. 272.] Available at http://narovol.ru/Person/barannikov.htm.

for new experiences, for danger. For him the means was the goal: the nomadic life, the strain of physical labor, the novelty of every day.

In a letter to his relatives he expressed his disdain for their routine lives in comfortable, predictable settings.

> The very thought that I could lead my life the way you lead yours horrifies me. No, happiness lies not in quietness but in struggle; it does not come unsolicited, one must catch it, and blessed is he who caught it!!![2]

After his "going into the people," Barannikov suddenly decided to leave Russia for Chernogoria (Montenegro) to participate in the war against Turkish occupation raging there. His motivation was apparently the same as that for his participation in activism: he sought new and exciting experiences. For about six months Barannikov was a guerilla fighter in the mountains of Chernogoria; then he returned to St. Petersburg. His arrival coincided with a wave of student demonstrations, some of them in the wake of Vera Zazulich's attempted assassination of General Trepov. Arrests and subsequent public trials followed one after another. Newspapers dedicated front pages to defendants' speeches.

In this highly charged atmosphere Barannikov felt himself to be at the right place at the right time. To avenge harsh sentences of their comrades, People's Will planned assassinations of high-ranking officials; Barannikov was a part of several of these plots. One resulted in the assassination of General Mezentsev, chief of the Third Section of police with responsibility for investigating political crimes. The general himself was not notorious for excessive cruelty, but he represented the division of the government that was the direct enemy of People's Will and so was deemed a useful target of terrorism.

As Mezentsev was taking an evening walk with a friend, a young man came from a dark alley and stabbed the general in the stomach before the eyes of shocked pedestrians. The general's friend, who, like the general, was an older man and unarmed, screamed and chased the attacker, striking at him with an umbrella. A shot in the air stopped the pursuit. The terrorist lookout who fired the warning shot, described by onlookers as young and handsome, was Barannikov. He galloped away from the scene astride a beautiful horse. The daring nature of this

---

2. Фигнер, В. Н. (1935). *Народоволец А.Баранников в его письмах*. Изд-во Всесоюзного общества политкаторжан и ссыльно-поселенцев. [Figner, V. N. (1935). *People's Will member Barannikov in his letters*. Soviet Society of Political Prisoners and Exiles Press.] Available at http://narovol.narod.ru/art/lit/bar1.htm.

murder occurring in the center of the capital city on a popular boulevard inspired multiple recapitulations and speculations in the press. Soon young men seeking easy fame were telling their friends in secret that they were in fact the horseman in the assassination. Arrests followed, but the true identity of the terrorists was not discovered until years later.

Barannikov himself was never one to boast about his adventures. He mentioned his time in Chernogoria only briefly in a letter, and aside from that nobody recalled personal accounts of this time in his life. He pursued experiences, their thrill, danger, novelty, for their own sake, not for fame. He later said of himself,

> ... I possess an ability to unmistakably gauge the importance, gravity, loveliness of every minute. When I felt that a happy moment approached I always said to myself, "This is life, use it; pull everything that's great out of it; don't miss anything, or life will pass and not come back."[3]

Barannikov's famous terrorist act inspired another young man to join the ranks of terrorists. Whereas Barannikov sought thrill and adventure, Leon Mirsky was primarily interested in fame.

Climbing the Social Ladder

Mirsky was a son of a Polish nobleman, refined, vain, and full of himself. He felt challenged when he heard his girlfriend admire the audacity and bravery of the assassins who had killed General Mezentsev. He was already a member of student activist circles but could boast of no daring escapades. It was clear to him that he required the fame and admiration that the unknown horseman received following the assassination of General Mezentsev. With that determination he sought an audience with Michailov, the head of the People's Will Executive Committee. At the meeting, Mirsky outlined a plan for an assassination; his selected target was Police Chief General Drenteln. In his pitch to Michailov, Mirsky insisted that he be the only party in the assassination; the fame was to be his alone, not to be shared with anyone. Michailov did not raise any objections.

On the day of the assassination Mirsky rented an English racehorse, dressed elaborately in beautiful clothes, and went riding along the path

---

3. Ibid.

of General Drenteln's usual route. He looked so magnificent astride his beautiful horse that women turned their lorgnettes to gaze at him. As Drenteln's carriage made its way along the street, Mirsky sped up. His horse overtook the carriage, and Mirsky turned around. To the shock of the bystanders, he whipped a gun out of his clothes and shot at the man in the carriage! After a second Mirsky realized that he had missed his target and fired again, and again missed. Then he fled the scene. Turning the corner, he dismounted and handed the reins of his horse to an idle policeman calmly saying, "My good man, do hold on to my horse for me as I need to get a change of clothes." Mirsky's arrogance and noble appearance put the policeman in a compliant mood. When the authorities arrived, the policeman was still holding the horse's reins, and Mirsky was long gone.

Unlike his inspiration Barannikov, however, Mirsky was unable to contain himself: he told everyone who would listen that he was the attempted assassin. Soon the Third Section of police began receiving reports that a certain young man was telling in convincing detail that he was the criminal they were looking for. Mirsky was arrested. His manner at the arrest and during his initial stay in jail was cavalier. He requested a tailcoat for his court appearance. Guards, laughing, brought it to him; they knew that he would not be using it for years.

Only a few weeks later, Mirsky was already betraying his comrades from People's Will and writing humble petitions to the czar. His loyalty to the radical movement evaporated completely; there is even evidence he was recruited to serve as an informant for the prison authorities. When his trial date arrived some two years after his arrest, Mirsky, sick with scurvy, a shadow of his former glamorous self, looked ridiculous in the tailcoat over his worn, baggy pants. Instead of the expected death sentence, which would bring some measure of the fame that he had sought, he was committed to life in prison. The czar wrote across Mirsky's police file a laconic summary: "Acted under the influence of babes and literary types."[4]

The Allure of Risk and Status

Our two Russian examples feature two kinds of motive for radical political action. Barannikov liked the thrill of physical risk taking. Mirsky

---

4. Радзинский, Э. С. (2007). *Александр II: жизнь и смерть*. Москва: АСТ.
   [Radzinskij, E. (2007). *Alexander II: Life and death*. Moscow: АСТ, p. 345.]

sought status, especially in the eyes of women. It is easy to imagine that status seeking and risk taking are unrelated motives. Were not Barannikov and Mirsky looking for very different kinds of reward? But in fact these two kinds of motive are often linked in experience and can be linked in theory as well.

To some, the idea of risking life or freedom, or engaging in violence, for thrill and status may seem preposterous: a seemingly trivial gain for a potentially great loss. But to a certain kind of person, the gain may not seem trivial, and the loss may not seem threatening. A young African American growing up in a run-down neighborhood of Detroit, a son of illegal immigrants from Mexico on the streets of Los Angeles, a rural runaway who never finished high school—these young men can find it natural to engage in risk taking and violence just for fun, for "homeboys'" respect, for admiration in the eyes of the girls. Two important questions can be raised: first, is it true that the disenfranchised, the marginalized, the young, and the restless are more likely to engage in violence and risk taking for thrill and status? And, a second question: if this is so, then why?

The answer to the first question is a simple "yes." Research in both criminology and psychology finds that involvement in risk taking and violence is much more prevalent among young men than in any other demographic group. This pattern obtains not just in the United States but in every country for which data are available. Here we will make the case with U.S. data.

Disproportionate involvement in risk taking and status seeking is particularly true of those young men who come from disadvantaged family backgrounds, have lower IQ levels, are of lower socioeconomic status, and who therefore have less opportunity to succeed in society along a traditional career path. These young men are more likely to be involved in gang activity, violent crime, drugs, and other high-risk behavior.

Margo Wilson and Martin Daly analyzed all violent homicides committed in the city of Detroit in one year (1972). They found that the majority of crimes were committed in the course of "social conflict" where status was at stake. Participants in these homicides (both victims and perpetrators) were predominantly young males, unemployed and single. The researchers analyzed each case and found that more than half were what criminologists call "trivial altercations," including "escalated showing-off disputes." Here is an example that the researchers offered of such a conflict resulting in homicide.

Case 121: Victim (male, age 19), offender (male, age 23) and others had been drinking together. Victim was a boxer and was talking about his fights. Offender showed off with his nightstick by placing it between the victim's legs and lifting him in the air. Victim was embarrassed and asked offender to let him down. Victim accused offender of tearing his pants and told offender to pay for them. Offender and others were laughing at victim. Victim hit offender and both were told to leave. Victim left first, then stood on the porch. Offender says victim hit him again when he came out, so he shot him.[5]

The authors note the critical role that witnesses play in such disputes, by their very presence raising the stakes of the competition. An important component of these altercations is the status that each participant is trying to project to observers. Once an individual has been challenged, backing off is equivalent to losing face; escalating the conflict is the only alternative.

Wilson and Daly draw a parallel between these types of conflict and gambling. Gambling is predominantly a male activity, and the higher the stakes, the more males are at the table. Here, too, presence of other players can raise the stakes: blackjack players make higher bets against the house when others are at the table. The implication is that losing face can be more threatening than losing money.

Driving is another domain in which young men take more risk than others, especially if there are male observers of their behavior. Insurance companies charge higher auto insurance premiums to younger than to older drivers and to male versus female drivers of the same age, reflecting higher rates of car accidents that result from young men speeding, chasing, tailgating, and cutting off other drivers. As with violent crime and gambling, research has found that the presence of witnesses can increase risk taking: a male driver with male passengers is especially likely to hazard a turn across oncoming traffic.

Military service offers both risk and status. The U.S. volunteer army began in 1973, and, since 2005, military service in the United States has been open to both men and women between seventeen and forty-two years of age. Yet the U.S. Army reports that the ratio of men to women

5. Wilson, M., & Daly, M. (1985). Competitiveness, risk taking, and violence: The young male syndrome. *Ethology and Sociobiology* 6: 59–73, p. 64.

among recent recruits is 7:1. Minorities comprise a disproportionate number of recruits; most recruits have no college degree, and two-thirds are under thirty years of age. Demographic research finds that U.S. Army recruits are more likely to come from lower-income families than nonrecruits, and to list pay and college benefits offered by the Army and "being away from home" as reasons for joining.[6] Here, too, it is young men with less opportunity who decide to join a group that has, for most Americans, the higher status associated with accepting risks in defense of the country.

The answer to the second question, why is it that young men with fewer opportunities should engage in more risk, is more complicated. A distal explanation comes from evolutionary psychology; a proximate one comes from psychoendocrinology.

Evolutionary Perspective on Status and Risk Taking

Evolutionary psychologists argue that not only our bodies but our psychology has evolved to maximize chances of reproducing and passing on our genes. Unlike physical attributes, psychological traits are usually a result of both genes and environment, but many psychological reactions clearly echo our ancestral past. For instance, most babies develop fear of heights at about the age when they can crawl, clearly an adaptive reaction. Similarly, most people feel attraction to individuals of opposite gender who show signs of good health. The attraction, evolutionary psychologists claim, is a product of ancestral history during which those who preferred partners too weak to reproduce ended up childless.

According to evolutionary psychologists, individuals are driven by preferences that maximize reproductive success. For men success can mean more children with more women—quantitative success. For women, who are limited in how many children they may have over a lifetime, reproductive success can mean quality: children with the best possible partner, one who can provide good genes as well as material support for mother and baby. To maximize reproductive success, both men and women need to appeal to the widest audience of potential partners—the more women are attracted to a man, the more children he can father, and the more men are attracted to a woman, the better her choice to father her children. What makes women attractive to

6. Hosek, J., & Totten, M. E. (1998). *Does perstempo hurt reenlistment? The effect of long or hostile perstempo on reenlistment*. Santa Monica, CA: Rand, p. 78.

men, and what makes men attractive to women? What characteristics would they need to play up to appeal to potential partners?

Because men pursue quantity in their mating strategy, they would be most interested in a woman's physical attributes that signal that she is fertile. Good physical health and appropriate hormonal status (after puberty, before menopause, low testosterone) are most important for women's fertility. As it happens, these are well reflected in a woman's appearance: secondary sexual characteristics, smooth, glowing skin, appropriate fat distribution with wider hips and narrow waist.

Psychologists predicted that men, regardless of culture or even historical period, would be universally attracted to these characteristics. To study their hypothesis, they asked men in different cultures what they valued most in a woman, and they compared classified ads from different countries. They also looked at depictions of beauty from different historical periods. They found that everywhere men valued physical beauty above other personal characteristics; in particular, they valued those physical traits that signal fertility.

Women, on the other hand, are much less interested in the physical beauty of their long-term partners. And rightly so, say evolutionary psychologists. What good is a pretty boy who is unable to protect and support his partner and children? Choosing a mate based on looks could only be a liability for a woman if she becomes pregnant and is then abandoned by the child's father. Vulnerable and unable to provide for herself and the child, she is more likely to lose the child to disease, starvation, predators, or infanticide, having wasted a significant portion of her reproductive life cycle. Thus, women are genetically predisposed by their evolutionary history to pay less attention to beauty and more attention to traits that make a man a better protector and provider.

Among these, status is the most important. A woman who is favored by a high-status man, whether tribal leader or wealthy businessman, is protected from many of life's hardships, and her child is likely to receive food, shelter, and other benefits from the father's status.

Consistent with this prediction, in surveys and in classified ads from around the world women say they prefer men with high status—high income and a good job—or a potential for high status signaled by intelligence, ambition, and education. ("A good sense of humor" is often cited by Western women but not so often by others.) More evidence in the same direction comes from experiments: women rate the same man as more physically attractive when he is wearing markers of high status such as a Rolex watch and a suit than when he is wearing a KFC

(Kentucky Fried Chicken) uniform. The same experiment conducted with males found no difference in attractiveness of a woman wearing a business suit and the same woman wearing a KFC uniform. In general, research shows that men's preferences disregard the social status of potential girlfriends and wives.

Status is a more complex characteristic than beauty. For one thing, it can change dramatically within a short period of time, so it requires more maintenance and more signaling (the Rolex watch and the suit). Additionally, status is easier to fake than beauty (at least it was until recent advances in plastic surgery). Anyone can say he has a good job, put on an expensive watch (possibly a fake Rolex), and be king for a day. This means women need to be much more discriminating about the signs of status that men display, lest they be fooled by a sheep in wolf's clothing.

For this reason men seek to signal high status to potential mates in ways that prove that the status is indeed genuine and that they are likely to retain it. In the animal kingdom males establish status by displaying their health (elaborate mating rituals that require skill and endurance) and dominance (by contesting other males). Both are what evolutionary theorists call "honest signals," in that the signaler pays a real price for the signal: mating rituals require real time and energy expenditure, and fighting between males can result in real injury or death. A faker could not endure the exhausting ritual or risk fighting a stronger opponent. Females can be reasonably confident in those who do.

The gold standard of a man's status is his status among other men. Respect and deference from other men is almost impossible to fake, and thus a reliable signal of status. The importance of this signal in relation to mating opportunities means that male motivation for attaining status among other men can develop to the point that it no longer depends on the presence of women. Indeed, male competition for status may even be exacerbated in all-male situations such as prisons and gangs.

Risk taking is then an honest signal of status in humans. By engaging in high-stakes activity, a man displays courage, self-assuredness, and strength, conveying to his audience—perhaps especially to other men—that he is the better man. Risk taking is an action that speaks louder than words.

Each risk carries potential losses and potential rewards. Someone of high status—someone with a good education, a good job, a BMW, and a Rolex—has a lot to lose and little to gain by getting involved in a bar fight. On the other hand, someone with no job, no education, and no prospects has more to gain and less to lose by taking this risk. With his inability to compete for status on other criteria, risk taking—in particular physical aggression—may be the only domain where a poor man stands a chance to gain status over rivals.

Evolutionary psychology can make sense of the different patterns of male and female partner preferences, patterns presumed to reflect the effects of natural selection over thousands of human generations. But the evolutionary account says nothing about what differences in the psychology of living men and women are producing gender and risk-taking differences in present-day behavior. For this more proximate explanation of status seeking and risk taking we turn to the hormone testosterone.

"The Big T"

Biologists and psychologists have known for a long time that aggression and dominance in animals are related to testosterone, a hormone that males produce in considerably larger amounts than females. Dominant males have higher levels of testosterone, and they establish their social position—status—through aggression against other males who may challenge them. It helps that testosterone makes muscles bigger and skin tougher.

In humans also, aggression has been empirically linked to testosterone. Males imprisoned for violent crime have higher levels of testosterone than those imprisoned for other crimes. While in prison, those with higher testosterone levels break more rules and get involved in more fights. Among college students, members of more rambunctious fraternities—with more police calls to the fraternity house, more violence in the fraternity house—have higher levels of testosterone.

But social status in humans is not always a direct result of physical aggression. Successful bankers, politicians, or lawyers have high status, but usually this is not achieved through violence. Supporting this observation, researchers Dabbs and Morris measured testosterone and antisocial behavior, including aggression, in a large sample of men. They found a strong correlation of testosterone with aggression but only among males of low socioeconomic class. Among men from high socioeconomic class, high testosterone was not a good predictor of aggression. For men of higher status, there are other avenues of risk taking and status seeking: for example, litigation lawyers (higher status) show higher levels of testosterone than patent lawyers (lower status).

More generally, Sapolsky has argued that testosterone levels are a biological readout of social status. Higher-status men stare longer at photographs of threatening faces (potential status challengers) than they do at nonthreatening ones, and they stare longer at threatening faces than do men with average testosterone levels. Men with low testosterone levels tend to avoid looking at threatening faces. When put in a low-status position in an experiment, men high in testosterone show greater emotional arousal, more concern about their status, and more distraction from a cognitive task than men low in testosterone. This pattern supports the idea that higher-testosterone men are more concerned about maintaining status and more distressed by loss of status.

Testosterone levels can change drastically when status changes, as can happen often and sometimes unexpectedly in sports. Thus, winners of sports matches show higher testosterone levels than losers. If winners feel the victory was a result of luck rather than skill, the elevation in testosterone is less, reflecting realization that an elevated status was a fluke and is therefore unstable. Elevations in testosterone occur in winners of both physical sports such as soccer and nonphysical ones such as chess.

Perhaps surprisingly, identification with a team can produce the same pattern of testosterone effects that team members experience. Sports fans, feeling elevated by their team's win or embarrassed by their team's defeat, show corresponding changes in their testosterone levels. This result indicates the power of group identification described in chapter 3.

In sum, testosterone appears to be an important driver of status seeking, whether it is through violent or nonviolent means. Young males (between ages sixteen and twenty-five) have the highest levels of testosterone of all demographic groups, making them especially attracted to status seeking. For lower-socioeconomic-class, undereducated males, who have little chance of achieving high status in society, elevated testosterone is associated with more physical risk taking and physical aggression. Through aggression these young males attempt to gain status that they could not achieve through academic, business, or professional success. For more educated and better socially positioned men, higher testosterone leads to risk taking and status seeking in nonviolent ways, as trial lawyers, athletes, or stock traders.

The psychology of thrill seeking and status can be seen at work in our Russian terrorists. With no money and no connections, Barannikov was facing a life of boredom as a low-ranking officer stationed in a provincial Russian town; he chose instead to turn to physical risk taking in terrorism for thrill and adventure. When he was arrested (to be imprisoned for life) at the age of twenty-three, Barannikov had already been married and estranged from his wife. Despite the fact that he had no money, he was enjoying great success with women, some of whom were conspicuously devoted to him. Risk taking, honest signaling of high status, earned him their attentions.

Mirsky came from an aristocratic and wealthy family, with the nineteenth-century equivalents of a BMW and a Rolex watch. But a woman he wants to impress challenges him with Barannikov's example (more evidence that Barannikov succeeded in gaining high status from risk taking). In evolutionary terms, she challenged the authenticity of the status Mirsky inherited from his family: "Is that your Daddy's BMW?" His honor at stake, Mirsky followed Barannikov into terrorist violence.

A similar emphasis on risk taking is evident in the student terrorists of the 1970s. The two most famous terrorist groups that emerged in Europe were the Italian Red Brigades and the German Red Army Faction. Della Porta provides excerpts from interviews that show some of the thrill value of violence and the special attraction of guns as instruments of dominance and violence.

> Thus the Italian militants also glorified the idea of an adventurous and active life. The dangers involved in participating in a terrorist organization were considered "the expression of a dynamic and interesting life," a contrast to the dullness of ordinary life.
>
> Both Italian and German militants had "very special relationships with guns." Guns held a particular glamour: "the gun ... gives you more strength," one militant explained ...; "arms have a charm ... that makes you feel more macho," said another.... You can feel "very secure of yourself because you keep a gun in your hands ... [they give you] a crazy self-confidence."[7]

The search for status and risk taking can be unrelated to any sense of grievance or ideology. An example of how far the separation between

---

7. Della Porta, D. (1995). *Social movements, political violence, and the state: A comparative analysis of Italy and Germany*. Cambridge, UK: Cambridge University Press, pp. 172, 176.

politics and radical action can go was recounted to one of the authors in a government-sponsored meeting. A young Iraqi had been captured trying to place an improvised explosive device (IED) on a road traversed by U.S. forces. When interrogated, he showed surprisingly little animosity toward Americans. Placing IEDs was a high-status, well-paid occupation; he was saving his money to get to America.

A Bad Boy, Looking for a Good Fight

The United States placed a price of $25 million on his head—the same bounty offered for Osama bin Laden. At the onset of his criminal career, nobody would have thought that Ahmad Fadeel al-Nazal al-Khalayleh, later known as Abu Musab al-Zarqawi, could gain such prominence on the international stage.

Born in 1966 he grew up in a middle-class family in a suburb of Zarqua, Jordan. His school performance was weak, and he dropped out of high school in his final year, refusing to undertake vocational training or to continue his studies. He was not interested in religious studies either and did not attend religious services. Instead, he got involved with other neighborhood troublemakers, quickly creating a reputation for himself as an aggressive and dangerous thug—not because of his extraordinary physical strength but because of his bad temper. He took one unskilled job after another, only to be fired for neglecting his duties and inciting fights. In 1986 a mandatory two-year military service took him away from the street career he was building, but he came back with the same drive for intimidation and domination.

His contemporaries recall that at this time he drank too much and earned a nickname, "the green man," for the numerous tattoos he acquired (a practice condemned by Islam). He liked to stand out in other ways too: in several cases, he became involved in altercations with local police, repeatedly causing his father the embarrassment of picking him up from the police station. In 1987 he stabbed a local man, earning a two-month prison sentence, which was eventually substituted by a fine. Numerous arrests followed—for shoplifting, for drug dealing, and for attempted rape. Although the authorities did not approve of Ahmad's behavior, there were plenty of admirers. Neighborhood young men feared and respected him, and he began frequenting a Palestinian enclave where he became a leader for young Palestinian refugees.

To keep him out of trouble, his mother enrolled Ahmad in a religious school at a mosque in the center of Amman. There, among

Islamic radicals preparing for jihad in Afghanistan, he realized that his talents might best be applied in war. Hoping to be sent to the front of the fighting, he submitted to the most basic requirements of Islam by beginning to attend sermons and abstaining from alcohol. In 1989, with a group of peers, Ahmad finally set off on the road to Afghanistan.

To his dismay he arrived too late: the war against the Soviets was already over, and he could only join the fighters in celebration. But the region was in ruins, the situation was chaotic, and Ahmad thought he might yet find his adventure. He decided to stay for a while. On his many trips between war zones in Afghanistan he met and befriended individuals who became influential in the radical Islamist movement. One such meeting, with charismatic Islamist ideologue Mohammad Taher al-Barqawi (Abu Mohammed al-Maqdisi), became a close friendship. It was on Maqdisi's recommendation that the barely literate Ahmad was hired as a reporter for a Peshawar-based journal, *Al-Bunyan Al-Marsus*, an ideological outlet for al Qaeda.

The war with the Soviets was over, but a civil war was just beginning in Afghanistan. Wasting no time, Ahmad joined the majority Pashtun side and gave up journalism for his true passion—fighting. This was an opportunity to learn from the best. Ahmad attended several training camps, learned to use automatic weapons and rocket-propelled grenades, and absorbed the politics and practices of war, including rape and beheading. According to a biographer,

> "In Afghanistan, he filled himself with the spirit of *jihad*, no matter what the cause: for the liberation of Afghanistan, for Islam, for the liberation of Iraq, or on any other grounds. Zarqawi discovered in himself the personality of a fighter."[8]

In 1993 Ahmad returned to Jordan. Here the police and intelligence services began to take great interest in the "Afghans"—individuals who came back from the war in Afghanistan—as potentially destructive forces and a threat to the regime. This attention was warranted since the returning veterans actively recruited young Jordanians and offered them both military training in the desert and rhetorical ammunition against Israel and the Jordanian government (which was at the time involved in peace talks on the U.S. side).

Of those under suspicion, Ahmad was already well known to the local police for his prewar delinquency. Now steeped in the Islamic

---

8. Brisard, J.-C., with Martinez, D. (2005). *Zarqawi*. New York: Other Press, p. 26.

ideology he had absorbed in his Afghan years, he started to "act locally," first subjugating his immediate family to the strict and arbitrary rules he thought important. Suddenly his family was alone in town wearing traditional Afghan clothing, and his brothers were forbidden to watch television.

Once Ahmad had subdued his family, he moved on to larger domains. He went into crowded streets and the marketplace and shouted out his call to embrace jihad—this in a city where public sermons were forbidden. Feeling the limits of his own rhetorical skills, Zarqawi turned to the one whose words and ideology he had himself found convincing: Maqdisi. His friend agreed to come and give religious courses to potential followers and to teach Ahmad one-on-one the ideas behind jihad.

It was around this time that he adopted the new name, al-Zarqawi—clearly aiming to expand his influence far beyond his hometown. The two friends—the bully and the ideologue—joined about three hundred other Afghan veterans to form a terrorist cell. But being a part of a larger organization was not enough for Zarqawi. This organization became the launching ground for Zarqawi's own terrorist cell, Bayt Al-Imam, funded in part by Osama bin Laden. Maqdisi and Zarqawi went from home to home, and from one mosque to another, one preaching and convincing, the other inspiring with his fearful presence and interpersonal intensity. Zarqawi was overshadowed by his smarter, more learned friend, "... it was Maqdisi who served as the group's mentor, while Zarqawi took charge of military operations."[9] Zarqawi's chance for new power came when Bayt Al-Imam was dissolved and the leaders arrested and imprisoned in 1996.

Zarqawi, Maqdisi, and some other members of Bayt Al-Imam were sent to the maximum-security prison Suwaqah. Here, among the worst offenders, not only political prisoners but also felons and drug dealers, intellect and well-delivered sermons were less impressive than heavy fists. Zarqawi quickly established his status by beating up those who challenged him. His strategy was the same for intellectual as for physical challengers: when a prison newspaper printed articles critical of Zarqawi, he pummeled the authors.

Building up his main "arguments" for status, he lifted weights obsessively, becoming beefier and stronger than he had been before prison. He told stories of his heroic role in the Afghan war (the war that he

---

9. Ibid., p. 37.

missed) to impress other prisoners. He demanded complete obedience from those who wanted to be under his protection. They had to wear what he told them, read what he approved, and get his permission for any activity, even a visit to the infirmary. Violators were brutalized.

Observers recalled that he could give orders to his followers with only a blink of his eye. In addition to the sticks, Zarqawi had carrots: he distributed food rations to his followers and on occasion even cared for those who were sick or injured. But what won them over most was his overt defiance of prison authorities. He refused to wear a prison uniform and demanded that his sidekicks be allowed the same laxity. The army had to intervene to enforce the rule, and when Zarqawi realized he had no chance against the armed troops, he shouted insults in soldiers' faces.

On several other occasions he tried to organize prison uprisings, and when the head of prison security summoned him, Zarqawi never once looked away from his eyes. Over months and years, the prison authorities came to fear and avoid conflicts with this berserker. Eventually, Zarqawi and his gang gained special status. The whole prison wing where former Bayt Al-Imam members were held was excused from morning rounds and, eventually, from wearing a uniform.

> In 2004 his friend Maqdisi formally ceded his authority to Zarqawi. He wrote, "The brothers chose me as emir [chief]. I remained in that role unwillingly for a year before dedicating myself to the religious sciences. I decided to give my position to Zarqawi. Contrary to what certain people have written, [this] was not the result of a quarrel between us, but the result of an agreement, so that we could speak with one voice to the heads of the prison."[10]

In prison, for the first time in his life Zarqawi found the status he sought. He was more powerful than anyone. He got to this position through brutal force and unyielding defiance of authority. When in 1999 King Hussein died and Zarqawi was released in an amnesty, he had served only five years of his fifteen-year term. But it was the best five years of his life, so much so that he later told his friends and relatives that he had not really been glad to be released. He told his brother-in-law that life behind bars was much more enjoyable to him than his uneventful life as an average Jordanian. He even stayed an extra night in prison after being released.

---

10. Ibid., p. 44.

Once out of prison Zarqawi did not wait long to leave Jordan in search of further adventure. He wanted to connect with bin Laden himself and went looking for him, first in Pakistan, then in Afghanistan. He brought with him his faithful followers, some from Bayt al-Imam, some from prison, and some recruited on the way. In 2001, already a trusted member of al Qaeda, Zarqawi took the oath of allegiance to bin Laden.

Being a part of a larger organization did not suit Zarqawi's grand ambitions, and he moved away from al Qaeda's main ground in Kabul to Herat, stirring anxieties in the terrorist leadership about his autonomy and unruliness. In 2003 the United States began its offensive against the Saddam Hussein regime in Iraq. By August influential radical clerics announced that there was no difference between the U.S. war in Iraq and the USSR invasion of Afghanistan, calling on all good Muslims to join arms in jihad against the infidels. Zarqawi saw a great chance to make Iraq his own battleground, out from under the leadership of al Qaeda.

The world soon learned his name and saw his face in connection with multiple kidnappings and brutal beheadings of U.S. and allied forces' contractors in Iraq, most notably his videotaped beheading of Nicholas Berg. In addition Zarqawi began a campaign of violence against the Shi'a of Iraq, with the goal of eliciting Shi'a reprisals against Sunni that would rouse the "inattentive" Sunni to jihad against both Western invaders and heretic Shi'a (see chapter 11). Video beheadings and attacks on Shi'a civilians were bad publicity for al Qaeda, and Ayman al-Zawahiri, al Qaeda second-in-command, wrote a letter to Zarqawi, asking him to moderate his bloody violence because his tactics were alienating support for al Qaeda among the broader Muslim base.

But pressure from authorities had not stopped Ahmad on the streets of Zarqua, had not stopped him in prison, and did not stop his bloody campaign in Iraq. Al-Zawahiri's political plans and calculations were of little consequence to Zarqawi. All he had ever wanted was power and the thrill of violence, and he got both from his violent operations in Iraq.

In 2006 a U.S. air strike destroyed a house where Zarqawi was hiding. He died shortly after being discovered in the rubble.

Looking Further

Albert, D., Walsh, M., & Jonik, R. (1994). Aggression in humans: What is its biological foundation? *Neuroscience & Biobehavioral Reviews* 17: 405–425.

Archer, J. (1991). The influence of testosterone on human aggression. *British Journal of Psychology* 82: 1–28.

Bernhardt, P. C., Dabbs, J. M., Fielden, J. A., & Lutte, C. D. (1998). Testosterone changes during vicarious experiences of winning and losing among fans at sporting events. *Physiology & Behavior* 65(1): 59–62.

Cornish, D. B. (1978). *Gambling: A review of the literature and its implications for policy and research.* London: Her Majesty's Stationery Office.

Dabbs, J., Jr., Frady, R., Carr, T., & Besch, N. (1987). Saliva testosterone and criminal violence in young adult prison inmates. *Psychosomatic Medicine* 49: 174–182.

Dabbs, J., Jr., & Morris, R. (1990). Testosterone, social class, and antisocial behavior in a sample of 4,462 men. *Psychological Science* 1: 209–211.

Dixson, A. (1980). Androgens and aggressive behavior in primates: A review. *Aggressive Behavior* 6: 37–67.

Ehrenkranz, J., Bliss, E., & Sheard, M. (1974). Plasma testosterone: Correlation with aggressive behavior and social dominance in men. *Psychosomatic Medicine* 36: 469–475.

Elias, M. (1981). Serum cortisol, testosterone, and testosterone-binding globulin responses to competitive fighting in human males. *Aggressive Behavior* 7: 215–224.

Lindgren, E., Youngs, G. A., Jr., McDonald, T. D., Klenow, D. J., & Schriner, E. C. (2005). The impact of gender on gambling attitudes and behavior. *Journal of Gambling Studies* 3: 155–167.

Mazur, A. (1976). Effects of testosterone on status in primate groups. *Folia Primatologica* 26: 214–226.

Mazur, A., Booth, A., & Dabbs, J., Jr. (1992). Testosterone and chess competition. *Social Psychology Quarterly* 55: 70–77.

Mazur, A., & Lamb, T. (1980). Testosterone, status, and mood in human males. *Hormones and Behavior* 14: 236–246.

McCaul, K., Gladue, B., & Joppa, M. (1992). Winning, losing, mood, and testosterone. *Hormones and Behavior* 26: 486–506.

Rose, R., Bernstein, I., & Gordon, T. (1975). Consequences of social conflict on plasma testosterone levels in rhesus monkeys. *Psychosomatic Medicine* 37: 50–61.

Sapolsky, R. (1998). *The trouble with testosterone: And other essays on the biology of the human predicament.* New York: Touchstone.

Stradling, S. G., & Meadows, L. M. (1999). Highway code and aggressive violations in UK drivers. Paper presented to the Aggressive Diving Issues Conference, Ontario Ministry for Transportation, Toronto.

Sullivan, A. (2000). The he hormone. *New York Times Magazine*, April 2.

Tessendorf, K. S. (1986). *Kill the tsar!* New York: Atheneum.

CHAPTER SEVEN

Unfreezing

*Loss of social connection can open an individual to new ideas and new identity
that may include political radicalization.*

Vanechka

For many individuals, the path to radicalization is blocked by prior
routines and responsibilities. Supporting a family, building a career,
and attachments to friends and neighbors are all jeopardized by committing time and energy to political activism; joining an illegal and
dangerous organization costs even more. But what if everyday commitments and attachments are lost? Perhaps parents die suddenly or a
spouse unexpectedly departs. Or an individual moves from home to a
remote city or a foreign country and has to begin again with no social
ties and few resources. Or civil war ravages the country, destroying
families, jobs, and social networks; streets become dangerous, and fear
follows people home. Disconnected from everyday routines and relationships, an individual becomes an easy prospect for any group that
offers friendship and security. If the new group comes with an ideology, new ideas may be embraced along with new friends.

The content and quality of these new ideas can be less important
than who holds them. A new group member cannot shut out the messages of new friends, especially if friendship comes with everyday

necessities of food and shelter. Gratitude, as well as the desire to establish and maintain strong ties with new friends, opens the individual to new ideas and actions. In 1870s Russia, radical student circles organized communes where kind words, as well as food and a bed for the night, were readily available to anyone in need. As Ekaterina Breshko-Breshkovskaya recalled in her memoirs,

> In the seventies, relationships among comrades had a truly brotherly feel. Simple, from-the-heart interaction was usual not only among socialist youth, but also among students in general. If someone got into a troublesome situation on the street, or in travels, he looked whether there was a student around and could be absolutely certain that he would receive any help that he needs. In that time students did not wear uniforms, but one could easily tell them apart by wide-brimmed hats and plaids. They were friends of humanity, responded to questions of inexperienced comrades and answered calls for help. Such trusting, kind relationships existed also among female students, and the same friendly spirit got inside prisons.[1]

At a time when many were in dire need, radical student circles stood to gain new members simply by offering them a helping hand. One example of such radicalization is "Vanechka"—Sophia Andreevna Ivanova.

Vanechka was from a provincial town, one of ten children of a noble army officer. When she was nine years old her father died, leaving her mother with Vanechka and three younger sisters to fend for themselves. Vanechka's seven older brothers were already studying in military academies across the country. Unlike her sisters who were interested in social gatherings, knitting, and cross-stitching, Vanechka preferred playing active games with her brothers or reading books from her father's library. The eclectic collection of reading material, from Dickens to random issues of contemporary liberal journals, opened her eyes to the life outside of their small military post. The life she read about offered exciting ideas and opportunities, but at home all she could aspire to was marriage to an officer.

Vanechka's mother died when she was sixteen, and she immediately asked one of her brothers to help her get out of the boring provincial town. As she recalled in her autobiography, "my image of Moscow was

---

1. Брешко-Брешковская, Е. (2006). *Скрымые корни русскои революции; Отречение великои революционерки*. Москва: Центрполиграф. [Breshko-Breshkovskaya, E. (2006). *Hidden roots of Russian revolution: Abdication of a great revolutionary.* Moscow: Tsentrpoligraf, p. 144.]

something fantastic: it seemed to me to be inhabited by some special, ideal people."[2] She also hoped to attend a gymnasium or some other higher educational establishment, of which she held similarly idealistic views. Her brother, approving of Vanechka's ambitions for higher learning, agreed to help her move to Moscow.

Upon her arrival, Vanechka's image of Moscow and Muscovites was confronted with a sobering reality. Moscow turned out to be a bustling, unfriendly place, and most Muscovites she encountered were materialistic and boring people resembling those she knew back home. What was more troubling still was that the brother, whom she expected to find in Moscow, was not there: he had been sent to work as an army doctor in a small town outside of Moscow. He provided an apartment and a little bit of money for her, but he could not help her further.

Vanechka applied to a nursing school but was rejected because of her young age. Her brother advised her to study for entrance exams into a teaching academy. Unfortunately, these plans were curtailed by his sudden sickness: he contracted tuberculosis and had to move to the south of Ukraine for treatment. With her brother and his help gone, Vanechka was left completely alone in a big unfriendly city with no money and no place to live. She had no education or skills, and her job opportunities were limited.

She tried working as a seamstress, but the job paid so little that Vanechka had to choose between paying her rent and eating. She lived on an ascetic diet while working from 8 a.m. to 8 p.m. under a despotic boss. Someone suggested to her a job at a printing workshop. To be around books that she loved so much, to see how they are made—that sounded perfect. By chance Vanechka applied to a workshop operated by Myshkin—a member of activist circles and later of People's Will. In a secret room the workshop printed forbidden literature: radical pamphlets, propagandistic handouts, and forbidden books.

---

2. Якимова-Диковская, А. В. (ред.) (1929). *Народовольцы. 80-х и 90-х годов: Сб. ст. и Материалов, составленный участниками народовольческого движения*. Москва: Изд-во Всесоюзного общества политкаторжан и ссыльно-поселенцев. [Yakimova-Dikovskaya, A. V. (ed.) (1929). *People's Will members of the 80s and 90s: Collection of articles and materials contributed by participants in People's Will movement*. Moscow: Izdatel'stvo Vsesouznogo obschestva Politka-torzhan I Ssyl'no-Poselencev.] Available at http://elib.shpl.ru/ru/nodes/5019-narodovoltsy-80-h-i-90-h-godov-sbornik-statey-i-materialov-sostavlennyy-uchastnikami-narodovolcheskogo-dvizheniya-m-1929-istoriko-revolyutsionnaya-biblioteka-kn-39#page/1/mode/grid/zoom/1. Accessed May 2 2016.

As Vanechka knew nothing about printing, she became an apprentice to two women who were "typical nihilists of that time, dressed carelessly, with short hair and a stern look."[3] They were a part of a student circle that had come together from the remote Russian town of Arhangelsk. Vanechka and her two teachers quickly became good friends. She was entrusted with working in the secret room, printing secret literature. Soon she realized what was going on, but she felt honored to be given such responsibility.

> When her miserable circumstances became known to her co-workers they decided to organize a commune within the printing workshop. In the building taken up by the workshop a few rooms remained empty, and the workers moved into these rooms together. They shared a common pool of money for food, clothes, and other necessities, cooked in turns in the communal kitchen, and otherwise supported one another. The workshop commune attracted visitors from the underground world who fell on hard times and needed a bowl of soup or who were in Moscow on revolutionary business and needed a discreet place to stay. Vanechka, of course, was right there: observing, taking in the whispers and innuendoes.
>
> At one point Myshkin took her aside to ask whether she understood the danger that she was in by associating with the radical workshop. But she felt it was "... ridiculous and incredible that I could be arrested. I saw myself as such an insignificant person. 'Who would need to take me in?' I thought. 'Especially in contrast with my comrades,' to whom I looked up, considering them very smart and important people."[4]
>
> Vanechka was part of the workshop commune for only a few months when it was shut down by the police. Myshkin, the owner, eluded capture, but the workers were arrested and imprisoned. Vanechka had already been primed by her teachers on how to behave once arrested. "The oldest among us, Supinskaya, prior to arrest, taught us, 'Don't forget that you would be taken by the enemy. Be ready for anything and keep your mouth shut.'"[5]

Vanechka took these words to heart and kept quiet during interrogations. She spent seven months in jail before her brother found a sponsor to pay her bail and petitioned for her release.

When Vanechka was finally released, she found that all her friends from the print shop were behind bars. She was once again all alone in

---

3. Ibid.
4. Ibid.
5. Ibid.

Moscow with no job, no money, and no place to live. Vanechka moved to St. Petersburg, where she knew her friends from the commune were imprisoned and awaiting their trial. During prison visiting hours, which she frequented, she befriended many young radicals, both imprisoned and still at large. Their help was once again instrumental in getting her life back on track. In a few weeks in the capital she found a new printing job.

In St. Petersburg Vanechka's political views, to some degree formed in her first commune in Moscow, were sharpened through her new friendships and participation in student activities and protests. In one of these protests Vanechka was arrested and sentenced to a Siberian exile.

In Siberia she was placed under the care and surveillance of two "unreformed" Orthodox women—themselves victims of the government repressions against religious minorities. They were supposed to report to the police if their tenant did anything out of the ordinary. Instead, they soon offered Vanechka help to escape from Siberia. They connected her with a reliable peasant who, in exchange for the horse she bought him, drove her west to another town. From there she hired the first of a series of carriages that took her back to St. Petersburg. The money for this journey had come from her comrades before she left St. Petersburg, and clever Vanechka had found ways to save during the months of her exile so as not to use up her comrades' gift. For six days after she left, her "guards" staged the appearance that Vanechka was still with them, lighting candles in her room after dark. When they finally told the police, Vanechka was already back in the capital.

This idealistic young woman later joined People's Will and rose to the exclusive ranks of its Executive Committee. Her expertise proved invaluable for organizing and running an underground printing press. She married a convicted terrorist, Kvyatkovski, and when he was sentenced to death along with several of their comrades, she, the mother of a toddler, petitioned the court that she be granted the same sentence as her husband. Instead, she was sentenced to four years of hard labor. Her young son, whom she left with relatives, died while she was serving her sentence. In her autobiography printed in the collection *Members of People's Will of the '80s and '90s* (*Народовольцы. 80-х и 90-х годов*), her son's name never appears.

Vanechka lived a long life, surviving the horrors of her imprisonment as well as the Bolshevik revolution, and died in Moscow in 1927.

Unfreezing: Radicalization to Escape Fear and Pain

There is an easy path to persuasion through pain and fear. If you give me bone-jarring shocks or keep me awake for forty-eight hours or bring me near to drowning on a waterboard or chill me two-thirds of the way to a hypothermia in which gums retract, teeth fall out, and bones are broken by shivering muscles, I am very likely to tell you what I think you want to know. This kind of treatment is sometimes called *torture*. To the extent that the treatment aims at internalized persuasion—change in values that lasts beyond the torture—it is called *brainwashing* or *thought reform*. Although often generalized to mean any kind of heavy persuasion, brainwashing properly refers to the procedures applied to U.S. soldiers captured by the Chinese during the Korean War or more generally to Chinese and Western civilians in Chinese prison cells. These procedures begin with captivity, threat, fear, and pain.

Research on brainwashing suggests that it produces mostly compliance—behavior required to stop the pain and fear—with little effect or even boomerang effects once the pressure of pain and fear is withdrawn. But political radicalization and especially terrorism require more than compliance. Trust is the key to terrorist cooperation in action, and individuals who want to betray their comrades have many opportunities to do so. Brainwashing, properly understood as coercive persuasion in which threat, pain, and fear unfreeze old commitments, does not usually produce political converts.

Another kind of pain and fear is the experience of a failed state. When government monopoly of violence fails, streets and countryside are at the mercy of armed bands, who may be criminal gangs or political militants or some combination of these. Insecurity of this kind has been all too common in recent years in Colombia, Somalia, Bosnia, Chechnya, Iraq, and Afghanistan. Unfreezing occurs as fear drives individuals to seek new routines and new connections that can provide safety. For individuals stuck in these conditions, joining a group with guns can look safer than traversing the streets alone.

A failed state is not the only state that can provide an occasion of political radicalization to escape threat. The czarist state was not a failed state, and most of the states in which jihadist terrorists have emerged are not failed states. A powerful state can produce its own version of unfreezing when activists or radicals anticipate capture and interrogation by the police or security services. Student radicals in the United States (Weatherman), Italy (Red Brigades), and Germany (Red Army Faction) often went from communes to underground cells when expecting the police at their doors. Most Weatherman members, for instance, went underground only after an accidental explosion in a New York City townhouse alerted police and the FBI that "bringing the war home" had taken a more serious turn. Again, this form of radicalization is relatively rare, and we focus instead on a much more common contribution to radicalization: unfreezing by social disconnection.

Unfreezing: Radicalization to Escape Disconnection

Where do human values come from? Some would say from childhood experience and family values, but many parents have noticed that their success in imparting values to their children is partial and uncertain. Social psychologists starting with Kurt Lewin have argued instead that values are anchored in groups.

In 2010, when everyone around us agrees that smoking is dangerous, it is easy to be confident that smoking is dangerous. In the 1950s, when everyone in the United States agreed that ashtrays were a sign of civilization, it was equally easy to be confident that smoking was sophisticated. Then and now, few study the evidence to make an individual decision about smoking; the group norm was and is clear enough.

Confidence about our value judgments depends on a stable network of others who agree with us (this idea is expanded in section 2). If we leave our daily round of connections, or if our connections leave us, we are opened to new connections and new values. Following Kurt Lewin's 1947 model of unfreezing, social psychologists distinguish three phases: first unfreezing of old connections and ideas; then development of new connections and new ideas; and finally refreezing in a new social network that provides the confidence of consensus for new values and new actions. Notice that, in this model, changes in values that are not anchored in a new group must remain unstable and liable to further change or reversion to older forms.

A concept very similar to unfreezing has been advanced in social movement theory. *Biographical availability* is defined as "the absence of personal constraints that may increase the costs and risks of movement participation."[6] Personal constraints may include, as already noted,

---

6. McAdam, D. (1986). Recruitment to high-risk activism: The case of Freedom Summer. *American Journal of Sociology* 92: 64–90, p. 70.

spouse, children, and a full-time job; individuals with these constraints are expected to be less available for the commitments required to participate in political activism. In general, younger people and perhaps older retired individuals may have fewer constraints; university undergraduates living away from home may be particularly available for political action.

Survey data indicate that unmarried students without a job are more likely to say they would march or demonstrate to protest a government decision they disagree with, but the strongest demonstration of the power of unfreezing and biographical availability comes from studies of cult recruiting. These studies indicate that conversion to an intense religious group requires that the potential convert meets members of the group at some kind of turning point in life. Unfreezing, biographical availability, and turning point—all three of these appear in recruitment to the Unification Church.

Unfreezing in Recruitment to the Unification Church

Jerrold Post appears to have been the first to recognize that cult recruiting can provide a useful model of terrorist recruiting. The analogy begins by noting that individuals who join either a cult or a terrorist group are likely to be characterized as "crazy." Both a cult and a terrorist group require a level of commitment that most people find difficult to comprehend. Also, much has been written about how to define a cult, especially about how to distinguish a cult from other kinds of religious groups, paralleling a similar uncertainty about the definition of terrorism, especially about how to distinguish terrorists from guerillas and freedom fighters.

Here we focus on recruitment to the Unification Church (UC) of the Reverend Sun Myung Moon. The UC is generally regarded as a cult, and, more important, there is an unparalleled research literature for this group.

A 1965 report by Lofland and Stark[7] titled "Becoming a World Saver" chronicled the beginnings of the UC in America, and the surprise value of the report was its emphasis on the importance of social networks in religious conversion. The first UC missionary came from Korea to begin work in Eugene, Oregon, in 1961, and her first convert contributed a social network that was soon exploited for additional recruits. Indeed,

---

7. Lofland, J., & Stark, R. (1965). Becoming a world-saver: A theory of conversion to a deviant perspective. *American Sociological Review* 30: 862–875.

"the great majority of converts in Eugene were linked by long-standing relationships prior to any contact with Moon's movement."[8]

The importance of this social network was made plain to Lofland and Stark when the group left Eugene for San Francisco and stopped growing for lack of social ties to potential recruits in the Bay Area. Recruiting efforts during the early 1960s in San Francisco were weak, haphazard, and bumbling. Improvement was more the product of trial and error than any theory, but eventually "lovebombing"—intense, positive, and personal attention focused on potential converts—was developed as the means of creating instant connections with strangers, especially newcomers to the Bay Area. The focus on newcomers made recruiting slower than if each new convert brought a local acquaintance network that could be tapped for additional converts. Compared with geometric progression in Eugene, recruiting in the Bay Area was reduced to arithmetic progression.

The emphasis given by Lofland and Stark to social networks was a watershed in the study of cults. The established view had pointed to the match between the needs of the individual and the ideology of the group to explain why some people and not others join a cult or sect. This view assumed that a deviant group would attract individuals with a grievance or deprivation for which the group offers some interpretation and remedy. In retrospect the deprivation explanation was always too broad because most individuals who suffer a particular deprivation do not ever join a deviant group. Thus, Lofland and Stark did not so much contradict the established view as complement and focus it. Deprivation and grievance establish a pool of potential converts for a particular cult, but social networks determine who among the many in the pool are likely to be among the few actually recruited.

The interaction of deprivation and social networks in predicting cult recruitment is well represented in some remarkable studies carried out by an investigator with the cooperation of UC leaders. Galanter and his colleagues obtained 237 completed questionnaires from a representative sample of UC members living in the church's residences in a large metropolitan area.[9] Most were unmarried, white, and young.

---

8. Stark, R., and Bainbridge, W. S. (1980). Networks of faith: Interpersonal bonds and recruitment to cults and sects. *American Journal of Sociology* 85: 1376–1395, p. 1379.
9. Galanter, M., Rabkin, R., Rabkin, J., & Deutsch, A. (1979). The "Moonies": A psychological study of conversion and membership in a contemporary religious sect. *American Journal of Psychiatry* 136: 165–170

Consistent with the deprivation hypothesis, most had been at least moderately committed to their family's religion before the age of fifteen but had lost this commitment. Half reported some previous commitment to a political party or movement. A majority had attended college, although only a quarter held degrees. Thirty percent had experienced emotional problems leading them to seek professional help, and 6 percent had been hospitalized for such problems. This is a picture of individuals dissatisfied and seeking, and indeed most seem to have found some help in the UC, reporting less psychological distress after joining than before.

The same membership study also shows the importance of interpersonal bonds during the conversion period. Over 60 percent reported having felt during this period much more than usual "a great deal of respect for another person," and about half felt more than usual "close or intimate with another person" and "cheered up."

Another study by Galanter provides questionnaire and outcome data for 104 individuals who began the twenty-one-day sequence of lectures and group activities that ends with deciding whether or not to join the UC.[10] Most of these individuals had been invited by a UC member they had met in some public place. Questionnaires showed that the 104 individuals who attended the first weekend at a rustic center outside a metropolitan area in Southern California were very similar to the 237 individuals in the above study of UC membership. Despite this similarity, seventy-four guests left at the end of the first weekend. Those who left differed from those who stayed in reported feelings toward "the ten or so people from the workshop [from outside the workshop] you know best," with dropouts reporting both less feeling for insiders and more feelings for outsiders. Dropouts also reported less acceptance of UC religious beliefs.

Of the thirty guests who stayed at the center past the first weekend, only nine ultimately joined the church on day twenty-two. The late dropouts did not differ from joiners in positive feelings toward workshop members or in acceptance of UC beliefs, but they did report more positive feelings toward the ten people they knew best from *outside* the workshop. In other words, it was weakness of interpersonal attachments outside the church—unfreezing—that predicted who would finally join the UC.

---

10. Galanter, M. (1980). Psychological induction into the large group: Findings from a modern religious sect. *American Journal of Psychiatry* 137 (12): 1574–1579.

And what keeps recruits in the cult? As already indicated, UC members report feeling less stressed than they were before joining. In this sense the UC experience is not a fraud and does fulfill the promise held out to recruits. Friendships inside the UC are evidently key to keeping members as well as the key to recruitment. But here we want to underscore that there are also very concrete and material rewards of membership. Groups that live communally, such as the UC and the Hare Krishnas, provide not just values and connections but everyday necessities such as clothing, food, and shelter.

Even this brief review indicates a number of obvious parallels with what is known about recruitment into terrorist groups. Both pull mostly from the ranks of youth who are often middle class. Both depend for recruits on a pool of seekers or sympathizers much larger than the numbers actually recruited. Both require a socialization period during which recruits are brought to full commitment, with a constant flux of dropouts from the path that leads to full commitment. Commitment may happen faster for cults than for terrorist groups, but this quantitative difference is easily attributable to the greater barriers to both entrance and exit for terrorist groups. Higher barriers for terrorist groups reflect the fact that terrorists more than cults violate the norms and laws of the larger society.

In terms of group dynamics, both cults and terrorist groups offer a full array of rewards to members: affective, social, cognitive, and material. Chief among these rewards for both groups are powerful interpersonal bonds among group members. Particularly susceptible to the sense of community offered by both cults and terrorist groups are those who have lost or never developed close ties to others. The importance of unfreezing in radicalization to terrorism is examined in the next section.

Radicalization of Muslim Immigrants in Western Countries

Marc Sageman has focused on international terrorists, those who attack the United States and its allies. Starting with the nineteen terrorists of September 11, 2001, Sageman has accumulated data on an expanding network of jihadists that by 2008 totaled more than 500 individuals. A striking commonality of these individuals is that they come from the Muslim diaspora: over 80 percent are either Muslim immigrants to a Western country or the children or grandchildren of Muslim immigrants to a Western country. Sageman interprets this commonality in terms of the social and value opening that we have called unfreezing.

Unfreezing occurs when young Muslim immigrants in Western countries are lonely and disconnected from families and friends in their country of origin. Homesick, lonely, and marginalized—perhaps after trying the Western lifestyle without relief—they seek companionship in and around mosques. There they form like-minded groups; focus on victimization of Muslims represented in news and videos from Iraq, Afghanistan, and Israel; interpret this victimization as a war on Islam that also makes sense of their own experience of discrimination against Muslims in Western countries; and then, if they can connect with al Qaeda or another source of training, turn to terrorism. In this account, group ties (Sageman's "bunch of guys" formulation) come first. Then a group develops outrage for group and personal grievances and accepts "war on Islam" as the interpretation of their grievances, and group polarization (see chapter 8) moves the group to terrorism if it can find access to weapons or bomb-making skills. Sometimes, as with the case of Muhammad Bouyeri considered later in this chapter, the weapons can be more primitive than bombs.

Sageman's account of radicalization of second- and third-generation Muslim immigrants is similar.[11] Born and raised in a Western country, they have learned the language and ambitions of their country but experience discrimination as "foreigners." They do not fit into the country their parents or grandparents came from, and they do not fit into the country they were born in. So they drop out, join gangs, get involved in petty crime and drugs, and then sometimes turn to radical Islam as the explanation of their plight. Again the group ties come first, the group develops outrage and the interpretation that there is a war on Islam, and group polarization pushes the group toward political radicalization and violence.

Whether for immigrants or the children of immigrants, Sageman's account of radicalization begins with feelings of disconnection. For immigrants, the disconnection is more about loneliness in separation from friends and family at home, whereas for the children of immigrants loneliness is not an issue but the experience of discrimination separates them from identification with their country of birth. In either case Sageman believes that isolation and alienation open the door to

---

11. Sageman, M. (2008). *Leaderless jihad: Terror networks in the twenty-first century.* Philadelphia: University of Pennsylvania Press.

radicalization for young Muslims living in Western countries, especially in Europe. It is important to note that unfreezing can facilitate many new identities, but for a Muslim living in a non-Muslim country, shared religion is likely to be a high-salience source of similarity and support.

Muhammad Bouyeri

To illustrate how unfreezing works in a particular case, we reproduce below a profile of Muhammad Bouyeri developed by Petter Nesser for the Norwegian Defence Research Establishment.[12] On November 2, 2004, Bouyeri killed filmmaker Theo van Gogh—shooting him eight times, trying to behead him, then pinning a jihadist statement to his chest with a filleting knife. The statement was an open letter to Ayaan Hirshi Ali, a woman born in Somalia who became a feminist writer, activist, and politician in the Netherlands. The letter assails Hirshi Ali as a critic of Islam and author of the screenplay for Van Gogh's film *Submission*, which Bouyeri and many other Muslims felt to be insulting to Islam.

> Muhammad Bouyeri was born and raised in the suburb Slotervaart, West of Amsterdam, dominated by Moroccan and Turkish immigrants. Muhammad's parents came as immigrants to Holland from Morocco. He and his three sisters were born in the Netherlands. The publicly available sources about his family and his upbringing are relatively scarce and based on interviews with friends, colleagues, school personnel, and neighbors. The family has not talked to journalists, and many of his closest friends were detained after the murder of van Gogh. Neighbors have described the family as "quiet" and said they prayed in a moderate mosque. The young Bouyeri has been described as "a good boy," "gentle and cooperative," and as "a promising member of the second generation of Moroccan immigrants to Holland."
>
> He went to the local Mondrian College, and his teachers have described him as a "B-level student." He went on to study accounting and information technology at a technical educational institute in the town of Diemen south of Amsterdam. While studying, he is said to have spent

12. Nesser, P. (2005). The slaying of the Dutch filmmaker—Religiously motivated violence or Islamist terrorism in the name of global jihad? Kjeller, Norway: Forsvarets Forskningsinstitutt [Norwegian Defence Research Establishment], FFI/RAPPORT-2005/0, pp. 11–13. Available at https://www.ffi.no/no/Rapporter/05-00376.pdf.

much time on the streets of Slotervaart. Some of his friends have told a Dutch newspaper he was arrested and imprisoned for seven months due to a "violence-related crime." Bouyeri was known to have problems controlling his temper, and this was not the only time he had been arrested for violent behaviour. His friends said he was angry and frustrated because of political issues such as the conflict in Palestine. He supported HAMAS, and studied their suicide operations in detail. Bouyeri's friends believed he became more religious and fundamentalist during his imprisonment, and that the death of his mother from breast-cancer possibly contributed to his radicalisation. The September 11 attacks in the U.S. have also been cited as a possible source of inspiration. He started to wear traditional Islamic clothing and grew a beard in order to emulate the Prophet Muhammad and the Companions. He also became increasingly engaged in social activism and community work.

When he had served his time in prison, he started to study social work instead of accounting and became a volunteer worker for the Stichting Eigenwijks community centre. One of the workers at the centre has highlighted one event staged by Bouyeri in February 2002 in which local politicians had to face neighbourhood youths and listen to their political opinions and views. He has been described as an idealist, staging several events for youths, such as a soccer tournament, a neighbourhood clean-up campaign, in addition to writing for the centre's bulletin "Over 't Veld" (Over the Fields). It has also been said he had a dream about establishing a youth centre in his home community. He lobbied for support of this idea in the Dutch parliament and the Amsterdam city council, but did not receive the necessary financial support.

Bouyeri gradually became more radical, and focused on Iraq. According to the *Washington Post*'s backgrounder, his change was reflected in his writings for "Over 't Veld." The earliest articles called for cross-cultural and cross-religion understanding and tolerance, whereas articles from early 2003 appeared more fundamentalist and aggressive. For example, he reportedly compared Dutch police with Nazis, he used "sexual insults" when referring to American troops inside Iraq, and said they deserved to be beheaded. In the summer of 2003 he wrote the following in the bulletin: "the Netherlands is now our enemy, because they participate in the occupation of Iraq. We shall not attack our neighbours but we will those who are apostates and those who are behaving like our enemy. Ayan Hirshi Ali is an apostate and our enemy."

It appears he increasingly interlinked grievances related to the treatment of Muslims in Holland with the "global war on terrorism" and the invasion of Iraq. In line with his gradually more fundamentalist and intolerant approach, Bouyeri wanted to ban the sale of beer at the community centre he worked for, and he also "discouraged women from attending the events he organized." As this was not acceptable to the centre's staff he stopped working there and moved to Amsterdam.

In Amsterdam he was recruited by a group of Islamist militants. The group later convened regularly, twice a week, in the house Bouyeri rented at Marianne Philipsstraat in the district of Geuzenveld-Slotermeer in Amsterdam.... Exactly how Bouyeri was recruited to the Hofstad Network remains unclear. Seemingly, his way to jihadism resembled patterns of recruitment seen in the other thwarted terrorist conspiracies in Western Europe and the U.S. The typical pattern is that radical recruiters have approached alienated young Muslims in transitional phases of their lives, often after some kind of personal crisis, or failed ambition....

In a 2003 report the Dutch secret service Director Sybrand van Hulst stated that Islamist militants impress youth with a "certain fascination" with terrorism. According to the Associated Press, the report described the recruitment process like this: "After striking up a friendship, militants tell youths that modern mosques are too lax and take them to isolated, sect-like surroundings to convince them that taking part in *jihad* is a Muslim duty, with martyrdom the highest achievement." Quoting analyses based on the intelligence report, Associated Press continues, "They watch *jihad* videos with each other and go to readings, congresses and (Muslim) summer camps.... In addition, they participate in Internet chat rooms that discuss *jihad* and Islamic martyrdom." In the final phase of the training the young recruits are asked to write a martyr's testament similar to the one found in Bouyeri's pocket when he was arrested.

This account includes a history of cumulating disconnection that began with seven months in jail. Going to prison is a major separation from friends and family. Bouyeri seems to have become more religious in prison, but many who find Islam in prison lose it again after release ("prislam"). At about the same time, he lost his mother to cancer, and some of his friends date Bouyeri's radicalization from the time of her death. In a farewell letter written to his family before he killed van Gogh, Bouyeri says of himself, "You can't have failed to notice that I have changed since my mother's death."[13] Indeed, he appears to have gone from selfish interests to looking for something larger than himself. After release from jail he turned from studying accounting to

13. Benschop, A. (2005). Chronicle of a political murder foretold: Jihad in the Netherlands. Available at http://www.sociosite.org/jihad_nl_en.php#abu_zubair.

studying social work. He worked at a community center and developed programs for young Muslims; he dreamed of opening a new youth center in his home community. But his proposal for the new center did not succeed, and during 2002 his writing moved from promoting tolerance to inciting hostility against those he saw as threatening Islam. His growing fundamentalism got in the way of his work at the community center, and he lost his position there.

Adding up the damage, Bouyeri suffered multiple disconnections and losses in a short period of time: seven months in jail, his mother's death, the failed proposal for his own center, and his job lost. By the time he encountered those who became known as the "Hofstad Group," his life was coming unglued. There are many other elements to the story, some of them already familiar: grievances relating to Dutch participation in the war in Iraq and to perceived discrimination against Muslims in the Netherlands and love for new friends in the Hofstad Group. But the speed with which Bouyeri moved from tolerance and social work to intolerance and murder is an indication of the importance of the kind of opening to new people and new ideas that we have called unfreezing.

Looking Further

Beyerlei, K., & Hipp, J. R. (2006). A two-stage model for a two-stage process: How biographical availability matters for social movement mobilization. *Mobilization: An International Quarterly* 11 (3): 299–320.

Galanter, M. (1980). Psychological induction into the large group: Findings from a modern religious sect. *American Journal of Psychiatry* 137 (12): 1574–1579.

Galanter, M., Rabkin, R., Rabkin, J., & Deutsch, A. (1979). The "Moonies": A psychological study of conversion and membership in a contemporary religious sect. *American Journal of Psychiatry* 136: 165–170.

Lifton, R. J. (1963). *Thought reform and the psychology of totalism.* New York: Norton. Chapter 1, What is brainwashing? Chapter 2, Research in Hong Kong; Chapter 5, Psychological steps.

McAdam, D. (1986). Recruitment to high-risk activism: The case of Freedom Summer. *American Journal of Sociology* 92: 64–90, p. 70.

Sageman, M. (2008). *Leaderless jihad: Terror networks in the twenty-first century.* Philadelphia: University of Pennsylvania Press.

Брешко-Брешковская, Е. К. (1929). Софья Андреевна Иванова-Борейша. В кн.: *Народовольцы 80-х и 90-х годов.* Москва: Изд-во Всесоюзного общества политкаторжан и ссыльно-поселенцев., с. 9–14. [Breshko-Breshkovskaya, E. K. (1929). Sophia Andreevna Ivanova-Boreisho. In: *People's Will Members of the '80s and '90s.* Moscow: Izdatel'stvo Vsesouznogo obschestva Politkatorzhan I Ssyl'no-Poselencev, pp. 9–14.]

Group Radicalization

In the run up to D-Day in 1944, twelve men are released from military prison to prepare what is expected to be a suicide attack on a French *chateau* housing important German officers. The twelve had been convicted of serious and mostly violent crimes, including murder and rape, and were facing sentences ranging from twenty years of hard labor to execution. The twelve then train together, bond together, and attack together; most are killed making their mission a success.

This is the storyline of *The Dirty Dozen*, a film directed by Robert Aldrich with a star-studded cast that included Robert Ryan, Ernest Borgnine, Lee Marvin, Charles Bronson, John Cassavetes, Richard Jaeckel, George Kennedy, Ralph Meeker, Telly Savalas, Robert Webber, Clint Walker, and Donald Sutherland. Based on a bestselling novel of the same name, the film was the top moneymaker in 1967, the year of its release. It even generated several made-for-TV sequels in the 1980s.

The surprising part of this success is that the premise of the story is absolutely false. It is not true that violent individuals make the best soldiers. Quite the contrary, numerous studies have shown that better-than-average performance in combat is associated with absence of criminal record and higher-than-average intelligence, education, and family stability.

The difficulty of turning criminals into an effective combat team becomes evident in the light of what is known about combat motivation: soldiers may sign up for patriotic motives, but they risk their lives for their buddies. Most soldiers try to do their duty because doing less will endanger their friends. Criminals, especially violent criminals, are likely to be below average in capacity to care about the welfare of friends.

groups not just sum of parts!! Despite its false premise, *The Dirty Dozen* was a great success, and its success is a tribute to the ease with which groups are seen as simply the sum or average of individual group members. What better group for a violent mission than a group made up of violent individuals? The assumption is so easy, so obvious, that it often disappears from view. We do not see the air we breathe; nor do we see how often we project individual-level characteristics and individual-level relationships to interpretations of group-level characteristics and intergroup relationships.

Sometimes the levels-of-analysis issue is more obvious. The pattern of line relations we call a square does not depend on whether the sides are matchsticks or yardsticks. A melody does not depend on the notes that make it up, since transposing can reproduce the melody with an entirely different set of notes. The same water molecules can be ice or steam, depending on the state of interactions among the molecules. Carbon atoms related in one way are diamond and in another way are graphite lubricant. A wave on the water's surface is not reducible to the up-and-down motions of water molecules that transmit the wave. More controversially, many would say that a language is more than the speech behavior of current speakers of the language and that culture is more than the thoughts and actions of living members of the culture.

The general issue here is that relationships among elements at one level can produce new properties and new phenomena at a higher level. The emergent properties cannot be reduced to the properties of the elements at a lower level because it is the relationships that are key to the new properties. Human physiology depends on chemistry; but our organs are related in ways that transcend chemical structure, and chemists are not qualified as physicians. Bridges depend on the physics of steel and concrete, but physicists are not qualified as architects or engineers. The micro–macro issue arises no less in the relation of individuals and groups, where group psychology—including the mechanisms of radicalization of interest in this section—is more than just an aggregation of the individual psychologies of group members.

Group Dynamics

Some groups are aggregations; some are dynamic systems. The people you share the elevator with are an aggregation, as are Toyota drivers and five-year-olds. A school of fish, flashing first in one direction then another, is more than an aggregation because no single fish matches exactly the heading or speed of the school. Human crowds, similarly, can appear to share a "group mind," although individual movements of crowd members can be highly varied.

More interesting for our purposes are groups where members share a perceived interdependence so that what happens to one member of the group is seen to have an effect on all. Sports teams, work teams, neighborhood associations, and problem-solving groups have perceived interdependence—as might the elevator aggregation if the lights were to go out and the elevator shudder to a stop between floors.

The mechanisms of radicalization considered in this section operate in small, face-to-face groups in which group members share a perception of group boundary and interdependence. Large aggregations can also share a sense of group boundary and interdependence and so become psychological groups—a nation, for instance, or an aggregation of Toyota drivers who learn they face a common danger in the course of a new recall announcement. Mechanisms of radicalization in mass publics are the focus of the third section of this book.

Research on small, face-to-face groups began in earnest during World War II, including both groups created by an experimenter and groups found in everyday situations of work or sport. Results of this research indicated that perceived interdependence produces something new, something more than just the sum of the characteristics and needs of individual group members. Group properties emerge from the interaction and organization of individual group members.

This interaction can be minimal. An experimenter's coin flip that assigns an individual to one of two groups can alone be enough to elicit (small) biases in which individuals distribute more reward to members of their own group (whom they have never seen). How does this happen? Some individuals infer from the coin flip that the experimenter must be planning to do something different with the two groups; in other words, they read into the arbitrariness of the coin flip a certain degree of perceived interdependence. Others seem to feel that a norm of favoring your own group applies no matter how minimal the group.

The first step in understanding group dynamics is to distinguish between two kinds of interdependence, one obvious and the other more subtle. The more obvious perceived interdependence occurs when group outcomes will affect all group members. Thus a gang provides security to all members wearing the gang "colors." A sorority tries to provide the rewards of congeniality to all its members. An honorary society or club confers status on all its members, and if the group loses status, all members lose status. In general individuals join and stay in groups for shared goals that include material rewards, status, and congeniality. If, childlike, you asked your grandmother, "Why do people join groups?" she could easily point you to just these kinds of group attractions.

The more subtle kind of interdependence is based in the human need for certainty, especially about issues of meaning and value. What is beautiful, and what is ugly? What is good, and what is evil? What is worth working for, or dying for? What does it mean that I am going to die? How does my life mean any more than the life of the dead squirrel I drove by on the way to work? Am I a good person, at least as good as others? These are questions of value, and no empirical science can answer them.

According to group dynamics theory, group consensus is the only source of certainty about questions of value. If all agree that a certain behavior is bad and disgusting, we are certain that it is bad and disgusting. The subtle interdependence then is the degree to which we depend on group consensus for our social reality, which, if the consensus is strong enough, makes value judgment seem as objective as the consensus about which tree is tallest.

The two kinds of interdependence, for obvious group goals and for the less obvious social reality, together determine attraction to a group. This attraction, often called *group cohesion*, pushes individuals toward agreement, especially on issues relevant to group goals, because disagreement threatens both the cooperation that can attain group goals and the consensus that gives certainty to value judgments. The higher the attraction to the group (higher cohesion), the stronger the pressure for group agreement around a group norm, which means stronger pressure on deviates from the norm. This pressure threatens deviates with loss of the material, status, or congeniality rewards of group membership and can include ridicule, exclusion from the group, and even violence.

A famous conformity experiment shows this theory at work.

Group Dynamics in Action: The Asch Experiment

Imagine yourself as a participant in a psychological study. You arrive at the appointed time to the lab and find seven other participants assembled, sitting in a row that faces the blackboard and the researcher. The only chair remaining is number seven, next to last at the right end of the row—that is where you will sit. The researcher explains that he studies visual perception, and for the duration of the experiment he needs all

(handwritten margin notes: "Need for certainty about meaning and value, with consensus being its standard")

the participants to call out loud, left to right at his direction, what they see in front of them at the board. For each trial the experimenter places in the chalk tray a card with a line marked "S"—for stimulus—and next to it a card with three lines of different lengths, marked "A," "B," and "C." One of the three lines matches the line of the stimulus, and the job of participants is to say which line that is, a kind of multiple choice test.

It is really easy to pick out the matching line, and on the first trial each participant, one by one, calls out the correct answer: "B." When the experimenter reaches you at the end of the table, you answer with no hesitation, "B." The same thing happens on the second trial: everyone calls out the correct answer, "A." Visual perception experiments are often very boring.

On the third trial the experimenter pulls out another card; you see immediately that the answer is again "B" and prepare to say it out loud when your turn comes. But something unexpected happens. The first participant the experimenter turns to gives an obviously wrong answer: "A." Then the second participant says "A" instead of the obviously correct answer, "B." One by one, each of the first six participants calls out the wrong answer. Now it is your turn—will you go with your own judgment or with the obviously wrong judgment of the other people in the experiment?

If you studied social psychology, you know the answer: about 75 percent of participants will go along with an obviously wrong majority in at least one of these "unanimous majority" trials. Only one-quarter of participants never conform. For the average participant, 32 percent of answers follow the majority. This result has to be considered alongside a condition in which participants performed the same line-length matching task alone. In this "control" condition, fewer than 1 percent of answers were incorrect. Similar results have been obtained for males and females, for older as well as college-age participants, and in many countries in addition to the United States.

You may have guessed the reason behind the group's unanimously false answer: the participants who arrived to the lab early were all accomplices of the experimenter instructed to play this trick on the unsuspecting last participant. The researcher who invented this conformity test, Solomon Asch, was surprised at the results of his studies: "Reasonably intelligent and well-meaning young people are willing to call white black."

Several of Asch's experimental variations produced important differences in yielding to the majority. If judgments are made from memory after the "S" card is removed, yielding increases. Yielding also increases if the A, B, and C lines are made more similar in length. If the minority of one is allowed to write judgments instead of calling them out loud, average yielding drops from 32 percent to 10 percent. If one confederate (calling out judgment before the naive participant does) is programmed to give always the correct answer, the naive participant's yielding drops to 7 percent.

Group dynamics theory accounts for these results as follows. Making the judgment from memory or with more similar choices raises uncertainty, attraction to the group for reducing uncertainty is increased, and the power of the majority norm is thus increased. Writing instead of calling out judgments protects the minority of one from fear of majority ridicule, that is, from threat to the deviate member's participation in group goals. So the 10 percent yielding in the anonymous condition shows the power of the social reality value of the group—the extent to which the minority of one really believes that the group judgment must be correct. About one-third of yielding in the Asch experiment (10 percent vs. 32 percent) is based on the social reality value of the group, and the remaining two-thirds (22 percent vs. 32 percent) is based on the attractions of group goals. Finally, a confederate who always gives the correct answer reduces yielding because the naive participant has an ally in facing the threat of ridicule and because the value of complete consensus is already lost when the confederate stands up to the bogus majority.

There is one more variation of interest. Asch placed a single confederate in a group of naive participants, and instructed him to give the same schedule of wrong answers that the bogus majority gave in Asch's standard experiments. Can you guess what happened? With each wrong answer, the six naive participants turned as one to laugh at the confederate. Asch, who had set up the scene, reports that he could not help but join in laughing at the confederate. It appears that insight into group dynamics does not eliminate their power.

In this section we examine three mechanisms that can move whole groups toward radicalization. *Group polarization* emerges from expanded consideration of in-group dynamics, *group competition* is about how outside threat changes group dynamics, and *group isolation* focuses on the added power of the group when group members have no other group to turn to. All three mechanisms depend on the relationship of perceived interdependence from which these mechanisms emerge. Taken together these mechanisms are an important part of how normal individuals become more extreme in beliefs, feelings, and action.

Looking Further

Asch, S. E. (1956). Studies of independence and conformity: A minority of one against a unanimous majority. *Psychological Monographs* 70 (Whole No. 416).

Back, K. (1951). Influence through social communications. *Journal of Abnormal and Social Psychology* 46: 9–23.

Hertel, G., & Kerr, N. L. (2001). Priming in-group favoritism: The impact of normative scripts in the minimal group paradigm. *Journal of Experimental Social Psychology* 37 (4): 316–324.

Rabbie, J. M., Schot, J. C., & Visser, L. (1989). Social identity theory: A conceptual and empirical critique from the perspective of a behavioral interaction model. *European Journal of Social Psychology* 19 (3): 171–202.

CHAPTER EIGHT

Group Polarization

*Discussion among like-minded individuals tends to move the whole group further
in the direction initially favored.*

The Age of Idealism

There has been an important commonality in the case histories of
Russian terrorists. At one point each revolutionary belonged to, or
frequented, a student commune or discussion group. Student circles,
student communes, student movements—these provided an extended
forum for airing ideas, critiquing literary works, and discussing economic and social problems. Living in a commune made participation in the never-ending discussions unavoidable. But even for those
students who lived outside communes, discussions came as a part of
daily routine: at street corners, in university hallways, at protests, demonstrations, and tea parties. They discussed everything: the scientific
method; the theory of evolution; economics and sociology; literary
works by Russian and European authors. With growing enthusiasm
they discussed political issues that related to students' lives. These
ranged from women's rights to overthrowing the Russian government.

Reflection and discussion are characteristic Russian social forms
and rituals. Popular wisdom holds that during Russian winters, when
much of activity outdoors ceases, even the least educated are forced

to spend hours talking or thinking (drinking may belong to the same causal chain). Whether this belief is well founded is less important than the fact that it gives misery—Russian winters—a higher purpose, always a welcome turn of events in Russia. But the reign of Alexander II saw an unprecedented proliferation of student discussion groups. There are several explanations for this development.

The Wind of Change

Russia was changing. Everywhere there were new laws, new customs. Serfs gained freedom. The military was no longer a death sentence for draftees. Railroads connected remote regions of Russia, allowing for rapid travel throughout the year and not just in the summer. Censorship was weakening, and a number of political publications sprouted. Travel abroad was allowed, and many students traveled to Europe to study there. Education was made accessible to the poor, ethnic minorities, and women. What used to be unthinkable was becoming a common reality.

Imagine being born at such an age. Imagine growing up with an ever-evolving sense of your country and your identity. Women, previously expected to stay home and raise children, now could become teachers or doctors. Children of serfs, previously confined to their master's village, subject to the master's orders and whims, now could travel and learn a trade. Jews, previously forced to live in designated rural areas, now were allowed to live in the major cities. It was both exhilarating and confusing. No expert could advise on the best way to think and to behave. Everything was new to everybody.

As new possibilities challenged old certainties, young people found themselves gravitating to their peers in quest for direction. They needed to understand change and to find their role in it. The insurmountable quantity of new information, both academic and political, required filtering and interpretation. Morality, values, and norms were being reformulated, and that, too, required input from others. No medium served these purposes better than a discussion group.

Educational Reform

Czar Alexander's education reform gave generous scholarships to talented but indigent students, greatly increasing the number of individuals able to attend university. In addition to growing in size, the student body became diversified when former serfs from remote villages were able to attend universities alongside the sons of nobility. The same reforms allowed Jews and other ethnic minorities to attend university. Despite restrictions on the percentage of minority students per year, university student bodies became more ethnically diverse.

Previously, students had come from the same elite background, and their education had only small impact on their lives and careers, which were determined by their parents' fortunes. They had minor ambitions, little motivation, and, as a result, few original ideas. Now, with the inflow of penniless talent who saw themselves as potential winners of life's lottery, the race to achieve "the Russian dream" was on.

They felt the world was their plaything, these children of slaves and ostracized peoples, suddenly given a chance at a life they had not dared to dream about. Now no dream was too grand for them. If they could go from being traded by their masters for livestock to being university students, why couldn't they invent new theories or a new social order? The older generation had nothing to teach them. What did their elders know—having lived as zombies for all those years of injustice and repression? It was from among the young that the young sought insight. They were their own inspiration, and so they got together and talked and talked and talked until they could not stay awake any longer.

An unexpected consequence of the arrival of lower-class provincial students to university cities was that the newcomers, torn from their social networks, could find social and material support only from other students. The problem of finding and financing room and board was solved by organizing into communes that lived and ate together. Thus, the infrastructure for discussion groups was created.

Golden Age of Russian Literature

Who knows how talent is born? What explains the synchronized emergence on the literary scene of such giants as Dostoyevsky, Tolstoy, Turgenev, and Nekrasov? Why, suddenly, was every student in Russia poring over the works of philosophers like Bakunin, Chernyshevsky, Dobrolubov, and Belinsky—works complex beyond an average reader's taste? The reign of Alexander II became known as the golden age of Russian literature. No historic period before or after could boast a comparable richness of social issues raised in such masterful language.

As the poet Nekrasov put it, "a poet in Russia is more than a poet." Indeed, there was no Walter Scott among the emerging literary geniuses, no Alexandre Dumas, no J. R. R. Tolkien. Russian literature of the time was not concerned with fairy tales, adventure, or fantasy. Instead it focused on problems of everyday life in Russia. Here, the heroes were those who challenged the accepted injustices. Dostoyevsky's Prince Myshkin is a challenge to the vanity and hypocrisy of society; Tolstoy's Anna Karenina is a challenge to the subservient and meaningless role of women. Nekrasov's entire life's work was a challenge to the misery of peasants' lives. Turgenev in his classic novel *Fathers and Sons* coined the term *nihilism*, a rejection of the accepted order, a challenge to the old society that became popular among Russian youth. The villains of this literature were those obstructing change to indulge their laziness, stupidity, selfishness, or corruption.

Although with weaker storylines and dialogues, Russian philosophers of the time did not shy away from writing fiction, most notable of which was an influential novel by Chernyshevsky aptly named *What's to Be Done?* With less subtlety than Dostoyevsky or Tolstoy about his book's ultimate lesson, Chernyshevsky called on youth to organize cooperatives and communes—to take responsibility for building the new Russia. His lack of subtlety was not a problem for his audience who looked to be both inspired and instructed. The book became a kind of bestseller; banned by the government shortly after publication, it was hand-copied or smuggled from abroad. There were popular student songs about *What's to Be Done?* and its author. Every student activist or terrorist read it. A more detailed description of the book and its author is in chapter 13.

With the plethora of literary works turning every social issue into a metaphor, a parable, a tragedy, or a triumph, the social conscience of impressionable youth was pinched to the last nerve. They turned to one another to reflect on their reading, to compete with one another in how well they had learned the books' lessons. They discussed, without a shade of skepticism, how to translate idealistic literary images into everyday Russian reality.

First Discussion Milestone: "Going into the People"

Whether it was the uncertainty of the historical moment, education reform with its many benefits and challenges, or the literary inspiration, discussion groups dominated the landscape of social life for young people. In 1875 the first crop of discussion groups arrived at an idea that electrified schools, universities, and communes: to go into the people. The idea was to become one with the peasants, to share their burdens, and to mobilize them for political action. Chernyshevsky's *What's to Be Done?* was instrumental in building this common goal. Hoping to become the "real people" that Chernyshevsky idealized, students began to seek training in peasants' occupations in preparation for "going into the people."

By this time discussion groups began organizing into a centralized hierarchy with headquarters in St. Petersburg and branches in major cities, including Moscow, Odessa, Harkov, and Kiev. The organization took the name "Land and Freedom" to reflect its goals of endowing peasants with more land to go with their newly acquired freedom.

The years between 1875 and 1878 were the testing ground for the strategy of "going into the people." The experience was disappointing; it turned out to be very difficult to live and work like peasants. Radicalization efforts ran into a stone wall of peasants' inertia and apathy. And it was boring: no peers to talk to about exciting new ideas, about the future that they were going to build together; no elevating conversations; no larger picture. It was dull routine, hard work, day after day. By 1878 young activists started packing up and going back to their student communes, to the discussion groups where they started.

In 1878 Land and Freedom also experienced a number of arrests and imprisonments. The government saw a threat in students' activism and arrested anyone who possessed radicalizing literature or who was witnessed attempting political conversations with peasants. Hundreds of activists were arrested and awaited trial, on average for four years. The hardships of life as a political prisoner in 1870s Russia are described in chapter 9.

Second Discussion Milestone: Propaganda by Fact

The tone of student discussions in 1878 had become more somber. There was less youthful enthusiasm, more skepticism and bitterness. It was obvious to many that radicalization of peasants alone was not going to bring social change. Something more drastic needed to happen to awaken peasants to the necessity of change and to move them to action.

Most Land and Freedom members leaned toward shifting the focus of propaganda and mobilizing efforts from peasants to factory workers. The latter were more easily accessible because factories were mostly located in urban centers, with workers housed in barracks and buildings nearby. There was no need to venture into remote rural locations, risking hypothermia and starvation on the way. Factory workers were also more worldly and less politically naive than peasants. Land and Freedom's new goal was to convince factory workers to fight for their rights by staging protests, demonstrations, and strikes.

But a faction of Land and Freedom members, outraged by the arrests of their comrades and disillusioned about the effectiveness of propaganda, felt that the only fruitful action was political terror. About a dozen individuals formed a secret group that they ominously called "Freedom or Death." The group's manifesto claimed the necessity of political terror for social change in Russia, and group members began acting separately, secretly, and sometimes in defiance of the official Land and Freedom leadership.

Part of the warrant for violence was the increasing threat of government repression: government spies had become more numerous and more deadly. Murdering spies was useful in two ways: averting danger to themselves as well as publicizing to potential traitors that their actions would be brutally punished. Another part of the manifesto argued for the need to communicate to peasants and others afraid of political action that opposing the government was possible. In social movement theory, McAdam has referred to this kind of recognition as "cognitive liberation." During 1878–1879 Freedom or Death debated a new strategy of "propaganda by fact" that would include high-profile assassination of government officials involved in oppressing students and peasants.

The attempted assassination of General Trepov by Vera Zazulich (see chapter 3) and the successful assassination of General Mezentsev (see chapter 6) initiated a transition from discussing propaganda by fact to accomplishing the fact—a widely publicized assassination of prominent officials. The transition was made possible by an important addition to the group. Freedom or Death discovered Nikolai Kibalchich, a former student and an activist who had spent three years in solitary confinement for his activism. Kibalchich was a whiz kid; a talented chemist and physicist, he designed explosives for the revolutionaries.

Third Discussion Milestone: Terrorism as Revolution

Inside Freedom or Death, discussion of violent tactics moved from punishing traitors and publicizing group goals to the ultimate goal of overturning the Russian government. Increasingly, consensus grew that the only way to achieve a change of government was to eliminate those in power—whether or not they personally oppressed students or peasants.

A vivid illustration of this change in rhetoric was the decision to kill Odessa police detective Baron Geiking. According to Lev Tichomirov, a member of Freedom or Death who later divorced from its radical agenda,

> ... the murder of Geiking was a big disgrace. That Geiking had done absolutely no wrong by the revolutionaries. He related to his work formally, without particular fervor, and granted various concessions to the political prisoners. He was generally liked by political prisoners, and Geiking felt he was safe without a doubt. But exactly because he was not guarded it was decided to kill him. There is nothing easier than to kill Geiking, who is known to everyone and walks down the street unguarded.[1]

The unfortunate baron fell prey to the new agenda of political change through targeted assassinations of public officials.

The discussions within Freedom or Death grew more intense. Conspirators felt that theirs was the only way to achieve Land and Freedom's goals. They became completely disillusioned in the activist agenda and wanted to abandon it in favor of terrorism.

However, they knew that a number of their peers from Land and Freedom were still very invested in activist work. Land and Freedom's leadership categorically denied requests to plan the czar's assassination, fearing that peasants who worshiped the monarch would attribute such an act to the revenge of retrograde noblemen bitter about the czar's liberation of serfs. The sharing of resources, both money and people, between the activist and terrorist purposes grew increasingly problematic. Already terrorist-leaning groups in the south of Russia engaged in assassinations unsanctioned by Land and Freedom. A crisis was imminent.

In order to bring the dilemma to discussion of the entire group, Land and Freedom resolved to organize a general assembly in the city of Voronezh, June 18–21, 1879, where delegates from all branches could express their opinions on the changes proposed by Freedom or Death. But just before the general assembly, Freedom or Death held its own meeting, unannounced to Land and Freedom, in Lipetsk, on June 15–17. Invitation to the Lipetsk meeting went to individuals known

---

1. Available at http://dugward.ru/library/xxvek/tihomirov_pochemu.html.

to be sympathetic to Freedom or Death proposals, both members of Land and Freedom and others unassociated with the organization. One of the outsiders invited to the Lipetsk meeting was Andrei Zhelyabov.

According to participants, there were about fourteen people at the Lipetsk meeting. These individuals later formed the kernel of the People's Will Executive Committee, the elite and secret governing entity for Russia's most notorious terrorist organization. Here, at the very first discussion, the group's program of action (*Program of the Executive Committee of People's Will*) was formulated and unanimously accepted. Betraying the authors' romantic roots in literary discussion circles, the program vowed to "fight in the manner of Wilhelm Tell,"[2] arms in hand. In a more pragmatic turn, the program also explained that, because the government imprisons and confiscates revolutionaries' property, they should feel entitled to similarly confiscate anything that belongs to the government.

At the same meeting, the revolutionaries began discussing the code of the Executive Committee. The first item in the code asserted that the only person eligible to enter the Executive Committee is one ready to give it everything, including life; therefore, it was impossible to exit from the Executive Committee.

At the third and final discussion in Lipetsk, Alexander Michailov (unrelated to chapter 4's Adrian Michailov) gave a long accusatory speech against Alexander II. He concluded it by listing the names of those comrades who had suffered from state repressions. He then asked his audience whether it was reasonable to forgive all the suffering caused by the czar for all the good that he has done and received a unanimous answer, "No." The first operation of the Executive Committee, and the goal of its future actions, was assassination of Alexander II.

Fourth Discussion Milestone: Fission

At the Land and Freedom meeting in Voronezh, the members of the newly formed Executive Committee privately tried to agitate some of their ambivalent friends to join their faction. Andrei Zhelyabov was particularly interested in converting Sonia Perovskaya. Despite his

2. Morozov, N. (Ed.) (1979). *Program of the Executive Committee of People's Will*. June 15–17, Lipetsk. Available at http://narovol.narod.ru/document/progamIKmoroz.htm.

charismatic personality and articulate speeches, he failed at this time to bring her over to the terrorists' side (see chapter 5).

The Voronezh assembly counted over two dozen delegates present, and some others sent letters to express their positions. They convened for group discussions twice a day for four or five days. The assembly, careful not to stand out in its activities, picked remote locations in parks and forests for their meetings.

The rift between terrorists and activists made the general atmosphere of the meeting tense, with each side fearing conflict with the other yet unwilling to compromise. The discussion went round and round with neither side giving in. Finally, George Plechanov, the leader of the activist faction of Land and Freedom, declared that Land and Freedom did not exist as an organization anymore since the views of both the radicals and the activists deviated significantly from the original organization's position.

Plechanov henceforth headed the activist group that became known as Black Repartition, referring to the group's goal of redividing "black" or fertile land to benefit the peasants. Those who accepted the proposed terrorist platform formed People's Will. The Executive Committee of People's Will was formed of the radicals who had come to Voronezh from Lipetsk. The proposal to assassinate Alexander II was again raised to the now-larger group that composed People's Will. Here they started plotting the first in a series of terrorist acts that made the name of People's Will synonymous with political violence for generations of Russians.

Group Polarization

Each milestone of students' discussions moved them toward more radical positions. They went from talking about social change to trying to radicalize the peasants by personal discussion and radical literature. When this goal failed, discussions resumed, and two directions emerged. Land and Freedom continued to advance the idea of peaceful propaganda and mass mobilization—but this time among factory workers. Those who became disillusioned in mass mobilization and sought revenge for their imprisoned comrades formed the secret faction Freedom or Death. Their tactic became propaganda by fact, where instead of talking with peasants, occasional assassinations of government officials were meant to demonstrate the irrelevance and vulnerability of the political system.

The third transition, to terrorism as a primary tactic, took place when Freedom or Death, in defiance of Land and Freedom leadership, engaged in a campaign of violence against anyone who represented the government, regardless of his role in the social problems that the group set out to solve.

The final transition, to violence against civilians—including family members of the czar, involuntarily drafted soldiers, and innocent bystanders—took place after days of intense discussions at the meetings in Lipetsk and Voronezh. The terrorist group that crystallized at the end point of these four transformations was drastically different from the group that had started out as a literary discussion circle, though it included many of the same people. This trajectory of radicalization is not as surprising as it may seem.

There is an experimental model of group radicalization through discussion that has been referred to variously as "risky shift," "group extremity shift," or "group polarization." Groups of strangers brought together to discuss issues of risk taking or political opinion consistently show two kinds of change: increased agreement about the opinion at issue (see introduction to section 2) and a shift in the average opinion of group members. The shift is toward increased extremism on whichever side of the opinion is favored by most individuals before discussion. If most individuals favor risk before discussion, the shift is toward increased risk taking. If most individuals oppose American foreign aid before discussion, the shift is toward increased opposition to foreign aid.

The shift is not just a matter of "go-along-to-get-along" compliance; each group member gives both prediscussion and postdiscussion opinion on a questionnaire that only the researcher sees. Thus, discussion among individuals with similar values produces an internalized shift toward more extreme opinions; when asked after the discussion has ended, individuals show more extreme opinions.

There are currently two explanations of group extremism shift. According to *relevant arguments theory*, a culturally determined pool of arguments favors one side of the issue more than the other side. For instance, risk taking in Western culture is considered a desirable trait, and, as discussed in chapter 6, risk taking among males is often associated with higher social status. Among Russian students in the 1870s, the culturally favored opinion was supporting an active intervention toward peasants' well-being and government reform.

Before discussion, an individual samples from the culturally determined pool in reaching his or her individual opinion, then in discussion hears new arguments from others, which, coming from the same pool, are mostly in the same direction as the individual was leaning. Individuals are then persuaded by the imbalance of new arguments heard in discussion. In the Russian student discussion circles, the preponderance of arguments was that the situation was intolerable, something had to be done.

A second explanation for group polarization is *social comparison*. Opinions have social values attached to them. Individuals more extreme in the group-favored direction—the direction favored by most individuals before discussion—are more admired. They are seen as more devoted to the group, more able, more moral—in sum, as better people. This extra status translates into more influence and less change during group discussion, whereas individuals less extreme than average in the group-favored direction have less influence and themselves change more. No one wants to be below average in support of the group-favored opinion, and the result is that the average opinion becomes more extreme in the group-favored direction.

Both relevant arguments and social comparison are necessary to explain the pattern of experimental results. In support of relevant arguments, research shows that manipulating arguments (giving participants written statements reportedly from other group members but in fact selected by experimenters to favor one side or the other) can change the size and direction of the group shift. In support of social comparison, research shows that knowledge of others' opinions even without knowledge of others' arguments (for instance, giving participants a tally of others' opinions) can produce group shift. The two explanations are complementary rather than redundant. Both conduce to increased similarity and increased extremism in a group of like-minded individuals.

Student discussion circles started out with most participants favoring social change through active personal involvement. Some individual participants came to the circles already radicalized enough to favor illegal action and violence. Such an individual was Andrei Zhelyabov (see chapter 2). These more extreme individuals gained higher status and more influence over their discussion groups. Over time less radical participants gravitated toward the extremism of the higher-status individuals—those willing to give more, to dare more—for the sake of the peasants. Repeated discussions brought out more and more extreme arguments in favor of "going into the people" to achieve radical change.

When "going into the people" failed, more extreme proposals were argued and accepted by a number of Land and Freedom members. This newly formed faction continued their discussion in secret, becoming progressively radicalized over time. When the meeting in Voronezh was called, in an attempt to reconcile the differences between Land and Freedom and Freedom or Death, it was already too late. Each group had veered off into a direction that departed from their original common goal, as Plechanov noted at the meeting. At the end, a small part of the group that had started as a literary discussion circle became a terrorist organization, with those having the most radical convictions holding the most influential positions.

There is an important limitation of research on group polarization. The experiments that demonstrated extremism shifts in group discussion asked about group members' opinions, but they did not ask about actions. Opinions and attitudes are not always good predictors of action. Of all those who might say they want to help starving children, how many would actually donate to UNICEF or work in a local soup kitchen? But for the Russian students of the 1870s, radicalization in opinion was often associated with radicalization in action. How are we to understand this unusually high consistency between opinion and behavior?

One possibility is the degree to which the era was swept up in a culture of change. Tectonic plates of Russian society were shifting, and the young generation who grew up amidst this change, themselves beneficiaries and victims of new hopes and new norms, felt that it was their job to rewrite history.

Social psychologist Robert Abelson advanced a similar perspective in relation to student activism in the United States. Abelson reviewed evidence that beliefs are not automatically translated into feelings, and feelings are not automatically translated into behavior. He then identified three kinds of encouragement for acting on beliefs: seeing a model perform the behavior; seeing oneself as a "doer," the kind of person who translates feelings into action; and unusual emotional investment that overcomes uncertainties about what to do and fear of looking foolish. Abelson brought these ideas to focus on 1970s student activism in the United States:

> ... it is interesting to note that certain forms of activism, for example, campus activism, combine all three of the above types of encouragement cues. Typically, the campus activist has at least a vague ideology that pictures the student as aggrieved, and provides both social support

and self-images as doers to the participants in the group. A great deal of the zest and excitement accompanying the activities of student radicals, whether or not such activities are misplaced, thus may be due to the satisfaction provided the participants in uniting a set of attitudes with a set of behaviors.[3]

As U.S. students of the 1970s discussed, dared, and modeled their way to the excitement of linking new ideas with new behaviors (see chapter 9), so too did Russian students of the 1870s.

Prison Universities

There are two approaches to investing. The first, recommended by all the experts, is diversification: putting money in many different stocks, bonds, and financial instruments so that failure of any one investment will be only a small loss. The second is concentration: putting money into just a few excellent stocks.

The second approach is famously associated with Warren Buffet, the most successful investor of the last fifty years. The "Sage of Omaha" makes relatively few but very large investments; that is, he puts all his eggs in a single basket and watches the basket very, very carefully.

The same choice is faced by governments holding terrorists: whether to spread them out in the general prison population, which means putting a few in many different prisons, or to concentrate them in one prison. Most governments seem to prefer putting all the terrorists in one place—placing all the bad eggs in one basket. The Israelis concentrate Palestinian terrorists, the French concentrate Islamic radicals, the United Kingdom concentrated Republican terrorists in Northern Ireland, and the Turks concentrated Kurdistan Workers' Party (Partiya Karkerên Kurdistanê , PKK) terrorists. One reason for concentration is the higher security needed for prisoners who have friends outside willing to risk their lives in prison breakouts. There may also be a fear of contamination: terrorist "rotten eggs" giving new ideas to criminal *yeggs*.[4]

The downside of placing all the terrorists together is the group polarization that occurs when like-minded individuals interact in prison.

---

3. Abelson, R. (1972). Are attitudes necessary. In B. T. King and E. McGinnies (Eds.), *Attitudes, conflict, and social change*. New York: Academic Press, pp. 19–32.

4. Safecrackers.

Over time, the group becomes more committed to the terrorist cause—more extreme, more radical—than the individual group members were when they entered prison.

The aspect of this problem that has been given the most attention is the mutual learning that terrorists profit by in *prison universities*. They have time to go over the operations that brought them to prison. What mistakes were made? How was security breached? How did an informant get in? They have time to improve their tradecraft. What are the best ways to reconnoiter a target? How best to manufacture bombs? How does state security operate? How can terrorist security be improved?

Another aspect of the problem is ideology. Those who join a radical group for personal grievance, love, thrill, or social connection may arrive in prison without much ideology. They may have only a slogan or two to connect with sectarian theology or Marxism or national self-determination. But with plenty of time for discussion, prisoners can learn the concepts and arguments that justify terrorist actions.

More important than new skills or new ideology, however, the prison university provides new connections. Groups of like-minded terrorists form in prison, mirroring the terrorist factions at large. *Terror behind Bars*, a video report from *60 Minutes*, shows Palestinians in an Israeli prison divided among Hamas, Fatah, and other factions. Similarly, the Republican prisoners in Northern Ireland's Long Kesh prison (later Her Majesty's Prison Maze) replicated various militant factions, notably the Provisional IRA (PIRA) and the Irish National Liberation Army (INLA). In other words, a single prison can house multiple terrorist universities.

With new skills, new ideology, and new attachment to a prison group, terrorists in prison can be radicalized to new levels of extreme behavior. In 1981 Republican prisoners in Long Kesh organized a sequence of hunger strikes in response to authorities' efforts to take away their status as "politicals" and treat them as ordinary criminals. The story of these protracted suicides, eight PIRA men and two INLA men, is told in the book *Ten Men Dead*. Similarly, PKK prisoners in Turkish prisons went on a hunger strike in 1996 when authorities tried to move them from communal housing (dormitories) to solitary cells. The strike lasted sixty-nine days; twelve died before the authorities gave in to most of the prisoner demands.

Suicide by hunger strike is difficult. It is relatively easy to press a button and detonate the explosive vest that ends life in this world. One decision, one press, and the job is done. Much more difficult is to choose every minute of every day to refuse food. In starvation, the body digests the internal organs. Starvation does not end pain; it extends pain. Hunger strikes by political prisoners are testimony to the power of group radicalization that can move individuals to persevere in a protracted and painful death.

One might argue that the terrorists in prison are already at such a high level of radicalization that there is little room for further radicalization. Even if terrorists become more extreme in prison together, perhaps the difference between 98 percent extremity and 100 percent extremity is not worth worrying about.

Unfortunately, identification of terrorists is not an exact science. Behavior can be misinterpreted. Informants can make mistakes, or they can lie to advance their own interests. The result of inadequate or incorrect information is that governments lock up a wide range of individuals as terrorist suspects. Some are indeed active terrorists, some are small-scale supporters of terrorism, some sympathize with the terrorist cause but have never participated in illegal action, and a few have no sympathy for either terrorists or their cause. Imperfect intelligence guarantees that there is a range of sympathy and support for terrorism among those in prison for terrorism.

Despite this range, most prisoners will be like-minded to the extent of feeling some hostility toward the government that locked them up and some sympathy for the terrorists who oppose the government. This agreement determines the direction of group polarization. Prison groups start with a range of opinion and commitment, but biased arguments and high-status extremists produce group polarization. Individuals who came to prison with little commitment to terrorism can leave prison with extreme commitments anchored in attachment to their prison friends.

The threat of terrorist mobilization in prison universities led to a change in penal policy in at least one country. In the beginning of its conflict with ETA (*Euskadi Ta Askatasuna*, Basque Homeland and Freedom), the Spanish government concentrated ETA suspects and convicts in only a few prisons. After 1986, ETA people were dispersed widely throughout the Spanish prison system. The dispersal policy seems to have had some success: some observers report that more prisoners resigned from ETA and that ETA control and organization of its people in prison was reduced.

There is a potential downside to dispersing terrorist prisoners, however. Short-term gains in reducing terrorist organization in prison must be weighed against the possibility that the government may one day want to negotiate with the terrorists. Disorganized terrorists are difficult to negotiate with; there is no central power on the terrorist side that can negotiate and then enforce a deal. Dispersing terrorist prisoners reduces the power of a terrorist organization, but the danger is that a weak terrorist organization can reduce the chances of negotiated peace.

Looking Further

Beresford, D. (1987). *Ten men dead: The story of the 1981 Irish hunger strike.* London: Grafton Books.

Brown, R. (1986). *Social psychology* (2nd ed.). New York: Free Press. Chapter 6, Group polarization.

McAdam, D. (1982). *Political process and the development of black insurgency, 1930–1970.* Chicago: University of Chicago Press.

O'Leary, B., & Silke, A. (2007). Proposition 15. Concentrated incarceration creates "insurgent universities"; dispersed imprisonment disorganizes insurgents but, in consequence, makes them less negotiable. In M. Heiberg, B. O'Leary, & J. Tirman (Eds.), *Terror, insurgency and the state: Ending protracted conflicts.* Philadelphia: University of Pennsylvania Press, pp. 411–413.

People's Will. (n.d.). History and documents. Available at http://elib.shpl.ru/ru/nodes/5019-narodovoltsy-80-h-i-90-h-godov-sbornik-statey-i-materialov-sostavlennyy-uchastnikami-narodovolcheskogo-dvizheniya-m-1929-istoriko-revolyutsionnaya-biblioteka-kn-39#page/1/mode/grid/zoom/1/. Assessed May 10, 2016.

CHAPTER NINE

Group Competition

Groups are radicalized in competition with other groups.

The Czar's Reforms

Groups define themselves in comparison with other groups. Earthlings might develop a sense of common identity if aliens from outer space appeared (as many science fiction authors have suggested), but without aliens humans remain a category, not a group. Americans feel common ties with other Americans when they travel abroad, suddenly surrounded by members of comparison groups. Back in the United States citizenship fades in importance as other contrasts—religion, ethnicity, accent—become salient.

A particularly powerful form of comparison and contrast is provided by intergroup competition. As anyone who has played a pickup game of basketball or soccer can attest, competition is often sufficient to create powerful group identities even if the individuals involved were strangers before the game started. When it is "us against them," the "us" is endowed with a powerful emotional appeal. For young activists and radicals in nineteenth-century Russia, "them" in the daily competition for rights, security, and status was the Russian government—which was of two minds.

The reforms instituted by Alexander II liberated the serfs, established an open judicial system, and gave the press an unprecedented freedom. This sudden liberation was in stark contrast to the brutal and autocratic regime of Alexander's father, Nicholas I. But most officials serving the more liberal administration had started as servants to an ultraconservative one—and they were not enthusiastic about the changes. Just a few years before, a nobleman could be flogged for a dissenting or simply careless remark; now university students were shouting their criticisms of the government in city squares. Not only were noblemen deprived of their birthright, the slaves who had supported their families for generations, and not only were their land endowments reduced in favor of their former slaves but, most insulting, now these former slaves, sitting in the same classroom as noble children, dared to accuse and criticize their former masters.

Alexander II did not have much support among his ministers: the great majority of them formed the retrograde party that opposed the reforms and warned of mass protests and civil unrest. In Alexander's own family, his second son (who later became Czar Alexander III) took the side of the retrogrades. Stuck between his beliefs and ambitions and the waning loyalties of those around him, Alexander II chose to be careful. The annals of the Romanov family included many bloody endings to monarchs' lives, always at the hands of noble ministers unhappy with the czar. Therefore, while advancing his liberal agenda, Alexander II was forever trying to please his opponents. The result was often a compromise that made neither side happy.

A stark example of troublesome compromise was land reform. Alexander realized that to liberate serfs and not give them any land would lead to a revolt by 28 million homeless and indigent people. But to give them enough land to satisfy their needs would mean completely alienating already aggrieved noblemen who viewed the land as theirs. In the end, the land endowments to liberated serfs were too small to allow them to rise beyond poverty. In addition, peasants were forced to pay heavy mortgages to their former landowners.

Peasants and Students Respond: Dissent and Protest

In the best traditions of Russian culture that idolized the monarch, peasants began circulating rumors that evil noblemen had corrupted and misused the czar's generous and benevolent reform. Here and there, a literate peasant (a rarity) claimed to know the true meaning of the reform: all land was granted to the peasants. Scores of pilgrims in search of a fairer deal flocked to these "heralds of truth." The response by local noblemen was predictable: unarmed peasants were shot by the hundreds.

In this tragic historical moment, young liberals, some of them former serfs themselves, took to debating the reform and its consequences. They gathered at universities, in their rented apartments, and on the streets; they published their thoughts in newly liberal and uncensored print. Alexander II was furious: What? They, the direct beneficiaries of his reforms, were complaining more than his nobles? He would show these ingrates!

Government Reaction: Crackdown and Repression

Resorting to the tactics favored by his late father, Alexander II appointed generals and admirals as ministers of education and university presidents and gave them power to institute whatever order they deemed appropriate. Among the generals' ideas for fighting dissent in universities was the canceling of scholarships for poor students, which left 65 percent unable to return to universities. For those of means, the right to attend was made contingent on carrying at all times a "matricular"—an identifying document in which all information about the student, including grades, attendance, and disciplinary measures, was recorded. All gatherings of three or more students were strictly forbidden. This repression set off a trajectory of competition between the government and the students.

At first there were mass student protests. Students marched toward the houses of university officials demanding explanations for the oppressive policies. The officials sent for the military. Soldiers, happy to indulge their class hatred for the long-haired, privileged, too-smart-for-their-own-good students, beat them with sticks and arrested hundreds. The protests spread from the capital, St. Petersburg, to Moscow and provincial towns. Everywhere, army units beat and arrested protestors. Russian prisons were overwhelmed by new arrivals. Inside the prisons students continued to discuss the government's policies, sometimes producing proclamations that called for radical action. With bribes to guards, these provocative proclamations made it outside of prison and eventually to the czar's desk.

At the same time, in the summer of 1872, Moscow suffered from a series of arson attacks, although no culprit was ever detained. The official version of the events held that disgruntled students were responsible for the fires, but equally likely is another account that puts the responsibility with members of the nobility, who seized the moment to reinforce the czar's anger and instigate more repression. Repressions did follow.

For those who could no longer attend the university, there was a choice. They could return to their villages or slums on the outskirts of the city and try to fit in with the lifestyle of their parents. They could try to forget the ideas and the excitement that they had experienced at the university, forget the dreams of a better future for themselves and their country. Alternatively, they could join the ranks of "former students," working as tutors and living in communes where, for a small fee, they could count on a bed to sleep in and a mostly vegetarian diet from the communal kitchen, occasionally spiced up by slaughtered horse meat. The main attraction of a commune, however, was in hot discussions that could run all night long, in books that students shared with each other, and in new ideas to ponder. For most, the choice was clear: they joined student communes.

Student Reaction: The Birth of Activism

It was in such communes that the idea of activism was born (see chapter 8). Former students decided to actively seek a fairer deal for the peasants and at the same time to seek a number of other reforms from the government, including a constitution and an elected legislature. Their plan was to radicalize the peasants for antigovernment protests. They reasoned that with the vast number of peasants backing up students' liberal ideas, the government would not be able to respond with repressions. The czar would be forced to cooperate.

The problem was that the peasants were illiterate and misinformed about political issues. Worse, they were too overwhelmed with their daily struggles to pay attention to politics. Former students resolved to address both issues at once. They would train in occupations that could ease peasants' lives: nursing, teaching, and manual labor. They would work for minimal or no pay, travel to remote villages, help the most needy and underserved. At the same time, they would talk to the peasants, popularizing new ideas. They would teach peasants to read using political pamphlets as texts.

One of the first organizers of the activist movement, Ekaterina Breshko-Breshkovskaya, described these preparations for "going into the people":

> In different parts of town workshops were formed where young revolutionaries learned to become smiths, carpenters, shoemakers. They were all very proud of their accomplishments. Young women, especially students, looked for factory jobs. . . . Most of the participants were 16 to 20 years old, others—between 20 and 25. The latter were called "old men."[1]

Breshko-Breshkovskaya's memoirs of her own experiences "in the people" are typical. Together with two or three commune friends, she traveled from one village in Ukraine to another. The friends' fake documents stated they were from a provincial Russian town, and they claimed to be wandering service people: mending shoes, sharpening knives, sowing, or painting cloth. When they met a peasant interested in their services or hospitable enough to offer them an overnight stay at his or her house, they attempted to discuss political issues. Mostly they encountered no interest or even resistance to their activist efforts. Occasionally they came across peasants who sympathized with their ideas but who were too afraid to do anything that might anger the authorities. The brutal sanctions against earlier revolts were still vivid in the peasants' memories.

Activists who "went into the people" stood out as foreign. Their clothes were inappropriate, as when they wore Russian-style clothing in Ukraine. Their accents and elaborate manner of speech betrayed their noble origins. And of course their biggest giveaway was that they could not perform the jobs that they claimed were their specialty. Their "shoemaker's" patches came off on the first wearing, the "carpenter" could not work with basic tools, and the "peasant" did not know how to plow. No wonder that local police were quickly on their trail. Breshko-Breshkovskaya was apprehended at a busy market, and a search of her bag revealed antigovernment proclamations. She was thrown into jail for her activism, as were many of those who "went into the people" in the early 1870s. Imprisonment was the government's response to student activism, and that response was disproportionately brutal.

---

1. Брешко-Брешковская, Е. (2006). *Скрытые корни русскои революции; Отречение великои революционерки*. Москва: Центрполиграф. [Breshko-Breshkovskaya, E. (2006). *Hidden roots of the Russian Revolution: Abdication of a great revolutionary*. Moscow: Centrpoligraf, p. 28.]

Government Reaction: Imprisonment

Breshko-Breshkovskaya describes her first prison, in the small town of Bretslavsk, where she was kept in solitary confinement (a practice that was often employed with political inmates for fear of their escape and political agitation). Like many political prisoners, she refused to say her name or give any answers and thus was categorized as a peasant—the lowest category of prisoners for whom almost nothing was provided. She wrote,

> They brought lunch—a slice of bread and a plate of clear pinkish water in which swam a small white stick. "What's this?" I asked. "Borscht" was the answer. I tried it. The water was a bit sour, a bit salty, and a stick turned out to be a bit of beet. . . . Time went by slowly. The cell was dark, and it stunk monstrously. The variety of insects stunned imagination. . . . There was no bench, no conveniences of any kind. The floor was covered with waste . . . I got tired of standing and sat on the floor, leaning against the door . . . but in a few minutes I jumped on my feet. I was covered in bugs: my body itched from head to toe. It was impossible to sleep, or even just stand.[2]

After some weeks in her first prison, Breshko-Breshkovskaya heard a commotion in the common courtyard. It turned out that the roof over some cells had collapsed, killing two and injuring others—the prison was over a century old and had never been maintained. All prisoners were to be moved to another prison. No transport was provided, and prisoners, young and old, men and women, healthy and sick alike, had to walk for 100 miles chained to a metal rod that forced them to walk in a thin line. Many women had their children with them in prison, and children had to walk beside their mothers. In October, nighttime temperatures already fell below freezing, but most prisoners had only rags for clothes. It did not matter. The authorities were not concerned if prisoners got sick or died on the way. Breshko-Breshkovskaya, during her initial imprisonment, developed a "slight paralysis of the right side, with weakness of the right arm and leg, and the right eye saw worse. It remained bad forever."[3]

In the new prison, Breshko-Breshkovskaya was placed under the supervision of a cruel guard who hit defiant women with his huge set

---

2. Ibid., pp. 74–75.
3. Ibid., p. 82.

of keys, placed them in solitary confinement for extended periods of time, and generally treated them as slaves. It was now November, and since her arrest in the summer, Breshko-Breshkovskaya had not had an opportunity to wash herself. Her repeated demands for a bath were denied; she was treated by the same protocol as peasant prisoners. Lunch soup was served to her in a big wooden bowl that was kicked into the cell by the guard. Trying to stir the soup, Breshko-Breshkovskaya discovered that the bottom of the bowl was covered with a thick layer of foul-smelling dirt; she was afraid to eat it. She lived off rye bread and water, which came from the well in the courtyard. Waste seeped into the well water, and prisoners developed stomach infections. No medical assistance was given to them.

In the common cell where nonpolitical female prisoners were kept, there were always fights. Children as young as five or six took part in them, defending their mothers and screaming obscenities at the top of their lungs. When the cruel guard died and was replaced by a young, nicer, and inexperienced one, instead of enjoying their new freedom, the inmates caused constant disturbances, finally broke out of their holding cell, and chased the new guard, hitting him over the head with the same set of keys that the brutal guard had used against them. The nice guard was replaced. The romantic image of innocent peasants cultivated by young activists was fading with each day of imprisonment alongside them.

After a while, the authorities had enough information about Breshko-Breshkovskaya to figure out her real name and noble status. They threatened to call for her parents. At this point she confirmed what they already knew and was moved to the "nobles'" quarters of the prison.

Here the situation was far better. In the cell stood a table and chair. The bed was covered with sheets and a blanket. Lunch consisted of two servings: soup and grits. She gained access to books and magazines. Very soon she began receiving messages lowered to her window by a string from a cell above hers where another political prisoner was being held. She could talk with him during hours of guard shift change. Every prison she moved to—Kiev, Moscow, and St. Petersburg—from now on placed her in the "political quarters."

Prisoner Reaction: Group Cohesion and Radicalization

Political prisoners were usually located in the same part of the prison, and they developed ways of communicating with each other. Some guards could be bribed into passing notes or even letting one prisoner visit for a brief time in another's cell. Sometimes, windows of one cell were directly facing windows of another, allowing for conversations among prisoners. Finally, the plumbing pipes that ran from top-floor cells to lower ones carried sounds, and prisoners developed a version of Morse code that allowed them to communicate without guards' assistance. This method of communication became so widespread that prisoners had to knock with different objects (hands, pencils, or feet) and against different surfaces (table, windowsill, or toilet) to differentiate their messages from the many messages simultaneously coming from neighboring cells. They communicated the news from the outside about their comrades, some imprisoned and some still at large. They told each other what they knew of the authorities' case against them. All of them were awaiting their trials for two, three, and even four years.

Breshko-Breshkovskaya recalls her experiences in prison this way:

> The monotone of solitary confinement slowly eats up the powers of any prisoner. All five of his senses lack stimulation, and besides he experiences spiritual hunger. His eyes see only the gray walls of the cell; his ears hear only the clicks of keys in the lock. Tasteless and sometimes harmful prison food kills his appetite, and the stuffy, stinky air dulls his sense of smell. Even his sense of touch atrophies because of lack of normal movement and fresh air. He is overtaken by sleepiness and apathy.... Night and day he [lies] in bed. Ulcers develop on his famished body; he barely eats and gets up with difficulty ...
>
> In prison every tiny piece of news—every hint of news—attained an extremely exaggerated meaning. Like the moon rising over the horizon in the desert seems huge, so is every event, happy or sad, without a measure against which its significance could be gauged, also inflated filling the tiny space of the prison world. It raises prisoners to the sky or completely closes off the light of life for them, forcing them into suicide.[4]

The prisoners developed strong bonds with others through their communications. These messages were the only ray of light in the darkness of their imprisonment. These people shared their dreams and hopes, not only for themselves but for their country. In addition, they shared their pain, their anger at the unfair and cruel treatment they

---

4. Ibid., p. 109.

all experienced at the hands of the authorities. No matter how hard the guards tried to silence prisoners' knocking, they were unsuccessful. Breshko-Breshkovskaya recalls that political prisoners became a tight community with emerging leadership, even though they never saw each other face-to-face. They played chess on imaginary boards, exchanged news from the outside, and discussed books that they had read.

Having friends in prison meant having friends outside. Only relatives were allowed to visit prisoners, but many prisoners came from noble families who did not want any part of their criminal life; others were too far from their family to hope for a visit. However, for a small bribe, a document certifying a valid relationship could be obtained, and so members of student communes became sisters, sisters-in-law, brides, aunts, or cousins of prisoners, enabling them to provide brief company and necessities such as food, clothes, medicines, and money to the prisoners. Among those actively involved in helping prisoners was Sophia (Sonia) Perovskaya, a noble-born activist later turned terrorist. Among those receiving help inside prison was Andrei Zhelyabov, a former serf with radical ideas and charismatic personality. Later, Sophia and Andrei became lovers and helped organize the assassination of Alexander II.

As was discovered during the Trial of 193 of which both Breshko-Breshkovskaya and Andrei Zhelyabov were part, the average time spent in "preliminary confinement"—imprisonment before the trial—was four years. Most of the 193 defendants were acquitted. Many had been arrested at age sixteen or seventeen and at the time of trial were twenty or twenty-one years of age. The years they had spent as political prisoners were not wasted. They formed lifelong friendships with people who suffered alongside them. They learned rules of conspiracy and a secret language that definitively juxtaposed their community to that of the authorities. No longer could their noble parents appeal to their family ties in attempts to turn them around. They were NOT the same, not in their ideas, not in their community, not in their bodies—all of these bore marks of their incarceration. Political prisoners came to rely on the larger group of sympathizers with their cause for everything: the news, food and clothes, companionship, above all perspective.

Activists' goals—romanticized by their reading and midnight discussions at the communes—changed as they felt more embittered and entitled. They were still seeking a fair deal for the peasants, but now, enlightened by their experiences, they came to see peasants as apathetic, uneducated, cowardly, and self-serving. The hope of mobilizing this passive crowd for radical action had withered. Instead former students (turned activists and political prisoners) realized they would have to carry out the changes themselves. Obviously, peasants did not know what was good for them. They were too infatuated with the idea of a benevolent, omnipotent czar. To free them of their delusion, the czar would have to be eliminated. Without his halo obstructing their perspective, peasants would then spring to action and overthrow the regime that had dealt them such an unfortunate fate.

A new goal was born in the dark, damp, and fetid cells where they spent day after day: hungry, sick, lonely, repulsed at the dirt into which they were forced. The goal was to continue the opposition to the government relentlessly, until all the humiliations, all the suffering and disappointments were avenged. In prison, they heard their comrades scream in pain in adjacent rooms; many died with no helping hand offered to them. They heard the mumblings of young men and women who slowly lost their minds. They heard of those who, unable to take the hardships, had killed themselves. There was no turning back, no turning the other cheek. It was not their own life and not their own suffering—it was life and suffering of an entire generation—that called for revenge, and they were only too willing to respond.

Over a period of years, then, the seesaw of government repression and student reaction produced the hardened core of a more radical movement. For those who went through protests, arrests, and prisons, the bridges to normal life were burned (see chapter 7). They could not go back to universities, their families did not want them for the trouble they had caused with the authorities, and their only relationships and jobs were inside their activist circles. The government's sanctions insured that, for their every need, activists had nowhere to go except to one another. They became each other's family and university. They became lawmakers and executioners unto themselves. Their underground life became an underground universe. And in that universe, killing the czar became for many an absolute good.

When Groups Collide

Hostility toward a threatening group is the obvious result of intergroup competition and conflict, but equally important is the effect of threat on the interactions among those feeling threatened. Perceived interdependence within the threatened group increases as group members see they will share the consequences of the outside threat. They see, as Benjamin Franklin famously put it, "We must hang together, or assuredly we all will hang separately." Group competition and conflict are a powerful source of radicalization as a group facing threat moves toward the unity of thought, feeling, and action that prepares its members to fight the threat.

External Threat Produces Cohesion

Cohesion emerges when group members feel they share group goals and values. The most reliable source of cohesion, demonstrated in hundreds of small-group experiments, is intergroup competition. Whether athletic contests, intellectual contests, economic contests, or political contests—as soon as there are identifiable sides in competition, there is a big boost in cohesion.

The cohesion-building power of competition is consistent with the general theory of group dynamics described earlier (see introduction to section 2). Competition means that some kind of prize goes to the winner but not to the loser; and in many competitions the winning side gets no more and no less than the other side loses—a zero-sum game. The prize—money, land, medal—often has both material value and status value; that is, the prize has two of our three kinds of group goals. The third kind of goal is congeniality, the reward value of pleasant interactions with others; and as we will describe shortly, competition for a prize increases congeniality.

Striving for a group prize also answers, at least temporarily, questions of value. The primary group value is winning, which can submerge other and more divisive value judgments. In the film *The Dirty Dozen*, individual conflicts, including racism, were submerged when men trained together for a dangerous mission. Individual differences irrelevant to the mission, such as the fact that Telly Savalas is far from good-looking, disappeared from view. The primary source of status in a group in conflict is an individual's contribution toward group success.

The increased group cohesion produced by facing a common threat is expressed in three changes in the nature of relations within the group: increased respect for group leaders, increased idealization of in-group values, and increased sanctions for deviation from in-group norms.

The in-group effect of external threat was evident in the United States after the terrorist attacks of 9/11. National cohesion (patriotism) increased. Polls showed sudden and major increases in approval levels for the president, George W. Bush, and for the legislative and judicial branches of government as well. For instance, approval for how President Bush "has handled his job as president" went from about 55 percent just before 9/11 to about 85 percent in the month or two after 9/11. Public rhetoric invoking American values flourished ("They hate our freedoms . . ."). Muslim immigrants, perceived deviates from American norms, were subjected to some public hostility; perhaps a thousand were rounded up for interrogation.

Continuing Threat Produces Escalation

Competition usually produces some hostility toward the threatening competitor. Most of us have experienced reactions of fear and anger toward an individual or a group that threatens us. The bigger the threat, the greater the hostility. In sports, hostility directed against the competitor is checked by the fact that the material stake is relatively small even when the status value of winning and losing is large. The fact that sports competitors rotate also helps to control hostility.

But political competitions can persist for a considerable period of time with the same opponents. The Russian students' conflict with the czar went on for many years, and the conflict escalated as both sides moved from rhetoric to violence. A similar escalation is described by Stefan Aust in the history of the Red Army Faction in 1970s Germany: indignation turned to protest, protest to resistance, resistance to violence, and violence to outright terrorism. The psychology of escalation is a key part of political radicalization in intergroup conflict, and we know something about how it occurs.

One mechanism of escalation is *perceptual.* Things I do to punish you are likely to look a lot worse to you than to me. Things *they* do to *us* are likely to look worse to us than to *them.* This tendency is plain in the conflict between czar and students.

In freeing the serfs the czar was undertaking a difficult task against resistance from the nobility. The czar expected love, or at least respect, for his efforts but received only criticism. The students criticized the czar for not having given the serfs enough land to live on and to repay their mortgages to former masters. The czar then acted to shut down the criticism, a mild response compared with what his father would have done. The students saw any censorship as unacceptable and escalated to demonstrations. The czar put down the demonstrations, but with special prison accommodations for students. The students focused on the prison, not the accommodation, and escalated to trying to rouse the peasants ("going into the people"). They were arrested as activists and imprisoned, now with peasant accommodations for students who refused to give their real identities. Horrors experienced in prison cracked some of the students but hardened others who emerged ready for terrorism. At every step, the czar felt he was being moderate and generous and the students were biting his hand, whereas the students at every step saw the czar as a greater tyrant than before.

A second mechanism of escalation is a shift in the *nature of the prize*. At the beginning the conflict between students and the czar was about how best to help the serfs—a material prize focused on the welfare of peasants. But as the conflict escalated, the prize became status and power: whether the czar or the students should determine how to deal with the peasants and indeed whether the czar or the students should control the future of Russia. From a material issue with some potential for compromise, the issue evolved into a contest for power and status with no room for compromise. When the prize of group conflict is status and power, the conflict is a zero-sum game in which each side can only win to the extent that the other side loses. In a zero-sum game, the czar and his government were ready to use whatever violence was necessary. So were the students.

The third mechanism of escalation is a *sunk-costs framing* of the conflict. When many have suffered for a cause, and especially if many have died for the cause, giving up means disloyalty to those who have already sacrificed and suffered (see chapter 13). Giving up means our friends' sacrifices would be for nothing, and so would our own. In the conflict between students and the government, the students had suffered and to some extent so had police, government officials, and even the czar. The choice between giving up and escalating became a loyalty test, and escalation was the only loyal and moral choice available—for both sides.

The psychology of escalation therefore includes three mechanisms: an asymmetry in perception of harm, a shift from material prize to status and power prize, and a sunk-costs framing of the conflict. Together these mechanisms make each step in the escalation a reason to escalate further. Escalation is another kind of slippery-slope mechanism (see chapter 4), now at the level of intergroup relations rather than the individual level. Whereas Milgram's individual-level slippery slope ends in escalating levels of punishment, the slippery slope of intergroup conflict ends in the perception of a zero-sum game that cannot be escaped.

Boys Will Be Boys: An Experimental Model
of Conflict and Escalation

A famous demonstration of competition-threat mechanisms is an experiment conducted by Muzafer Sherif in 1961. Sherif invited twenty normal (no indication of aggression, typical intelligence, and physical ability) twelve-year-old boys to a three-week summer camp he had created in the Robbers' Cave National Park, Oklahoma. They were randomly divided into two groups of ten and placed in different areas of the park without exposure to or knowledge of the other group. The camp counselors were instructed to act as nonintrusively as they could so that the boys could be free to work out their own subcultures without outside influence.

The first stage of the experiment (week 1) allowed the boys to engage in normal group activities (hiking, playing sports and games). The groups developed informal leaders and different internal norms and cultures. The group that named itself the Rattlers was a "tough-guy" group that encouraged cursing; the other group, the Eagles, forbade cursing.

The second stage of the experiment (week 2) began with introducing the two groups as one group was allowed to find equipment left by the other at a baseball diamond. This was followed by a number of other activities aimed at highlighting the fact that the groups were in competition for limited resources. A tournament was initiated, composed of many different kinds of intergroup competitions. The boys got a look at the shiny new jackknives that were to be the prizes for the winners. A camping trip was planned with both groups, but the group that arrived second (by design of the experimenter) discovered that the group that arrived before them took the better camping spot and all the best of the food supplies.

During this second week, Sherif asked camp counselors to rate the boys' behavior toward their group as well as toward the rival group. He found that, as the tournament unfolded, the boys began to show signs of in-group cohesion and out-group hostility. They used mostly positive traits to describe their own group ("brave," "friendly") and mostly negative traits to describe the rival group ("sneaky," "stinky"). New leaders emerged—"war leaders"—and boys displayed more respect for the new leaders than they had for previous leaders. In addition to these direct measures, there were other clear indications of hostility and violence. At a picnic the two groups broke into a food fight. Each group stole and burned the other's flag and raided the other's bunkhouse.

Boys plotted "raids" and "counterraids" as hostility and threats of violence increased.

The third stage of the experiment (week 3) involved attempts to reduce the conflict produced in the second stage. The first idea tested was that simply eliminating competition and providing opportunities for peaceful contact between the groups would allow the boys to get to know each other better and reduce negative stereotyping and hostility. Each such attempt ended in conflict escalation rather than reduction of hostility, sometimes resulting in fights.

The second idea for conflict resolution was that if the two groups needed to pool their resources to solve a common problem, their conflict would decrease. To that end, Sherif staged a water-supply break, effectively turning off water to both camps and requiring the help of both groups to fix it. Next, the truck that delivered food to the camps "got stuck in the mud." One group of ten boys could not pull it out, so they had to join forces with their enemies.

Common goals indeed proved to be effective in reducing intergroup hostility. By the end of week 3, boys were using more generous terms to describe the rival group, and they could name some friends from the rival group as well as from their own. In addition, following a competition in which one group won a cash prize, they voted to share the money with the other group to buy snacks for everyone. All the boys went home on the same bus; peace had been restored.

Sherif's experiment with white, middle-class American boys shows the power of competition and threat to raise in-group cohesion and hostility toward the external threat. Idealization of the in-group and increased respect for leaders emerged. Escalation of hostilities toward the out-group threat occurred throughout the tournament in the second week. Sherif's experiment is a model of the in-group consequences of shared threat.

Three Kinds of Political Competition

Politically, an out-group threat has three salient forms. A nonstate group can challenge state power, as the student movement challenged the czar's power in the late 1800s. A nonstate group can challenge another nonstate group when both claim to represent some larger cause of movement. And two or more factions can compete for power within a nonstate group challenging state power. In this section we describe a modern example of each form.

In 1954, the U.S. Supreme Court determined that maintaining separate public schools for blacks and whites was unconstitutional. Thus encouraged, a broad civil rights movement developed that engaged both African Americans and liberal whites, with an early victory in the Montgomery Bus Boycott in Alabama (1955). The movement challenged Jim-Crow practices with a variety of organizations and tactics. Sit-ins and marches were often considered illegal trespass, but, at least on the activists' side, they were nonviolent.

The legal battle against racism was largely won by 1968: the Civil Rights Act of 1964 banned discrimination in employment practices and public accommodations, the Voting Rights Act of 1965 restored and protected voting rights, and the Civil Rights Act of 1968 banned discrimination in housing. The success of the civil rights movement made it a model for social change, especially for the mostly white students who came together to form Students for a Democratic Society (SDS). Indeed most of the leadership of SDS first became involved in activism in civil rights demonstrations.

The 1962 Port Huron Statement is generally regarded as the constitution of the SDS. It has been many things to many people, but in broad terms it began as an idealistic call to fight apathy, alienation, racism, imperialism, economic inequality, the Cold War and nuclear weapons, and the military–industrial complex. It points to a future where human needs rather than profit will allocate resources, a future of equality and abundance. It is anti-anti-communist: agreeing that Soviet communism has been authoritarian and repressive but maintaining that the socialist, communist vision is still viable in a new participatory democracy in America. Finally, it identifies universities and students as the future of the socialist revolution: organized labor had failed; students are the new proletariat.

It is important to recognize that the Port Huron Statement called for reform, not revolution. It sought an enlarged and socially conscious federal government, a people-power government that would replace corporate power in economic decisions and replace local government in decisions about education. Following the example of the civil rights movement, the Port Huron Statement embraces nonviolence:

> In social change or interchange, we find violence to be abhorrent because it requires generally the transformation of the target, be it a human being or a community of people, into a depersonalized object

of hate. It is imperative that the means of violence be abolished and the institutions—local, national, international—that encourage non-violence as a condition of conflict be developed.[5]

In 1969 a faction of SDS issued a new manifesto that took its name from a Bob Dylan song lyric: *"You don't have to be a weatherman to know which way the wind is blowing."* The Weatherman manifesto was an almost unreadable amalgam of Marxist–Leninist vocabulary and hatred for the "pigs" who uphold the government and its war in Vietnam. The first three sentences set the tone:

> The contradiction between the revolutionary peoples of Asia, Africa and Latin America and the imperialists headed by the United States is the principal contradiction in the contemporary world. The development of this contradiction is promoting the struggle of the people of the whole world against US imperialism and its lackeys. Lin Piao [Mao Tse-tung's best general], Long Live the Victory of People's War![6]

The next major statement was a *Declaration of War*, read by Bernardine Dohrn, Weatherman's leading lady, in a phone call to a radio station in May 1970:

> This is the first communication from the Weatherman underground.
>   All over the world, people fighting Amerikan imperialism look to Amerika's youth to use our strategic position behind enemy lines to join forces in the destruction of the empire.
>   Black people have been fighting almost alone for years. We've known that our job is to lead white kids into armed revolution. We never intended to spend the next five or twenty-five years of our lives in jail. Ever since SDS became revolutionary, we've been trying to show how it is possible to overcome the frustration and impotence that comes from trying to reform this system. Kids know the lines are drawn [and] revolution is touching all of our lives. Tens of thousands

5. Students for a Democratic Society (1962). *The Port Huron statement.* Available at http://en.wikipedia.org/wiki/Port_Huron_Statement.
6. Asbley, K., Ayers, B., Dohrn, B., Jacobs, J., Jones, J., Long, G., Machtinger, H., Mellen, J., Robbins, T., Rudd, M., and Tappis, S. (1969). You don't have to be a weatherman to know which way the wind blows. New Left Notes. Available at https://ia600207.us.archive.org/34/items/YouDontNeedAWeathermanToKnowWhichWayTheWindBlows_925/YouDontNeedAWeathermanToKnowWhichWayTheWindBlows_925.pdf.

have learned that protest and marches don't do it. Revolutionary violence is the only way.

Now we are adapting the classic guerrilla strategy of the Viet Cong and the urban guerrilla strategy of the Tupamaros to our own situation here in the most technically advanced country in the world.[7]

In the 1970s, the Weather Underground was responsible for dozens of high-profile bombings, including bombs placed at the Pentagon and the U.S. State Department. How did student idealists become underground guerillas? They came from middle-class and even wealthy families, some of the best and brightest of their generation. A surprising number came from Jewish families traumatized by the Holocaust twenty years earlier. As Mark Rudd describes, he and his friends had lost their Jewish faith but felt a moral obligation not to be the "Good Germans" of their generation.

The Weather people were personally attractive, and most were the kind of emergent leaders who could move a crowd. They went to elite schools, including Harvard, Columbia, the University of Michigan, Swarthmore, and Bryn Mawr. They were energetic and intelligent: almost every Weatherman leader later wrote a book, and today several are employed as university professors. But, beginning with civil rights demonstrations, they saw their interactions with police and government as a long history of abuses from a government they saw as controlled by a military–industrial complex.

Highlights of their litany of abuse included the following. "Peace Candidate" Lyndon Johnson was elected president, then sent increased numbers of U.S. troops to Vietnam and bombed North Vietnam (1965). Martin Luther King was assassinated (April 3, 1968). The antiwar sit-in at Columbia University was smashed with police violence (April 30, 1968). Protestors at the Democratic National Convention in Chicago were assaulted by police (August 1968). Later called a "police riot" by the Walker Commission, the Convention protest was captured in pictures and film of police beating students that brought a wave of sympathy for the antiwar movement.

On October 8, 1969—the second anniversary of the death of Che Guevara—the Weatherman faction of SDS initiated a "national demonstration" in Chicago to show the "pigs" that they couldn't get away

---

7. Dorn, B. (1970). A declaration of a state of war. From *The Berkeley tribe*, July 31, 1970. Reprinted in Jacobs, H. *Weatherman*. Palo Alto, CA: Ramparts Press, 1970. Available at http://www.lib.berkeley.edu/MRC/pacificaviet/scheertranscript.html.

with "fascist tactics." Later called "Days of Rage," the demonstration was a failure. The expected thousands of SDS members did not show up, but a few hundred Weatherman members went ahead anyway. When they attacked police with pipes and baseball bats, most were quickly subdued and jailed. This first effort to "bring the war back home" with violence on American streets was a failure. Black Panther leader Fred Hampton called the action childish.

Two months after the Days of Rage, Hampton was killed in his bed by police bullets. Coming on top of their weak showing in Chicago, Hampton's death convinced Weatherman leaders that violence was the only answer to violence. Their communes had been harassed and penetrated by the "pigs" (the FBI's illegal COINTELPRO operations against antiwar groups only came to light years later). Despite all they had done—years of petitioning, community organizing, sitting-in, marching, confronting police, jail time—racism and the military–industrial complex still dominated the United States. The war continued, and hundreds of thousands of Vietnamese and thousands of U.S. draftee soldiers were dying (the My Lai massacre was revealed in November 1969). As the Weatherman leadership saw it, there was no nonviolent alternative remaining, only a choice between being complicit in the violence of Vietnam or taking their best people underground for guerilla war.

In 1970 the group issued a "Declaration of a State of War" against the U.S. government, under the name "Weather Underground Organization" (WUO). Bombing attacks (carefully prepared and advertised to avoid human casualties) were undertaken, each justified as a response to a particular government action. The bombing at the U.S. Capitol on March 1, 1971, was "in protest of the US invasion of Laos." The bombing at the Pentagon on May 19, 1972, was "in retaliation for the US bombing raid in Hanoi." The January 29, 1975, bombing at the U.S. Department of State Building was "in response to escalation in Vietnam." The WUO goal was "bringing the war back home."

There is real irony in the Weatherman version of Marxist–Leninist class analysis that called for war against the "pigs" when in fact the police "pigs" were the blue-collar brothers of the U.S. draftees that Weatherman claimed to represent. The police felt anger and contempt for the draft-dodging, long-haired, foul-mouthed products of universities they themselves could never aspire to, just as the czar's soldiers and police of the 1870s felt anger and contempt for the long-haired, university-based revolutionaries they faced. More generally, revolutionaries in both czarist Russia and LBJ's United States came to violence over a long back-and-forth of government policy, student reaction, and government response. Police violence and the FBI's COINTELPRO are evidence that it is not only students who can be radicalized in the dynamics of conflict and escalation.

Group Radicalization in Competition for the Same Base: Outbidding

Groups advancing the same political cause can be in competition for the same base of sympathizers and supporters. As competing groups try different tactics, the competition may escalate to gradually more radical acts if sympathizers favor these acts—a competition described by Mia Bloom as "outbidding."

Analysts have suggested, for instance, that the 1979 assassination of Lord Mountbatten by the Irish Republican Army (IRA) was an effort to compete with escalated attacks by the Irish National Liberation Army (INLA). Similarly, the hijacking of the luxury liner *Achille Lauro* by the Palestinian Liberation Front may have been an attempt to gain advantage over rival Palestinian groups. Today it is common to see more than one group claiming credit for a particular terrorist attack, even for a particular suicide terrorist attack.

Radicalization by competition is particularly clear in the case of the Armenian Secret Army for the Liberation of Armenia (ASALA). ASALA first gained support of the Armenian diaspora by attacking Turks at a time when mainline Armenian organizations were only talking about retribution for the Turkish genocide of Armenians. One of the older organizations (Tashnaks) responded to the new competition by establishing its own anti-Turkish terrorist group, the Justice Commandos of the Armenian Genocide.

Similarly the Palestinian Front for the Liberation of Palestine (PFLP) resolved to take up suicide terrorism when the group began to seem irrelevant in the second intifada. True to its Marxist logic, PFLP at first would have nothing to do with the "false consciousness" of jihad and *shaheeds* (martyrs). Its standing in Palestinian polls dropped to near zero as suicide attacks brought increased support for Hamas and Fatah. In response, PFLP determined that it did after all support jihad, recruited its own *shaheeds*, and a few martyrdom operations restored PFLP's standing in the polls.

Of course it is possible for a group to become too radical and lose its base of support. The line between higher status from more radicalization and lower status from too much radicalization is fine and variable over time. That it is possible to go over the line is indicated by examples when the IRA expanded its targets beyond what its republican sympathizers would accept. After demonstration of Catholic outrage over an attack that killed women and children, for instance, the IRA apologized and narrowed its target range, at least for a period of time.

Similarly, Palestinian suicide terrorism attacks against Israel slowed dramatically in the period after the Oslo Accords. Hope of a peace agreement was associated with decreased support for terrorism, as reported in a polling of Palestinians. When the promise of the Oslo Accords was lost and the second intifada began, polls showed support for terrorism rising to new highs even as the number of terrorist attacks rose to new highs. It appears that terrorism varies with popular support for terrorism, but too often more extreme violence brings more status to a group competing with other groups to represent the same cause.

An often-overlooked aspect of competition for a base of support is violence against anyone resisting the authority of the terrorists. About one-quarter of the killing in Northern Ireland involved Republicans killing Republicans and Loyalists killing Loyalists. Both sides killed suspected informers or individuals resisting the discipline that the militants sought to impose. The IRA in particular attacked those in Catholic neighborhoods who ignored IRA strictures against selling drugs.

An extreme example of in-group violence comes from the Tamil Tigers (Liberation Tigers of Tamil Eelam, LTTE), who, in their rise to power, killed more Tamils than Sinhalese. The LTTE early wiped out competing Tamil militant groups and continued, until its defeat in 2009, to kill individual Tamils who criticized or otherwise opposed the LTTE. An example that penetrated the Western press was the July 29, 1999, suicide-bomb killing of Dr. Neelan Tiruchelvam. As a leader of the Tamil United Liberation Front and a Sri Lankan member of parliament, Dr. Tiruchelvam had been a leading critic of human rights abuses by the LTTE.

From a group dynamics perspective, threat from in-group competitors is much like threat from an out-group enemy in producing high cohesion, with resulting high pressures for conformity and strong sanctions against those who deviate from group norms. From an individual point of view high cohesion in an extended conflict can feel like this: when my friends and I are risking all for the cause, and especially after some of our friends have died for this cause, no one can be allowed to betray our sacrifices.

Group Radicalization in Factional
Competition—Splitting

The within-group competition for status represented in social comparison explanations of group polarization (see chapter 8) can produce intense conflict. The downside of conflating the personal and the political (see chapter 3) is that differences of political opinion can lead to personal animosities—and vice versa. This kind of infighting occurred in some of the SDS communes and even more intensely in Weatherman and Weather Underground groups. When who is sleeping with whom becomes a political question, the answer can raise political conflicts within the group. A group committed to violence is particularly susceptible to violent quarrels; one former militant has suggested that only common action against the state or another group can save a terrorist group from tearing itself apart.

There is currently no systematic review of radical group splitting, but examples suggest that intragroup conflict may often lead a terrorist group to split into multiple factions. The IRA provides an obvious example, with many competing factions—Official IRA, Provisional IRA, Real IRA, Continuity IRA, INLA—who sometimes targeted one another. Similarly the ASALA split into a faction led by founder Hagop Hagopian and a faction led by Monte Melkonian. The split was the occasion of torture and killing between former comrades.

Often enough the split seems to be about the use of violence or the escalation of violence. The Provisional IRA split off from the less militant Official IRA. People's Will condensed out of the less militant Land and Freedom group. Weatherman condensed out of the less militant SDS. The result of such splits is usually a smaller faction that develops toward increased violence, leaving behind a larger number unwilling to escalate.

Intragroup competition can go beyond killing. A threat from members of one's own group is likely to produce a feeling of contamination that requires not just death but obliteration (see chapter 12). Such was the fate, evidently, of fourteen members of the Japanese United Red Army who in 1972 were found dead and dismembered in a group hideout.

From a group dynamics perspective, the tendency toward splitting in radical groups should not be surprising. As already noted cohesion leads to pressures for agreement within the group. When, as in an already radical group, perception of external threat produces very high cohesion, the pressure for agreement is very high. An individual will seldom be able to resist the pressure of a unanimous majority, but a minority of two or more individuals may be able to resist by joining together to form a new faction. When the pressure for agreement is very strong, the minority is likely to be expelled from the group—or attacked.

Looking Further

Asch, S. E. (1956). Studies of independence and conformity: A minority of one against a unanimous majority. *Psychological Monographs* 70 (Whole No. 416).

Aust, S. (translated by A. Bell). (1985). *Baader-Meinhof: The inside story of the RAF.* New York: Oxford University Press.

Bloom, M. (2005). *Dying to kill: The allure of suicide terror.* New York: Columbia University Press.

Collier, P., & Horowitz, D. (1989). *Destructive generation.* New York: Summit Books.

de Antonio, E., Lampson, M., & Wexler, H. (Directors & Producers). (1976). *Underground: The film the FBI didn't want you to see* [Motion picture]. United States: Turin Film Corporation.

Della Porta, D. (1995). *Social movements, political violence, and the state: A comparative analysis of Italy and Germany.* Cambridge, UK: Cambridge University Press.

Dugan, L., Huang, J. Y., LaFree, G., & McCauley, C. (2009). Sudden desistance from terrorism: The Armenian Secret Army for the Liberation of Armenia and the Justice Commandos of the Armenian Genocide. *Dynamics of Asymmetric Conflict* 1(3): 231–249.

Fay, M. T., Morrissey, M., & Smyth, M. (1997). *Mapping troubles-related deaths in Northern Ireland 1969–1994.* Londonderry: INCORE, Table 12. Available at http://cain.ulst.ac.uk/issues/violence/cts/tables.htm.

Grant, P. R., & Brown, R. (1995). From ethnocentrism to collective protest: Responses to relative deprivation and threats to social identity. *Social Psychology Quarterly* 58(3): 195–212.

Green, S., & Siegel, W. (Directors). (2002). *The Weather Underground* [Motion picture]. United States: Free History Project.

Hoole, R., Bomasundaram, D., Sritharan, K., & Thiranagama, R. (1990). *The broken palmyra: The Tamil crisis in Sri Lanka, an inside account.* Claremont, CA: Sri Lankan Studies Institute.

Levine, R. A., & Campbell, D. T. (1972). *Ethnocentrism: Theories of conflict, ethnic attitudes, and group behavior.* New York: Wiley.

McCauley, C., & Segal, M. (1987). Social psychology of terrorist groups. In C. Hendrick (Ed.), *Review of personality and social psychology*, Vol. 9. Beverly Hills, CA: Sage, pp. 231–256.

Rudd, M. (2005). Why were there so many Jews in SDS? (Or the ordeal of civility). Talk presented at the New Mexico Jewish Historical Society, Albuquerque.

Available at http://www.markrudd.com/?about-mark-rudd/why-were-there-so-many-jews-in-sds-or-the-ordeal-of-civility.html.

Sherif, M., Harvey, O. J., White, B. J., Hood, W. R., Sherif, C. W. (1961). *Intergroup conflict and cooperation: The Robbers Cave experiment*. Norman, OK: Oklahoma Book Exchange.

Zavodny, J. K. (1983). Infrastructures of terrorist organizations. In L. Z. Freedman & Y. Alexander (Eds.), *Perspectives on terrorism*. Wilmington, DE: Scholarly Resources, pp. 61–70.

Радзинский, Э. С. (2007). *Александр II: жизнь и смерть*. Москва, ACT. [Radzinskij, E. (2007). *Alexander II: Life and death*. Moscow: ACT.]

CHAPTER TEN

Group Isolation

The power of group dynamics is multiplied to the extent that group members are cut off from other groups.

Underground

In the evolution of the Russian Land and Freedom to People's Will, from student discussion circles to terrorism, there are two distinct periods when the group became more secretive, more isolated, and more radical. In both periods, group radicalization was multiplied by the extent to which student groups became *totalistic groups*—isolated groups that were all and everything to their own members.

The first period coincided with the end of the "going into the people" era, when government repressions targeted anyone remotely related to the student movement. Even carrying political literature or discussing political matters with peasants was grounds for arrest. Four thousand students were arrested and imprisoned on suspicion of antigovernment activity. Dozens died of diseases or suicide during months and years of awaiting trial; only 193 of the prisoners were charged and brought to public trial, where most were acquitted (see chapter 9).

The experience of prison and the bonds forged there with other political prisoners transformed former students. The world outside prison lost its significance as they survived day after day in horrific conditions, often in solitary confinement. To connect with other political prisoners, they developed a secret knocking code that carried across prison cells through plumbing pipes and walls. The guards could not stop the knocking, despite their best efforts. In concert with the knocking system, the political views that landed former students in prison gained a new significance for the incarcerated. The long empty hours in dark and noisome cells were relieved by the possibility of discussing with other prisoners books they had all read, ideas they all believed in, people they all admired. They could ponder their common future in the political movement. Suddenly, they were more than individuals in the same unfortunate circumstances: they were a community. The prisoners' shared reality—loneliness, mistreatment, physical and psychological ailments—amplified their feelings of unity and camaraderie.

Solitary confinement and isolation of "politicals" from nonpolitical (criminal) prisoners were designed by the authorities to prevent radicalization, but they did just the opposite. Their secret language, their dependence on one another for everything from news to sympathy to smuggled food, nurtured a bond among the politicals unlike any these young people had known before. They established a hierarchy and planned strategies for resistance to the guards and for their defense at trial. Those who lived through this hardening came out completely devoted to the group and its ideals, ready to sacrifice everything for their comrades. In a totalistic group, anyone and everyone who counts is in the group; nothing outside the group is important.

Stalin learned many useful things in the czar's prisons (1902–1903; 1908–1909; 1910–1911; 1913–1916), among them how not to repeat the mistakes of his enemies. Wise to the radicalizing potential of segregating political prisoners, he did just the opposite to Soviet-era dissidents. Political prisoners under Stalin were sent to Siberian labor camps and put in barracks with the coarsest and most violent criminals, who were pleased to oppress their social superiors. There was no time in a labor camp to devise a secret language or to dream of the future. There was no prospect of forming a cohesive group of radicals amidst brutal criminals who were, as a rule, devoted to the "proletariat" government. When Stalin's purges in the 1930s landed millions of innocent people in labor camps, no radicalization, no People's Will, emerged.

Embracing Violence

The second period when secrecy and isolation grew dramatically was at the time when a more radical faction of Land and Freedom—Freedom or Death—decided to break from their activist past and instead pursue a decidedly terrorist agenda. The leader of this breakaway faction that later became known as People's Will was Alexander Michailov (unrelated to Adrian Michailov of chapter 4).

Michailov was a natural leader and a rebel, by his own admission and by numerous accounts of his contemporaries. Even in gymnasium he formed an editorial board to publish a secret political magazine and organized a collection of banned books and magazines that was then used in efforts to radicalize peasants. His childhood friend was Barannikov (see chapter 6), less politically inclined than Michailov and not at all interested in leadership but loyal and courageous. Both recalled later that it was Michailov who turned Barannikov to the revolutionary path and introduced him to People's Will.

As a university student Michailov began dreaming of a nationwide revolutionary organization with a single purpose of overturning the government and improving life for the poor. According to Lev Tikhomirov,

> [Michailov] was a rare leader. I had not seen a person who could with the same skill not only group people together but also lead them in the exact direction—even despite their will—where in his opinion they needed to head. He could rule, but he could also play the role of a subordinate; he could offer the appearance of leadership to a vain competitor.[1]

By chance, Michailov's arrival in St. Petersburg coincided with the formation of Land and Freedom, which he joined very soon after its inception. His role, increasingly central, was to be conspirator and organizer. According to Vera Figner, a devoted member and historian of People's Will, Michailov

> looked for traits in the habits, characters and temperaments of group members that obstructed expansion of the group and harmed its activity. He wanted to re-train the comrades and called on them to work on themselves so as to reduce carelessness, sluggishness and lack of

---

1. Тихомиров Л. А. (1927). *Воспоминания.* Москва: Литиздат. [Tikhomirov, L. A. (1927). *Memoirs.* Moscow: Litizdat, p. 182.]

self-discipline that could lead to arrests, attract attention of police and spies, and sabotage revolutionary efforts. Every step in everyday life of a revolutionary has to be weighed and thought out—he demanded— and one's behavior needs to be consistent.[2]

At the time, however, the organization was large and diverse, its plans and goals still unclear, and Michailov's demands for conspiracy went largely ignored. Like other members of the group Michailov spent over a year "in the people." After Land and Freedom's plan to radicalize the peasants failed, Michailov returned to St. Petersburg. There he found most of his comrades disappointed and unsure what to do next. Many were in prison or on the run from the government.

In the years that followed, persecution and espionage by security forces brought a special significance to Michailov's talents for conspiracy and organization. After the failure of "going into the people" and after the Trial of 193, Land and Freedom took a new direction that included targeted assassinations. The division created for this purpose was called Freedom or Death. Michailov naturally assumed responsibility of this new radical wing of the organization.

Every assassination, every bombing by members of Freedom or Death, was a result of Michailov's planning. With time terrorism became his central interest. As Figner put it,

> The views of Alexander Michailov underwent change since the spring of 1878, when he came to Petersburg totally invested in "going into the people." The mood for war overtook even those who used to stand to the side of the revolutionary movement. Michailov, as a member of the central group, constantly participated in activities that the group planned and executed. These acts of war, no doubt, transformed him, while the possibility of continuing the work "in the people" faded and grew distant.[3]

This was the beginning of People's Will, although neither the name nor the group that comprised it had yet been fully formed. Michailov's increasing pressure to mount more and more deadly attacks on authorities began to trouble other leaders of Land and

---

2. Фигнер, В. (1964). *Запечатленный труд. Воспоминания в двух томах*. Москва: Издательство социально-экономической литературы "Мысль" [Figner, V. (1964). *Commemorated work. Memoirs in two volumes*. Moscow: Social-Economic Literature Press.] Available at http://narovol.narod.ru/f13.htm. Accessed May 6, 2016.
3. Ibid.

Freedom, particularly Plechanov. In Plechanov's view, assassinations were detrimental to the original purpose of Land and Freedom. Not only did assassinations draw authorities' attention to the organization and its activities, making Land and Freedom's activity among peasants more dangerous, but, worse yet, assassinations turned the peasants against the organization. Attempts on the czar's life were particularly counterproductive, as Plechanov saw it. Peasants saw the czar as nothing short of a deity, and anyone attempting to hurt him was automatically seen as an enemy. The support for Land and Freedom among the elites was also waning as attacks became more indiscriminant and brutal.

But in Michailov's eyes, neither the peasants' nor the elites' opinion counted for much. The peasants were too ignorant and exhausted by their miserable lives to get involved in the revolutionary movement; the elites were too complacent in their decadent lifestyles built on the misery of the peasants. With a small group of sympathizers drawn from the ranks of Land and Freedom as well as from the larger student movement, Michailov formed the Executive Committee that became the elite and, with guidance and pressure from Michailov, ultrasecretive leadership of People's Will.

According to Ashenbrenner, a member of People's Will, "one of the most prominent founders of this party—Alexander Michailov—was the patron saint of his comrades. He knew the faces of the most dangerous security services spies; knew not only all back alleys of the city but also all cracks and secret passages, all topography of the landscape in detail."[4] For his careful attention to every detail, as well as for his relentless enforcement of discipline and conspiratorial rules Michailov earned a nickname "the Janitor."

Lev Tikhomirov explains,

> He understood very well that in Russia care, practicality, and discreetness comprised necessary conditions for a revolutionary organization. He demanded these qualities of every revolutionary. Himself extremely practical and careful, he constantly noticed mistakes of others, and pointed to them, of course. If these mistakes resulted from "leisure," from boredom or disinterest in attending to one's own every tiny step— then [Michailov], for whom no effort at self-improvement was too hard if "business" so required, simply became enraged. He considered this dishonesty, lack of devotion.

---

4. Ibid.

In later years (People's Will years) [Michailov] could not find cynical enough and rude enough words for one comrade who sometimes came to visit his wife, though it was known she was followed by the secret service. . . . Forever he was himself following other comrades in the street, to make sure they were being careful. . . . There was going to be trouble if someone had not noticed the tail. Accusations hit them like hail. [Michailov] practically nagged people every day and every minute for such failings.

Sometimes in the street he would surprise one of us by making us read street signs and look at faces at different distances. "If you can't read, brother, you need to get glasses." And then he won't let you breathe until you get the glasses. One myopic declared that doctors forbade him to wear glasses lest he lose what remained of his eyesight. Michailov did not show mercy. "Well, then recuse yourself from tasks where you need to visit undercover apartments. Do something else." Unfortunately, it turned out that the myopic was needed precisely for visiting undercover apartments.

"Then you definitely need eyeglasses, definitely."

"I have no desire to go blind, thank you."

"When you go blind, then you can go into retirement. We're not going to doom the organization over your eyes."

Then he turned to other comrades, "Make sure NN wears glasses."

That was Michailov's way of controlling comrades' lives. He would enter an apartment, and immediately look over all corners, knock on the wall to see how thick it is, listen whether the conversations in the neighboring apartment are discernable, come to the stairs. "You have so many people over, yet there is only one way out. It's unacceptable." It was worse if there was no water in the apartment: meaning that the plumber was due to visit any time. He especially followed the "signs"—signals of safety to be taken down if the apartment was in danger. "Your sign is impossible to see, it is not possible to put a sign up here at all, what kind of room is this? How are we supposed to come here?"

Michailov made a science out of conspiracy. He developed in himself an ability with one look to find familiar faces in a crowd. He knew Petersburg like a fish knows its pond. He had compiled a huge list of pathways through courtyards and buildings in the city (about 300), and he remembered them all by heart.[5]

---

5. Тихомиров, p. 190. [Tikhomirov, p. 190.]

At the Voronezh meeting Michailov and his comrades broke off from Land and Freedom and formed People's Will, whose primary purpose was assassination of the czar and as many governmental officials as possible. This dangerous mission required complete secrecy, and Michailov was there to ensure it was maintained. The members of the Executive Committee were the only ones to know who comprised it, and they were never to tell either friend (including members of People's Will) or foe about their membership in it. Michailov scouted useful people to infiltrate the government and was exceedingly careful to keep their names secret from other members of People's Will. Thus, one of People's Will's informants was employed at the Third Division, perfectly positioned to supply People's Will with useful information about who was under surveillance, who was to be arrested, and who was a spy. This informant's identity remained a secret to other People's Will members for years.

The assassination plans grew more complex, requiring participants to play roles of husbands and wives, poor peasants, government officials. They were required to rent houses under false names and establish contacts with locals to ease doubts about the legitimacy of their residence. Secret apartments were devoted to publishing proclamations and newsletters, others to making bombs. Members of People's Will were required to sever all ties with the world outside the organization if they were to outwit the government spies. They were to maintain constant vigilance.

Change in Priorities

Their publications, newspapers, and proclamations still painted them as representatives of peasants' rights and freedoms; but the members of People's Will were fooling themselves as well as their audience. In their growing self-reliance and self-isolation, in the constant threat of capture and death, they came to care much more for those who shared these burdens than for the peasants they were supposed to be helping. People's Will became for its members the alpha and omega of their existence. It represented all of their contingencies: they could be happy only if People's Will was successful; if People's Will failed, they would all perish. Everyone they cared for was in the organization; everyone outside was to be feared and distrusted. In truth, it was no longer the peasants' freedom they were fighting for, nor the peasants' pain they were avenging. Their fight was for themselves: their rights, their revenge for the pain of their friends.

This change in group focus precipitated a tactical change from "scalpel" attacks with guns to "hatchet" attacks with dynamite. In 1879 People's Will planned an attempt on the czar's life with the help of Halturin, a talented carpenter who became employed at the Winter Palace. The organization supplied dynamite to him in small installments over a period of time, until he had about seven pounds hidden in his clothes chest there. The planned location of the explosives was two stories below the czar's dining room. Unfortunately, just below the dining room and in the immediate path of the explosion was a guards' quarters. The guards were peasants, precisely the people for whose welfare People's Will claimed to stand. Yet no discussion about their welfare appears to have taken place during the planning of the attack.

On February 5, 1880, the dynamite was detonated as the czar and his family dined upstairs. The dining room lost electricity, the walls cracked, and the table jumped from the floor. But nobody in the room was hurt. On the other hand, fifty soldiers lay dead and maimed in the room below. Two days later, People's Will issued a proclamation saying, "We look with sadness at the death of the poor soldiers, these unwilling keepers of the crowned villain. But as long as the army remains the instrument of the czar's whim, as long as the army fails to realize that the motherland's need and the army's holy duty both require the army to take the side of the people against the czar, these tragic clashes are inevitable."[6] Apparently the former students, most of them of noble origins, were better representatives of "the motherland" and "the people" than were involuntarily drafted peasant soldiers.

This disregard for the welfare of innocent people unfortunate enough to be in the vicinity of People's Will attacks increased with time. At the last and successful attempt on Czar Alexander's life in March 1880, terrorists detonated a bomb on a crowded city bridge to stop the czar's carriage. Several minutes later, as onlookers gathered around the shaken monarch, the terrorists detonated a second bomb. A third bomb was in place to be detonated in case the first two did

6. Исп [олнительный] ком[итет]. (1880). г., 7 февраля. *Прокламация Исполнительного комитета по поводу взрыва в Зимнем* дворце Летуч[ая] тип[ография] «Нар[одной] воли». [Executive Committee of People's Will. (1880). *February 7. Proclamation of the Executive Committee regarding the explosion in the Winter Palace*. St. Petersburg: Flying Press of People's Will.] Available at http://narovol.ru/document/proklamWinter.htm. Accessed May 6, 2016.

not hit the target. As the mortally wounded monarch was taken away, scores of dead and wounded remained on the bridge—not only soldiers but women and children.

Almost the entire Executive Committee was arrested as a result of the assassination. Although Michailov was not initially captured, this paragon of tradecraft suddenly decided to visit a photographer where pictures for fake documents were usually taken, to pick up some photographs. In the photographer's studio a comrade intercepted him and gave him a sign that the police had set a trap there, and Michailov escaped. But the very next day, he came again. As one of Michailov's comrades recalled, there was no need for him to go to the photo studio: the photographs were not immediately needed, and someone else could have easily picked them up. And to show up the next day knowing that the place was under intense surveillance—that would be an act of stupidity even from a civilian unpracticed in the security measures that Michailov himself enforced in People's Will.

The only explanation is that he could not stand to be free when his comrades were captured. Their fate, the fate of the group, was more important to him than the organization, than the goals they shared, more important even than his own fate, as he was sure he was going to be sentenced to death. To his dismay, unlike most of his comrades, who were hanged, Michailov was sentenced to life in prison. He died a few years later of pneumonia.

People's Will: The Next Generation

His older brother Aleksandr was executed for a terrorist attack against a government official, but Vladimir Ulianov was only ten years old when People's Will finally succeeded in killing the czar. Years later he would continue the mission of People's Will, perfecting and implementing their ideas. Secretive to the point of looking ridiculous in a warm overcoat in July heat, changing pseudonyms and apartments several times a year, he understood the importance of keeping the peasants' cause on the party banner but did not let concern for the peasants get in the way of revolution. A rich nobleman himself (although he did not like to advertise it), Ulianov did not "go into the people," nor did he have any direct contact with peasants or factory workers. For years he lived off the proceeds of renting out the land on his country estate (instead of allowing peasants who lived there to have use of it). So removed from the Russian peasants was he that most of his revolutionary career was spent in European countries: France, Switzerland, Finland, and Belgium. He saw no need to get too deeply involved with the Russian folk or to risk prison time that might aggravate his mental condition that manifested in insomnia, seizures, and irritability.

Ulianov understood that caring about "the people," or expanding their rights and freedoms, had no bearing on carrying out a revolution in their name. Instead he put his efforts into developing a tightly organized party, with an elite membership dedicated to full-time organizational work. Maintaining discipline in underground party cells was a particular challenge, and his solution was that each cell should regularly read and discuss party documents and undertake criticism and self-criticism in relation to party goals. This form of party discipline continued until Stalin took power and denounced the "fetishism of study-circles."

Ulianov's combination of military-style hierarchy and cellular discipline was successful where the romantic idealism of his predecessors had failed. Without taking the trouble of reading Marx,[7] learning peasant occupations, or living among them, without the hardships of imprisonment, he did what People's Will wanted to do. Ulianov overturned the government and killed a czar, Nicholas II, and his entire family. He became famous under one of his aliases: Lenin.

Group Radicalization under Isolation and Threat

As described earlier in section 2, group dynamics theory holds that the only source of confidence in answering questions of value is consensus: agreement with others. Systems of meaning and values represented in religions and secular ideologies offer abstract answers to these questions, but the specifics for implementing these abstractions in relation to the current situation depend on group consensus. When an individual belongs to many different groups with competing values, any one group has little power over the individual. But when a group is isolated from outside influences, its power over individual members is unlimited.

The joining of cause and comrades in a high-cohesion group is the goal of military training in every nation. This is the combination that

---

7. Данилов, Е. (2007). *Ленин. Тайны Жизни и смерти*. Москва: Зебра Е. [Danilov, E. (2007). *Lenin. Mysteries of life and death*. Moscow: Zebra E, p. 153.]

brings individuals to the self-sacrifice required for combat. It is convergent evolution—not accident—that military training in every country takes young people away from familiar places and faces and then strips them of their individuality with new haircuts and new uniforms. Old connections must be broken, and new group loyalty must be built. Just as unfreezing (see chapter 7) opens individuals to influence from new attachments, group isolation opens groups to mutual influence in group dynamics.

Isolated groups—terrorist groups, youth gangs, religious cults, soldiers in combat—have unchecked power to determine value and meaning. Consensus power in such groups can justify and even require extreme beliefs, feelings, and actions against anyone who threatens the group.

The unchecked value-setting power of an isolated group is a multiplier, but it is not necessarily the propensity for illegal and violent action that is multiplied. In a monastery isolation can serve to multiply the intensity of religious fervor and prayer. Isolation of small groups in a cult can produce increased proselytizing and fundraising. Isolation of small groups in prison cells can produce religious or political conversion, including the special form of conversion that has been called *thought reform* or *brainwashing*. In whatever direction the group is likeminded (see chapter 9), isolation will push the group further and faster.

In an underground terrorist cell, however, isolation is likely to multiply the intensity of violence and justify escalation of violent tactics. A model for this kind of radicalization is the powerful cohesion that develops in small combat groups. Soldiers in combat are largely cut off from all but their buddies in the same platoon or squad. Because they depend on one another for their lives, extreme interdependence produces extreme group cohesion, a cohesion described as "closer than brothers." During World War II, thirty-two U.S. marines are known to have jumped on a grenade in order to save their buddies.[8] They did not think and then act; indeed, the rare survivor is likely to say that if he had thought about it, he wouldn't have done it. Putting the group first becomes automatic, a level of group identification in which group-interest rather than self-interest controls behavior (see chapter 3).

---

8. Smithsonian National Museum of American History. (2004). *Price of Freedom: Americans at War*. Washington, DC: Smithsonian. Available at http://americanhistory.si.edu/exhibitions/price-of-freedom. Accessed May 10, 2016.

When an individual's social world has contracted to just one group, a "band of brothers" facing a common enemy, the group consensus about issues of value acquires enormous power. The social-reality power of the group extends to moral standards that justify and even require violence against those who threaten the group. If the power goes awry—becomes detached from the cause the group is fighting for and focused only on the preservation of the group—the results can be ugly. "Fragging" officers who don't respect the group and "wasting" civilians who hide insurgents are signs of a military unit in which the welfare of the group has become the paramount value.

The power of group isolation is at work in many forms of persuasion. New recruits to the Unification Church are brought to live with the group—first for a weekend, then for a week, then for two weeks—before being asked to join (see chapter 7). Thought reform or brainwashing requires not just prison authorities coercing a confession but the mutual coercion of fellow prisoners who share the same cell for years. In a weaker form the same principle is at work in boarding schools, residential colleges, and corporate training programs that require students to leave their families and friends and move, at least for a time, into a communal life that can support new norms. The longer and more complete the detachment from the familiar, the more power a group will have over its members.

Indeed, isolation multiplies every group-level mechanism of radicalization that we have identified. The mechanisms of social comparison and relevant arguments that produce group polarization are made stronger, and the group becomes more extreme in seeing its own goodness and the evil of the enemy (see chapter 8). Similarly, the effects of group competition (see chapter 9) are multiplied, especially the in-group consequences of conflict: idealization of in-group values, respect for leaders, and readiness to punish those who deviate from group norms.

An important implication of this analysis is that something important happens when a radical group goes underground as a terrorist group. Forever vigilant about police and informers, the members of a terrorist group can trust only one another. The combination of isolation and constant outside threat makes group dynamics immediately more powerful in the underground cell than in the radical group that preceded it. The result can be the same kind of cohesion gone awry that occurs in "fragging" officers and "wasting" civilians. As the importance of group survival grows, the larger cause for which a terrorist group is fighting can recede into the background, maintained more as slogan than a goal of group action.

This is what happened to the Land and Freedom Party. The first step toward radicalization was the rise of student communes, where a small group shared a house and its expenses. Students far from home ate, slept, and debated together in a new family of equals. The second step was the common experience of repression and prison that marked the failure and the end of the movement to "go into the people." The third step toward radicalization was the formation of the terrorist cells of the Freedom or Death faction that became People's Will.

At the first step, like-minded students began to aggregate in communes, but "going into the people" dispersed students from communes to the countryside. Then government repression and shared prison experience as "politicals" brought renewed aggregation and isolation and a step toward totalistic groups. Then condensation of the Freedom or Death faction from the Land and Freedom Party brought new levels of segregation and secrecy and another step toward totalistic groups. From communes to prisons to underground cells, student groups moved toward increasing isolation and increasing threat from the authorities. The more totalistic the group dynamics, the greater the radicalization.

As student protest and activism evolved into terrorism, the welfare of the peasants became more a slogan than a goal. People's Will turned inward, as described in the section titled *Change in Priorities*. They focused ever more on themselves as a group. Their concerns were their comrades in jail. Their attacks were retributions for their own suffering. From precise assassinations using guns, terrorist tactics turned to bombings that killed peasant soldiers and civilian bystanders, including women and children.

Putting the group first was a political disaster. Elites and a growing middle class saw the bombings as a kind of madness; peasants saw the bombers as threats to the czar they loved. Plechanov was right, but Michailov won enough converts to form People's Will. As Figner said about Michailov, "These acts of war, no doubt, transformed him, while the possibility of continuing the work 'in the people' faded and grew distant."

After the czar was assassinated, People's Will was largely rounded up by the police. The next generation of revolutionaries started where People's Will had ended, with an underground elite focused on getting power. Lenin and his comrades were not interested in romantic ideas of reform or the welfare of peasants; they aimed to replace the czar's dictatorship with one of their own. They made explicit what People's Will had stumbled into but denied: the only morality is the good of the party.

Student Revolutionaries of the 1970s

The first thing to notice about the rise of the Red Army Faction (RAF) in 1970s Germany is that the terrorists emerged out of communes. Della Porta cites data indicating that 47 percent of those who joined the RAF had previously lived in a commune (*Wohngemeinschaften*), versus 15 percent of those of comparable age and background who did not become terrorists. Even more striking, 42 percent of those who later joined the RAF had lived in a more overtly leftist form of commune (*Kommune*), versus only 5 percent of the comparison group. Living together is the first step toward a totalistic group.

Similarly, members of the Red Brigades in 1970s Italy recall lives in which political action and political comrades drove out every other kind of interest and connection. Della Porta reports interviews in which terrorists look back on their days of radicalization with fond memories of street action together, parties together, and even—this is Italy—country or beach vacations together.

The extent to which the terrorist groups became totalistic is the extent to which the group came to take precedence over the cause. An obvious indicator is the effort and risk taking that went into avenging dead comrades. Della Porta in writing about the Red Brigades describes this kind of reaction:

> The death of a fellow member produced strong emotional reactions and the desire for "revenge," evident, for example, in this statement of an Italian rank-and-file militant: "The deaths of Matteo and Barbara [two very young militants shot dead by the police] had such a strong emotional impact. . . . [We then entered] a spiral of revenge and retaliation, because when you are in that game, you have to play it."[9]

Revenge is more about loyalty to the group than about advancing a political cause, and it may well undermine the cause with violence that puts off sympathizers with the cause. Similarly, efforts to

---

9. Della Porta, D. (1995). *Social movements, political violence, and the state: A comparative analysis of Italy and Germany*. Cambridge, UK: Cambridge University Press, p. 178.

free imprisoned group members can be an indicator that the group is coming before the cause. In May 1970 Ulrike Meinhof and two comrades engineered an escape for captured RAF leader Andreas Baader; a librarian and two police officers were wounded in the escape. Again, the resources and risks devoted to the escape indicate more concern for comrades than for advancing the cause.

More generally, Della Porta has noted that emotional connections between terrorists and their comrades in prison can get in the way of backing off from violence that isn't producing a useful political effect. For group members still at large, giving up violence becomes a betrayal of comrades who have already paid the price of violence in prison or death. For group members in prison, reflection and doubts about violent tactics must be suppressed while comrades outside are still fighting. A totalistic group puts connection with comrades ahead of whatever cause the group began with.

Weatherman Collectives

Although less deadly, the U.S. students who formed the Weather Underground Organization in the 1970s were in some ways more ideologically extreme than their Russian predecessors. People's Will claimed the right to kill the czar and the officers of his police and prisons, but they did not try to kill every trace of existing morality. The Weather Underground rejected not just the military–industrial complex they saw behind racism and imperialism but the whole middle-class morality they had been raised in.

> They threw themselves into Mao and Marx, they practiced karate and survived on brown rice diets, they tried abstinence (off and on) from drugs, alcohol, even pets. Accustomed property feelings had to be rooted out, so that no one felt attached to personal belongings, and in many cases Weathermen reduced themselves to a single set of clothes. Individualism and selfishness had to give way to a collective spirit, and this meant totally: nothing, including an individual's desire to leave the apartment for a walk, was to be decided without group discussion. The desire for privacy also had to be uprooted, smacking as it did of individualism and self-centeredness, and in several collectives no one was permitted to be separated from another communard (this had its security advantages, too, of course). Attitudes to wealth and materialism had to be challenged, eventually to the point of requiring the Weathermen to donate their personal savings to the collective, a

step many found difficult to take. . . . And accustomed sexual relations were to be scrapped in favor of a freewheeling partner-swapping that would allow people to concentrate on their particular jobs in the revolution rather than on the comforts or needs of any one individual. . . . Naturally this kind of collective pressure, the attempt to make instant communists, took its toll. Especially racking, apparently, were the "criticism–self-criticism" discussions, sometimes so brutal and probing that in some collectives they were given the name "Weatherfries."[10]

For the Weather people, rejecting middle-class inhibitions against violence was extended to rejecting middle-class ideas about sex and family life—"smashing monogamy." The logic of this rejection was that the group and its cause should come first; no personal attachments could be allowed to compete with devotion to the group. Spreading the intimacies of sex across all group members expressed and reinforced the primacy of the group. In terms of the sources of cohesion described earlier, "smash monogamy" meant eliminating attractions to individual group members in order to strengthen attachment to the goals and status of the whole group.

An FBI informant who penetrated the upper ranks of the Weather Underground, Larry Grathwohl, provides an insider's account of the group dynamics that produced personal transformation and commitment to violence. Weather people lived together in communities or collectives located in major cities, including New York, Philadelphia, Chicago, Detroit, Cincinnati, and San Francisco. There was a clear status hierarchy in which the national leadership, people like Bill Ayers and Bernardine Dohrn, were the elite; each city collective had leaders of its own, and only the most devoted and useful sympathizers and supporters were invited to join a collective.

Life in the collective was a constant round of meetings and discussions, including the kind of criticism and self-criticism that makes the personal political. Every aspect of group life and individual behavior was held up for criticism and self-criticism (see chapter 7). In these meetings relevant arguments and status comparison always favored the most extreme arguments and risk taking. Revolutionary morality, including separating lovers from one another and parents from children, was the extremity shift that emerged from extended and intense group discussions.

---

10. Sale, K. (1973). *SDS*. New York: Random House, pp. 583–585.

The group-before-cause totalism of Weatherman collectives emerged after the National Action or, as it came to be called, "Days of Rage" in Chicago in October 1969. Perhaps 300 of the Weather cadre and 300 others attacked police lines in Chicago. Despite padding, football helmets, pipes, and baseball bats, the rioters were beaten down by the police. That so few showed up for what had been billed as a "National Action" was a sign that violent revolution was not around the corner in the United States. Many Students for a Democratic Society chapters had refused to participate and moved quickly to separate themselves from Weatherman violence. It did not matter. Totalist dynamics made the Weatherman collectives impervious to criticism and failure, and they upped the ante with the bombing campaign that ended their political relevance.

Looking Further

Applebaum, A. (2004). *Gulag: A history*. London: Penguin.

Barker, E. (1984). *The making of a Moonie: Choice or brainwashing?* New York: Basil Blackwell.

Della Porta, D. (1995). *Social movements, political violence, and the state: A comparative analysis of Italy and Germany*. Cambridge, UK: Cambridge University Press.

Grathwohl, L., & Reagan, F. (1976). *Bringing down America: An FBI informer with the Weathermen*. New Rochelle, NY: Arlington House.

Lifton, R. J. (1963). *Thought reform and the psychology of totalism*. New York: Norton.

Sherman, R. (Director). (2008). *Medal of honor* [Motion picture]. United States: Florentine Films.

Whyte, W. K. (1974). *Small groups and political rituals in China*. Berkeley: University of California Press.

Данилов, Е. (2007). *Ленин. Тайны жизни и смерти*. Москва: Зебра Е. [Danilov, E. (2007). *Lenin. Mysteries of life and death*. Moscow: Zebra E].

Радзинский, Э. С. (2007). *Сталин. Жизнь и смерть*. Москва: АСТ. [Radzinskij, E. S. (2007). *Stalin. Life and death*. Moscow: ACT.]

Радзинский, Э. С. (2007). *Александр II. Жизнь и смерть*. Москва: АСТ. [Radzinskij, E. S. (2007). *Alexander II: Life and death*. Moscow: ACT.]

Тихомиров, Л. А. (1927). *Воспоминания*. Москва: Литиздат. [Tikhomirov, L. (1927). *Memoirs*. Moscow: Litizdat.]

Троицкий, Н. А. (1999). «Дворник» (Народоволец александр Михайлов). Освободительное движение в России. *Саратов* 17: 53–66. [Troickij. N. (1999). "The janitor" (People's Will member Alexander Michailov). Independence movement in Russia. *Saratov* 17: 53–66.]

SECTION 3

Mass Radicalization

By many accounts, Barack Obama's 2008 presidential campaign was one of the best-run campaigns in recent history. The one attack that put the brakes on Obama's rising popularity and—temporarily—gave hope to the McCain campaign was a television commercial that interspersed images of Paris Hilton and Britney Spears with those of Obama at campaign rallies.

Inside the McCain campaign, many believed that the premise of the ad—that there is something in common between Paris Hilton and Barack Obama—was implausible and that the public would dismiss it or even turn on McCain for it. Obama's campaign also dismissed the ad. But according to *Newsweek*, "it dominated the news cycle for several days, something McCain had failed to do for months. Obama did not get much of a bounce from the trip [to Europe, Afghanistan, and Iraq] despite the heavy, overwhelmingly admiring press coverage. The ad helped stall Obama's momentum and, with some voters, raise doubts about the depth of his experience."[1]

The success of the TV ad in raising doubts about a candidate who had withstood more substantive attacks is puzzling. Similarly, few would have predicted that photographs of U.S. soldiers' bodies dragged through the streets of Mogadishu would produce a national reaction that forced President Clinton to abort the U.S. mission in Somalia. Why was Martin Luther King's "I Have a Dream" speech the inspiration it turned out to be? How could a cartoon version of the

1. *Newsweek*. (2008). Special Election Edition: How he did it: The inside story of campaign 2008. November 17, 2008.

Prophet Mohammed in a Danish newspaper become an international crisis?

Current research in psychology offers relatively little insight into mass politics. Compared with small-group behavior, mass behavior is difficult to study. It is easy to assemble small groups and observe interactions within and between groups but not so easy to assemble a crowd—let alone a crowd reacting to government policies or police actions.

One alternative is to theorize what is special about a crowd or mass of people and try to instantiate this in small groups. This approach led to the study of *deindividuation*, a situation in which group members do not keep track of who says what or who does what—mimicking the anonymity and lack of accountability for individual actions in a crowd. Research found that groups where there is less memory of who says what are groups with less inhibition (saying more bad things about group members' parents, for instance).

Another way to study mass politics is to identify crowd or mass phenomena that are different from small-group phenomena. For instance, group psychology presented in the previous section includes a phenomenon that most participants could not predict beforehand: group polarization. Indeed study of group polarization began when social psychologists were surprised to find that discussion could not only make opinions more similar but move average opinion as well. Does polarization happen only to small groups, or does the same phenomenon occur at the mass level? So far as we are aware, no one has asked this question.

Still, there are a few examples of mass behavior that seem to go beyond what can be explained by scaled-up versions of small-group dynamics. A study of fifty-seven Christian revival meetings in Australia, for instance, found that the larger the crowd, the greater the proportion of "inquirers"—those who came down to register a "decision for Christ" at the end of the meeting. It would not be surprising if a larger number came forward from a larger meeting, but here a larger *proportion* came forward at larger meetings. So far as we know, there is no parallel to this result in studies of small groups.

Another issue that may distinguish group psychology and mass psychology is *meta-opinion*. Meta-opinions are opinions about the opinions of others. Some polls ask separately about opinion and meta-opinion, as follows: Do you feel positive or negative about candidate X? Do you think most Americans feel positive or negative about candidate X? The first is the opinion question; the second is the meta-opinion question.

Public opinion is often thought of as the average opinion of citizens polled, but, to the extent that politics is the art of the possible, public opinion also includes the average meta-opinion. For example less support is likely to go to a potential candidate perceived as having "strong negatives" for many voters. Unusual political shifts can occur when meta-opinion has been wrong about the actual distribution of opinion, if an event occurs that indicates the actual distribution. Winning even one primary can move a candidate from being seen as unelectable to being seen as a front-runner.

Our point here is that average opinion and meta-opinion are likely to be similar in a small face-to-face group. We are likely to know the actual opinions of our friends. But we can be mistaken about the actual distribution of opinion among a large and abstract group: our university classmates, members of our profession, co-ethnics, and fellow citizens. We might think, for instance, that most Americans favor a particular health plan, when in fact most oppose the plan. Meta-opinions can go wrong in a crowd or mass public in a way unlikely to occur in a small group.

A study at Princeton University focused on a case of mistaken meta-opinions in relation to alcohol consumption. Prentice and Miller asked incoming undergraduates to rate "how comfortable you personally feel about the level of alcohol consumption on campus" on a scale ranging from "not at all comfortable" to "very comfortable." On the same scale, undergraduates also rated how comfortable they thought the average Princeton student felt about alcohol consumption on campus. The estimate for the average student was at 7 on an 11-point scale—more comfortable than uncomfortable, whereas students actually put themselves at an average of 5—more uncomfortable than comfortable. The two-point disparity between what they thought an average student felt about alcohol consumption and what in fact the average student felt was meta-opinion error in the direction of the stereotype that undergraduates are big drinkers.

Two years later, the researchers asked the same undergraduates the same questions. The results were different for men and women. Men had become more comfortable with alcohol consumption (thus moving closer to the meta-opinion, which did not change over years). But women continued to hold private reservations that diverged from the meta-opinion. The researchers suggested that the gender difference occurred because males feel stronger social pressure to conform to social norms of alcohol consumption. For males but not females, initial discomfort associated with the meta-opinion not matching their own opinion seems to have led to changed opinion and, likely, changed behavior as males aligned with the perceived meta-opinion.

Although research on mass psychology is relatively weak, personal experience of mass psychology is strong. Anyone who has been at a packed stadium when an important game is playing, in a street demonstration or riot, or in a Mardi Gras festival can tell you: "You had to be there." When it comes time to make a "wave" at a stadium, start crashing windows and cars in a street demonstration, or break out in song and dance at a festival—most participants are ready to join the crowd. In this place, at this moment, individuals become part of something bigger than the sum of individual participants.

Mass psychology is important for understanding radicalization because perpetrators of political violence depend on a much larger group who sympathize with and support their cause or grievance. Most terrorist groups depend on a mass base for cover and information, for funding and material support, and especially for new recruits. Understanding mass psychology means understanding what moves a mass public to support for political and social action around a particular identity. How do external threats such as the 9/11 attacks unite an otherwise diverse and dispersed population of millions into a cohesive group? How do millions of people come to see the enemy as having an evil nature or spirit that is indelible and unchanging? How does a particular death come to be accepted as a group sacrifice—an act of martyrdom—and how does this sacrifice move others toward sacrifice? The three chapters in this section describe three mechanisms of mass radicalization: out-group threat, hatred based in essentializing, and martyrdom.

Looking Further

Cannavale, S., & Pepitone, A. (1970). Deindividuation in the small group: Further evidence. *Journal of Personality and Social Psychology* 16: 141–147.

Festinger, L., Pepitone, A., & Newcomb T. (1952). Some consequences of deindividuation in a group. *Journal of Abnormal and Social Psychology* 47: 382–389.

Kravitz, D. A., & Martin, B. (1986). Ringelmann rediscovered: The original article. *Journal of Personality and Social Psychology* 50: 936–941.

Kuran, T. (1995). *Private truths and public lies: The social consequences of preference falsification.* Cambridge, MA: Harvard University Press.

Newton, J. W., & Mann, L. (1980). Crowd size as a factor in the persuasion process: A study of religious crusade meetings. *Journal of Personality and Social Psychology* 39(5): 874–883.

Prentice, D. A., & Miller, D. T. (1993). Pluralistic ignorance and alcohol use on campus: Some consequences of misperceiving the social norm. *Journal of Personality and Social Psychology* 64: 243–256.

CHAPTER ELEVEN

Jujitsu Politics

Terrorists often count on government reactions to advance their cause.

Agents Provocateurs

The epoch of 1860s Russian terrorism gave birth to the notion of "political provocation" as a tactic of radicalization. The use of provocation became so widespread that terrorist groups were constantly employing it at the same time as they were falling prey to the same tactic used against them by the government. It took a political genius to come up with the idea and demonstrate its power.

Sergei Nechaev was a son of an alcoholic waiter and former peasant from a provincial town. He was uneducated, indigent, and alone when he first came to St. Petersburg. Yet only a few years later, supported by such great minds as anarchist philosopher Bakunin and literary publisher and liberal nobleman Gerzen, his evil deeds earned him an international reputation and inspired a central character in a novel by Dostoevsky.

Despite his plebeian and nervous appearance (he had a habit of constantly biting his nails), Nechaev was no ordinary person. His contemporaries recall the power of his gaze, both mesmerizing and terrifying. When he was finally imprisoned in 1872, the prison chief came to offer him a chance to spy in exchange for freedom. In response

Nechaev slapped the prison chief's face. And the chief, who could be expected to kill the prisoner then and there, got down on his knees to apologize for his offer, coming to his senses only after leaving the prisoner's cell. Later during his imprisonment, Nechaev so influenced the prison guards that they not only were passing notes between him and other radicals but even joined in plots to assist his escape and to join in his revolutionary movement. Only an embedded spy stopped the plan. What psychological power must an individual possess to so influence the most conservative and coarse members of society—political prison staff!

Aside from being able to move individuals, Nechaev had the power to influence groups. Unremarkable in stature and credentials, he cherished grand dreams of leading a revolutionary movement. For that, he needed status—such status, for example, as political prisoners gained among their free comrades for their suffering in prison. However, Nechaev was not interested in spending time in jail, and he managed to avoid capture on many occasions. To solve this dilemma in his characteristic Machiavellian way, Nechaev sent an anonymous letter to someone he knew to have ties to most radical circles. It said,

> When I was taking a walk today.... I saw a prisoners' carriage. From its window a hand dropped a note. I heard the following words, "If you are a student, deliver this to the address outlined." I am a student and feel it's my duty to follow through. Destroy my letter.[1]

Included with the anonymous letter was a note by Nechaev that said he was being held prisoner in Peter and Paul Fortress. Soon a rumor started circulating that Nechaev miraculously escaped from his captivity and was on his way abroad. An escape from the dreadful Peter and Paul Fortress was unheard of, and Nechaev became immediately famous both for his martyrdom and for his ingenuity, all without ever having to step inside a prison cell. His story was not a complete fiction: he did travel to Geneva shortly after sending the anonymous letter.

This trip was designed to do more than just solidify the fabricated story of his capture and escape. Utilitarianism was all the rage at the time. Chernyshevsky's *What's to Be Done?* (chapter 13) and many other

---

1. Лурье Ф, М. (2001). *Нечаев: созидатель разрушения*. Москва: Молодая гвардия. [Lurie, F. M. (2001). *Nechaev: Creator of destruction*. Molodaya Gvardia. Available at http://on-island.net/History/Nechaev/SNechaev.htm.

radical texts preached abandoning intangible values, morality, and religion and instead pursuing more pragmatic and material goals. Nechaev profited by these ideas to become a model of political efficiency. Armed with talent, ideas, and status, all he lacked now was money. He aimed to get it on his trip to Europe.

The Russian radical émigré community in Europe was headed by Gerzen, a nobleman who had been arrested in his youth for minor dissent and emigrated to London as a result. From his residence and with his family income he published *The Bell*, an influential journal. The journal was prohibited in Russia, meaning that it was readily available, smuggled or hand-copied, to anyone who was interested—and every young Russian radical was very interested. Gerzen surrounded himself with a number of liberal intellectuals including Karl Marx, Friedrich Engels, and Michail Bakunin. The latter was Nechaev's main hope for procuring the funds he required.

Known for his radical anarchist ideas as well as for his idealism, Bakunin was getting older, more desperate to see his ideas realized, and more myopic about the people around him. Here is Gerzen's letter to Bakunin shortly before Nechaev came to Geneva.

> Fifty years of your life you spent torn out of practical life. Thrown as a youth into German idealism, which time turned into creative realism, you have not figured out the essence of Russia either during your imprisonment or in Siberia. You were overflowing with the passionate thirst for charitable activity and living in a fog of ghosts, student pranks, daring plans, trifling decisions. After ten years of imprisonment you came out the same theorist with all your incertitude; a babbler without scrupulousness in money matters … with an itch for revolutionary action which only lacks revolution.[2]

This was the person that Nechaev aimed to use for his purposes.

And he quickly succeeded. Bakunin doted on Nechaev, whom he called "the tiger cub." He was touched by the story of Nechaev's imprisonment in the Peter and Paul Fortress (where Bakunin himself had spent some time during his turbulent youth). Another elaborate lie Nechaev fed him was about a countrywide network of sleeper cells, all reporting to a central Russian committee whose goal was revolution. But more than his claimed accomplishments, Nechaev's passion

---

2. Демин, В. (2006). *Бакунин*. Москва: Молодая Гвардия. [Demin, V. (2006). *Bakunin*. Moscow: Molodaya Gvardia, p. 272.]

for revolution appealed to Bakunin. Conveniently, Nechaev's vision of revolution much resembled that of Bakunin, especially where it came to destroying societal foundations by terror. Bakunin joined with another of Gerzen's colleagues—Ogarev—and convinced Gerzen to give Nechaev a significant sum of money for his revolutionary activities. With new support, Nechaev soon published what he called *Cathexis of a Revolutionary*, his radical rejection of conventional morality.

> There is only one goal: the most expedient and most certain destruction of this frigging order.... Moral for [the revolutionary] is everything that helps the revolution. Immoral and criminal is everything that impedes it.... When a comrade is in trouble, in deciding whether to help him, a revolutionary must consider not some personal feelings but only the benefit of the revolutionary activity. Thus he must weigh the utility that the comrade brings on the one hand, and on the other— the expenditure of revolutionary resources needed for his rescue, and whichever side weighs more, that's how it should be decided.[3]

Nechaev's *Cathexis* analyzed and divided society into six categories, each of which is prescribed a different treatment by the revolutionaries, from immediate death sentence for the first category of those "especially harmful to the revolutionary organization" to respect and reverence for the "absolutely ours" women of category 6.c (women of category 6.a are to be used and disposed of as needed; women in 6.b are to be radicalized by any means).

Notable also are prescriptions for the treatment of people in categories 2 and 5. Thus, in "category 2 are those who are allowed to live temporarily so that they, by a series of their horrific actions, bring the peasants to an inevitable revolt." In category 5 are "theorists, conspirers, revolutionaries, all empty-worded in their circles and on paper. They must be constantly pushed and pulled forward, into useful, frivolous statements, the result of which will be traceless death of the majority and a real revolutionary formation of the few."[4]

For Nechaev, both the peasants and their vocal defenders had to be constantly provoked into dangerous and, for most of them, deadly political action so that at least a few of them would become fully radicalized. This idea of political provocation had been developed by Nechaev even before his European tour. Thus, he explained to his

---

3. Ibid., pp. 291–295.
4. Ibid.

Russian audience before his trip that, although most first- and second-year students are politically active, with time they settle down, get married and involved with their careers, and abandon their radical roots.

> What must be done? Here I have only one, though strong, hope in the government. Do you know what I expect of it? Let it imprison more students, let students be expelled from universities forever, let them be sent to Siberia, thrown out of their tracks, be stunned by the persecution, brutality, unfairness and stupidity. Only then will they harden in their hatred to the foul government, to the society which heartlessly watches all atrocities of the government.[5]

And he began implementing this idea in Geneva. Together with unsuspecting Bakunin, he prepared radicalizing literature, including Bakunin's writings, that was sent to Russian addresses that Nechaev provided. These were addresses of "category 5" people, whom Nechaev deemed insufficiently radicalized and in need of governmental "hardening." What naive Bakunin did not know, and Nechaev knew full well, was that the letters would certainly be intercepted by secret police and that their content would lead to immediate arrest and prison terms for the recipients. Over 380 letters were indeed intercepted, and Nechaev's program of radicalization by provocation had enrolled its first class.

Russian prisons were horrific, especially for political prisoners. Poor nutrition and atrocious living conditions helped prisoners hate the government that put them there, usually without due process. Nechaev knew well to avoid prison. He also knew that those who landed there would either break or harden. This calculation suited him. Those who would break were of no use anyway.

One of the addressees of Nechaev's tainted correspondence was Vera Zazulich, whose act of lone-wolf terrorism is described in chapter 3. She was arrested as a result of receiving a letter from a known dissident and held prisoner without any charge for almost two years. When she was released for lack of evidence, instead of proffering an apology the government exiled her to a small Siberian town without right of return to St. Petersburg (or any other city). Nechaev's university, assisted by the Russian government's blind persecution, produced a model student in Vera Zazulich.

---

5. Лурье, Ф. М. (2001). Нечаев—«созидатель разрушения» Издательство АО. Москва: Молодая гвардия. [Lur'e, F. M. (2001). *Nechaev—"creator of destruction."* Moscow: Molodaya Gvardia, p. 123.]

Not stopping with his correspondence provocation, Nechaev convinced Bakunin to issue an executive order endowing Nechaev with the full power of the European Revolutionary Alliance. Such an organization did not exist. But Nechaev convinced Bakunin that it would be useful to create an illusion of a powerful European organization to radicalize Russian revolutionaries. And Bakunin himself wrote and signed the paper. With money and a mysterious powerful European organization backing him, Nechaev returned to Russia in 1869. His last provocation, however, did not go well for him.

Nechaev organized a group of Moscow factory workers into a revolutionary organization using his mandate from Bakunin as well as his own fame. The workers were impressed with his elaborate lie about the international reach and hierarchy of the new organization. In 1870 Nechaev told them that there was to be a revolt, and their job was to work toward it under his guidance. One of the less gullible members of the organization, Ivan Ivanov, began to raise doubts about Nechaev's tales. Nechaev's response was a variation of his genius radicalization technique, designed to kill two birds with one stone: to get rid of a dangerous dissenter (Ivanov) and to radicalize some members of his organization he thought were too soft.

He told four group members of the organization that Ivanov was sentenced to death, and their job was to "liquidate him." He said it was time for them to prove that they were ready to live by the laws of the revolutionary time, to do what they set out to do. Reluctant at first, they couldn't back out of the commitment they had made to the powerful European organization and to each other. With Nechaev, they lured Ivanov into a deserted park at nighttime and after some struggle killed him. However, they did a poor job of hiding the body, and the police investigation soon traced the victim to Nechaev and his gang.

Nechaev fled Russia even as eighty-seven of his comrades were rounded up by the police. The four murderers testified against him, and Switzerland, which did not extradite for political activity, gladly handed him over to the Russian authorities for murder. In 1872 he was publically tried and sentenced to life in prison, in the very same Peter and Paul Fortress featured in his earlier fictitious tale of escape. He died there eleven years later, of scurvy and tuberculosis. Dostoevsky was so shaken by the case that he wrote *Demons* to reflect the crime, with Nechaev as the novel's main character Petr Verhovensky.

The government took note of the value of provocation and successfully turned it against the radicals by embedding spies who suggested terrorist attacks that were then smashed by the authorities. The result was public acclaim and increased budgets for the authorities and prison for would-be terrorists. This tactic was particularly useful because the terrorists used fake names and documents and frequently changed their residences. To capture them at large was difficult, but to capture them in a government-directed plot was easy.

Later terrorists, for their part, took to heart Nechaev's call to radicalize the peasants by making their lives intolerable. For example, Stalin was known in his revolutionary youth for robbing trains and carriages that delivered workers' salaries from banks to factories. The money was then available for "revolutionary purposes," and the workers were more likely to revolt against authority after not having been paid their wages. Riches and radicalization—two birds with one stone—Nechaev would have been proud.

Jujitsu Politics

In asymmetric conflict it is sometimes possible for the weaker side to attack in a way that elicits an overreaction that helps the weaker and undermines the stronger. The strategy that aims to use the opponent's strength against him is what we call *jujitsu politics*. This strategy has been recognized explicitly for at least seventy years.

In his 1935 book *The Power of Nonviolence*, Richard Gregg talked about "moral jiu-jitsu" as the effect on perpetrators of violence against nonviolent opponents. Gregg described this effect as a kind of psychological unbalancing in which violence meeting no resistance boomerangs to harm the perpetrators.

The idea was extended by Gene Sharp in his 1972 classic *The Politics of Nonviolent Action*. Sharp, "the Clausewitz of non-violent warfare," included a chapter called "Political Jiu-jitsu" that distinguished three audiences who can be moved by government violence against nonviolent opponents: the government may lose sympathy and support among its own supporters, may lose sympathy and support among bystander groups and governments, and may stimulate increased resistance from those experiencing government violence.

One of Sharp's strongest examples was Bloody Sunday, January 22, 1905, a case of violent repression against peaceful demonstrators in St. Petersburg, Russia. Unarmed and peaceful factory workers marched to Czar Nicholas II's Winter Palace to present a petition asking for improved working conditions and an end to the Russo–Japanese War.

Many of the demonstrators brought their families with them in hopes of a glimpse of the czar. Instead guards opened fire on the crowds, killing and wounding hundreds. This incident undermined the faith of workers and peasants who had seen Nicholas as a kind of royal father, undermined support for the czar in foreign capitals, and stimulated worker and peasant support for a revolution that soon engulfed Russia. The fact that Nicholas was not in his palace at the time of the incident made no difference.

In this chapter we further extend the concept of jujitsu politics to include violence aimed at eliciting disproportionate or badly aimed government counterviolence. State response, to the extent that it hurts or outrages those less committed than the terrorists, does for the terrorists what they cannot do for themselves. Terrorists count on the response of the state to mobilize those who sympathize with terrorist goals, to move passive terrorist sympathizers into active terrorist supporters. The strategy of jujitsu politics has been recognized in one way or another by many students of terrorism, but it is only beginning to appear in the discourse of security experts, policy makers, and journalists.

Historically, there is some warrant for terrorist confidence in this strategy. In *Death by Government*, Rudolph Rummel provides disturbing estimates of political killing in the twentieth century: 34 million combatants killed in interstate and civil wars; 169 million civilians killed by governments. Enemy civilians killed during war amount to 39 million; civilians killed by their own government total 130 million. Civilians killed by nonstate groups, including terrorists, guerillas, and insurgents, total perhaps a half-million.

Given the preponderance of state killing over nonstate killing in recent history, terrorists may well expect that their small but high-profile attacks will draw massive government counterviolence and that this counterviolence will miscarry to mobilize new support for terrorism. This is the expectation that al Qaeda brought to September 11, 2001.

Why is government counterviolence so easy to elicit? Every state has a criminal justice system that deals with assault and murder between individuals. Violence between criminal gangs is also brought to book in the justice system. What is special about violence by a terrorist group, such as the Irish Republican Army or al Qaeda, that so easily leads to a military response aimed at a category instead of a criminal justice response aimed at individual malefactors? This is a question for another book, but we cannot resist offering a few suggestions.

One possibility is that terrorists aim to destroy state power, whereas criminals want only to evade state power. Criminals may even depend on state power to preserve the criminal monopoly of vice businesses such as gambling, prostitution, and drug dealing. Thus, citizens are used to thinking of the military as protection against threats to the state and thinking of the police as protection against threats that work within the state.

Another possibility is the special emotional effect of illegal political action and political violence. Eliciting fear may not be the most important goal of terrorism. Although often suppressed and little studied, emotional reactions to terrorism include anger, outrage, and humiliation. In asymmetric conflict, these emotions are part of the reaction of the stronger when the weaker mounts a successful attack. These emotions can then become part of a reaction that is at least as much revenge as security building.

A third possibility is that anger and outrage among the victims of terrorism are reinforced by violation of a human need to see the state as natural and inevitable, like the difference between red and green. By contesting the legitimacy of the state and the state's claim to a monopoly of violence, terrorists can make a particular government appear suddenly arbitrary and temporary. The government and its supporters then react with emotions appropriate to an existential threat, a threat to the naturalized social reality in which the nation gives meaning to life and immortality to those who sacrifice for the life of the nation.

al Qaeda's Jujitsu Politics

At home, Osama bin Laden and Ayman al-Zawahiri were political losers. Bin Laden challenged the Saudi royal family and had to flee, first to Sudan and then to Afghanistan. Zawahiri led one faction of an Egyptian terrorist group—Islamic Jihad—that challenged the Egyptian government and lost; he fled with the remnants of his group to Afghanistan. After failing to rally Muslims against the government in their home countries, bin Laden and Zawahiri joined their remaining forces in Afghanistan and turned to a new strategy: rather than attack the near enemy of corrupt Muslim governments, they would attack the far enemy supporting these governments—the United States.

In a political memoir and manifesto, al-Zawahiri has been remarkably frank about the logic of this strategy. Published in Arabic in London in 2001, *Knights under the Prophet's Banner* frames the strategy as follows.

> The masters in Washington and Tel Aviv are using the [apostate Muslim] regimes to protect their interests and to fight the battle against the Muslims on their behalf. If the shrapnel from the battle reach their homes and bodies, they will trade accusations with their agents about who is responsible for this. In that case, they will face one of two bitter choices: either personally wage the battle against the Muslims, which means that the battle will turn into clear-cut *jihad* against infidels, or they reconsider their plans after acknowledging the failure of the brute and violent confrontation against Muslims.[6]

A vivid version of this strategy was represented in a 2005 posting on the forum Risalat al-Umma by a jihadi analyst who calls himself Sayf Allah. According to the posting, al Qaeda has, and has always had, a specific aim: to arouse the sleeping body of the Islamic Nation—a billion Muslims worldwide—to fight against Western power and the contaminations of Western culture. In support of this aim, the 9/11 attacks were designed "to force the Western snake to bite the sleeping body, and wake it up."[7]

This is jujitsu politics in action. Attack the United States at home, the U.S. response will be to send troops to Muslim countries, and this "invasion" will mobilize Muslims against the United States. Muslims who did not support attacks on Muslim governments previously will soon join bin Laden and al-Zawahiri in jihad against Americans.

The jihad Zawahiri had in mind was the kind of jihad that had won against the Russians in Afghanistan. Muslim volunteers from around the world came together (with U.S. help Zawahiri does not mention) to fight the Russians in Afghanistan. The presence of Russian soldiers on Muslim soil had stimulated a successful jihad; U.S. forces on Muslim soil would do the same.

With this strategy, al Qaeda expected U.S. forces in Afghanistan and sent a suicide bomber to kill Ahmed Shah Massoud two days before the 9/11 attacks. Massoud was a charismatic leader who had resisted the

---

6. Aaron, D. (2008). *In their own words: Voices of jihad—Compilation and commentary.* Santa Monica, CA: Rand Corporation, pp. 196–197.

7. Ibid.

Taliban and was the obvious choice to lead Afghans who might join the U.S. against the Taliban and its al Qaeda guests.

In the event, the U.S. intervention in Afghanistan did not produce the jihad al Qaeda had expected. Most Muslims saw the attack on the World Trade Center as immoral because it violated the Koran's strictures against attacking civilians. In addition, the U.S. intervention was accomplished with only hundreds of Special Forces and CIA officers on the ground. Suitcases full of hundred dollar bills bought tribal warlords to fight against the Taliban who had suppressed them earlier, and the small U.S. force on the ground was sufficient to direct U.S. air power against the Taliban. A drawn-out ground war in Afghanistan seemed to have been avoided and with it the international jihad that al Qaeda hoped to lead.

Unfortunately, early U.S. success against the Taliban was followed by a new intervention in Iraq. The war against Iraq's military was quickly won, but the nation-building that followed has been slow and painful. In 2016, U.S. troops continue in both Iraq and Afghanistan, and polls show that many Muslims continue to believe that the war on terrorism is a war on Islam.

Are the terrorists really so clever? Perhaps not. Bin Laden and al-Zawahiri had at least two earlier opportunities to learn the value of jujitsu politics.

In 1986 the United States responded to Libyan-supported terrorism by sending fighter bombers over Tripoli, targeting Libya's leader, Muammar Gaddafi. The bombs missed Gaddafi but killed fifteen Libyan civilians. This mistake was downplayed in the United States but became a public-relations success for anti-U.S. groups across North Africa. Bodies of women and children killed by U.S. bombs were displayed in pictures and television footage. Libyans who had dismissed Gaddafi's talk of the United States as "the great Satan" were now ready to believe that Gaddafi might not be so crazy after all.

In 1998, the United States responded to al Qaeda attacks on U.S. embassies in Africa by sending cruise missiles against al Qaeda camps in Afghanistan and against a supposed bomb factory in Khartoum. It appears now that the bomb factory was in fact producing only medical supplies, and the cruise missiles did not kill bin Laden or al-Zawahiri. But the missiles landing in Afghanistan did blow off the table a deal in which the Taliban were to send bin Laden to the Saudis in return for Saudi economic assistance. Politically, the Taliban could not be seen negotiating with a U.S. ally while U.S. bombs were falling in Afghanistan.

There were then two opportunities for al Qaeda to learn jujitsu politics before 9/11. Gaddafi's support for terrorism elicited a U.S. attack that raised Libyan and, more generally, Arab support for Gaddafi. Al Qaeda's attacks on U.S. embassies elicited a U.S. attack that saved bin Laden from being deported into the hands of his enemies in Saudi Arabia. By the time al-Zawahiri was writing *Knights under the Prophet's Banner*, he did not need a scholarly search of Marighella's *Minimanual of the Urban Guerrilla* to realize the power of jujitsu politics.

Jujitsu Politics Builds Walls

An important part of the reaction to terrorist violence is to seek increased security. This can take many forms, including avoiding members of threatening groups, profiling members of these groups for additional surveillance and reduced legal protection, and increased hostility and even violence toward members of these groups. Psychologically and sometimes physically, jujitsu politics builds walls between groups.

In Iraq and in Afghanistan, shootings and bombings targeted those who work for the Americans, not only those recruited to American-supported police and military forces but those who work for the Americans as translators, drivers, or hotel keepers. Attacks on Americans and those who work for Americans help to separate Westerners from Muslims. As Dexter Filkins has described, when U.S. forces respond to these attacks, breaking down doors must substitute for language skills, and the result is increasing opposition from local Muslims. The alternative in Iraq has been for U.S. forces to retire to their bases and leave policing to Sunni and Shi'a forces. In Afghanistan, the alternative is to bring an Afghan "government in a box" from Kabul into towns liberated by U.S. troops. Either way, the answer is to keep U.S. troops away from Muslims.

In Western countries, the reaction to terrorism includes stereotyping and profiling. It should amaze us that nineteen Arabs attacking on 9/11 could produce a wave of hostility toward millions of U.S. Arabs and Muslims. More recently one failed Nigerian terrorist, Umar Farouk Abdulmutallab, the "Underwear Bomber," was enough to initiate new visa restrictions for Nigerians traveling to the United States. The search for security is understandable but unavoidably contributes to the power of jujitsu politics.

Sometimes the results of jujitsu politics are physical walls that reinforce psychological barriers of avoidance and hostility. Republican and Loyalist neighborhoods were walled off from one another in Northern Ireland, and in 2016 many of the walls are still standing despite the cessation of violence and new political arrangements. Israel's security wall reduces casualties but reinforces the poverty and hostility of West Bank Palestinians. Walls between Greeks and Turks on Cyprus, between North and South Korea, between Egypt and Gaza, between the United States and Mexico—all provide physical security and a barrier to the kind of mixing that might contaminate one ethnicity or nation with members of another. The reaction of hostility and separation that is elicited by terrorist attacks can be very useful for those who want to build walls.

Suicide bombing is an especially effective form of jujitsu politics because it makes every member of an ethnic or national group a potential threat. Distance becomes the key to security, and soldiers in doubt want to shoot first. Jujitsu politics is the strategy behind suicide attacks against Westerners from Morocco to Indonesia, the Philippines, and Malaysia—wherever Westerners and Western culture are penetrating the Muslim world. The Western response to jihadist suicide terrorism is withdrawal and increased security that builds a wall between Westerners and those Muslims who are, from the jihadist point of view, getting on too comfortably with Western culture and politics.

Looking Further

Crenshaw, M. (1995). The effectiveness of terrorism in the Algerian War. In
    M. Crenshaw (Ed.), *Terrorism in context*. University Park, PA: Pennsylvania State
    University Press.
Crenshaw, M. (2002). The causes of terrorism. In C. Besteman (Ed.),
    Violence: A reader. New York: New York University Press.
Cullison, A., & Higgins, A. (2002). A once-stormy terror alliance was solidified by
    cruise missiles. *Wall Street Journal*, August 2. Available at http://www.wsj.com/
    articles/SB1028236160532452080. Accessed May 10, 2016.
Dostoevsky, F. (translated by R. Pevear and L. Volokhonsky) (1995). *Demons*.
    New York: Vintage Classics.
Filkins, D. (2005). The fall of the warrior king. *New York Times Magazine*, October 23.
German, M. (2007). *Thinking like a terrorist: Insights of a former FBI undercover agent*.
    Washington, DC: Potomac Books.
Gregg, R. B. (2013). *The power of non-violence*. Redditch, UK: Read Books.
Higson-Smith, C. (2002). A community psychology perspective on
    terrorism: Lessons from South Africa. In C. Stout (Ed.), *The psychology of terrorism*.

Vol. 4: *Programs and practices in response and prevention*. Westport, CT: Praeger, pp. 3–22.

Louis, W. R., & Taylor, D. M. (2002). Understanding the September 11 terrorist attack on America: The role of intergroup theories of normative influence. *Analyses of Social Issues and Public Policy* 2(1): 87–100.

Lustick, I. S. (1995). Terrorism in the Arab Israeli conflict: Targets and audiences. In M. Crenshaw (Ed.), *Terrorism in context*. University Park, PA: Pennsylvania State University Press.

Marighella, C. (translated by J. Butt & R. Sheed) (1970). *Minimanual of the urban guerrilla*. Havana: Tricontinental. Reprinted in Marighella, C. (1971). *For the liberation of Brazil*. Harmondsworth, UK: Penguin Books, pp. 61–97.

McCauley, C. (2006). Jujitsu politics: Terrorism and response to terrorism. In P. R. Kimmel & Chris E. Stout (Eds.), *Collateral damage: The psychological consequences of America's war on terrorism*. Westport, CT: Praeger, pp. 45–65.

Rummel. R. J. (1994). *Death by government*. New Brunswick, NJ: Transaction.

Sharp, G. (1973). *The politics of nonviolent action*, 3 vols. Boston: Porter Sargent.

Ulph, S. (2005). Al-Qaeda's "bowing-out" strategy. *Terrorism Focus* 2(17). Available at http://www.jamestown.org/programs/gta/single/?tx_ttnews[tt_news]=567&tx_ttnews[backPid]=238&no_cache=1. Accessed May 10, 2016.

Гроссман, Л. П. (1935). *Жизнь и труды Ф. М. Достоевского*. Москва: Литиздат. [Grossman, L. P. (1935). *Life and work of F. Dostoyevsky*. Moscow: Litizdat.]

Щеголев, П. Е. С. Г. (1924). *Нечаев в Алексеевской равелине*. Москва: Красный архив. Т. 5. [Schegolev, P. (1924). *Nechaev in the Alexy Raveline*. Moscow: Krasnyj Arhiv.]

CHAPTER TWELVE

Hatred

In protracted conflicts, the enemy is increasingly seen as less than human.

Over There Are Monsters

In 1879 People's Will broke off from Land and Freedom as an independent party with a primary agenda of political terror. By then the conflict between student activists and the government had been raging for five years, and both sides had been hardened.

The czar saw the students as ungrateful brats to whom he had given both freedom and opportunity and from whom he saw nothing but criticism, protests, and terrorism. The students, for their part, saw the czar as "taking one step forward and two steps backward" in his reforms, making life even more difficult than it had been before reform. The police, in the middle of this conflict but loyal to the czar, took it upon themselves to enforce his authority over the arrogant rebels with fervor that went beyond the law.

In this atmosphere of hostility and misunderstanding the conflicting sides drifted farther and farther apart. Having started as members of the same social class, sometimes of the same families, former students and government officials came to feel that they shared nothing anymore—their goals for themselves and the country, their values and beliefs, put them on opposing sides.

Leo Tolstoy, on visiting the Peter and Paul Fortress in St. Petersburg and talking with its superintendent Major Maidel, made this note in his journal.

> To me, from afar, standing outside of the struggle, it is clear that the anger in the two parties toward each other became monstrous. For Maidel and others all these Bogolubovs and Zazulichs are such rubbish that he does not see people in them, and can't feel sorry for them. For Zazulich, in turn, Trepov and others are rabid animals that can be—and need to be—killed like dogs. Meanwhile both camps have people, and good people at that.[1] (March 1878)

Tolstoy's observation was correct: both the government and the terrorists had stopped seeing the other as humans. In a private conversation before he assassinated General Mezentsev, Kravchinsky said of his target,

> ... he is merciless as only a person who thinks that any atrocity can be repented by fasting and praying before the icons can be. He prays when he goes to work for the Third Division to imprison and exile people, and he prays when he comes back from his business. In his family he is kind; but his worldview does not reach beyond his family. It is a worldview of a tiger that attacks his victim from the jungle to carry it to his cubs.[2]

In fact there is no evidence that General Mezentsev was cruel or particularly hostile to the political prisoners. It was his position of heading the detective division of police that was responsible for capturing radicals that put him on their blacklist. Nevertheless, in their indiscriminate hatred they did not see him as a person, only as a representative of a hated class. No less than in private conversations, in public statements about the government People's Will relied on animal metaphors:

---

1. Толстой, Л. Н. (1984). *Собрание сочинений в 22 т.* Москва: Художественная литература, Т. 18, с. 838. [Tolstoy, L. N. (1984). *Collection of works in 22 volumes.* Moscow: Hudozhestvennaya Literatura, Vol. 18, p. 838).] Available at http://narovol.narod.ru/. Accessed March 5, 2010.
2. Морозов, Н. А. (1947). *Повести моей жизни.* В трех томах. Издательство: Издательство Академии Наук СССР. [Morozov, N. (1947). *Novels of my life.* In three volumes. Moscow: USSR Academy of Sciences Press.]

It's time to wake from your long sleep and inaction and bravely side with the socialists who decided that the predatory Russian government should not exist. Death to the czar's bloodline![3]

... Squeezing the whole country in its iron claws, suppressing all life, thought and initiative—our government is something akin to those fairytale monsters that had to be appeased with human sacrifices.[4]

Yet at the same time and in the same public outlets, People's Will painted itself as virtuous and enlightened, in stark contrast to its portrayals of the regime. "To you, Russian public of both privileged and humble origins, appeal we, Russian Socialists, protectors of truth and human dignity." And, in an apparent clarification for the drastic difference between their proclaimed moral and their official legal status, they proclaimed,

The history of Russian thought can hardly find a single person who served Russia's progress and who was not considered at one point a criminal. Always, everywhere, our government considered as a firm foundation for itself only sociopaths, fools and thieves; and any glimpse of intellect, conscience and talent it considered a sign of something hostile.[5]

Clearly, the terrorists saw themselves as the direct opposite of the regime, not only in their goals but also in their humanity. In their view, their own humanism was juxtaposed to the government's monstrosity; their intellect was faced with the government's ignorance; their selflessness and morality were opposed to the government's corruption.

On the other side of the divide, police detectives and other government officials felt just as strongly that the revolutionaries were beasts with no conscience. Thus, Detective Sudeikin wrote in a letter to a friend, that "Real revolutionaries are people, people of ideas, in contrast to the Russian revolutionaries ... what we have here is a herd.... A gang! And it's a gang with leadership."[6]

---

3. Proclamation (ca. 1879). Available at http://narovol.narod.ru/.
4. People's Will Newspaper, St. Petersburg, September 20, 1879. Available at http://narovol.narod.ru/
5. Ibid.
6. Лурье, Ф. (2006). Политический сыск в истории России, 1649–1917 гг. Москва: Центрполиграф. [Lurie, F. (2006). Political policing in history of Russia 1649–1917. Moscow.] Available at http://regiment.ru/Lib/A/53/3.htm. Accessed May 10, 2016.

Likewise, Minister Pobedonoscev wrote in a letter, "I have no doubt that all current terror is of the same origin as that of 1862, except conducted more elaborately; and our idiots, as always, follow as a herd of sheep." The minister followed up on this point by bringing up negative ethnic stereotypes—foreigners—to explain the origins of the terror: "The main conscious weapon are the Jews (Zhidy)—these days they are omnipresent as a weapon of revolution. Look—all these assassinations by means of riders with racehorses handy—doesn't all this carry the mark of a Polish invention? In press it is also the Poles who agitate."[7]

The idea of the opposing side as less than human and therefore unworthy of compassion and dignity was expressed in action. For terrorists this idea enabled them to plan assassinations coldly. When it came to the czar, they wanted to kill not only him but also his entire family, including his children. So evil was the nature of this beast, they felt, that his entire bloodline had to be eliminated.

Sentiment also ran high for terrorists' student sympathizers. F. A. Burdin wrote to his friend A. N. Ostrovsky about an incident he witnessed in 1879. At a restaurant, someone pointed out to students an agent of the Third Division of Police (security service), and the students started to hit him. The beating continued until the reported agent of police was half-dead, at which point he narrowly escaped through the back door of the restaurant.

On the other side, the police acted on their views of political prisoners through their inhumane treatment of them. According to the People's Will newspaper, one prison protest was followed by prison guards tying prisoners with ropes, then hitting and kicking them into unconsciousness. One victim could not get up for days afterward, yet no prisoner received medical treatment for open wounds and internal bleeding.

The students and the police each developed an idea of the opponent as fundamentally and irreparably immoral, unaware of its immorality, and evil in its core motivations and beliefs. Armed with such powerful images, each side felt itself licensed to employ any and all means to defeat the enemy. After all, laws are for people; beasts who pose a threat to civilization should not be protected by its legal system. They need to be eradicated.

---

7. «Пишу я только для вас . . . ». (1994). Письма К. П. Победоносцева к сестрам Тютчевым. Новый мир. № 3. 1994. с. 209. ["*I am writing only to you . . .*" (1994). Letters from K. Pobedonoscev to the Tutchev sisters. Novyj Mir, 3, p. 209.]

Hatred and Bad Essence

It is often observed that groups in conflict, especially if the conflict involves prolonged violence, become more extreme in their negative perceptions of one another. This tendency can progress, as described in the previous section, to the point that the enemy is no longer seen as human, or at least not fully human as we are. Della Porta quotes a Red Brigade militant as follows: "... enemies are in a category, they are functions, they are symbols. They are not human beings."[8]

A high level of hostility toward another individual or group is often described as hatred. Some theorists believe that hate is an emotion, perhaps a combination of anger, fear, and contempt. A more recent view is that hate is an extreme form of negative identification—a sentiment—that includes the idea that members of the enemy group share a "bad essence." In this view hate is not an emotion but the occasion of experiencing many emotions, depending on what happens to the hated target. As noted in chapter 3, positive emotions (pride, joy) are occasioned when bad things happen to the hated group, and negative emotions (fear, shame, anger) are occasioned when good things happen to the hated group.

The idea that enemy individuals share a bad essence can make sense of an impulse to attack all of them without regard for age, gender, or civilian status. A group's essence is the hidden something shared by group members that makes them what they are or, more specifically, gives them shared group characteristics. A group's essence is understood to be stable over historical time and immutable for the individual group member. If the essence is bad, there is nothing to be done—negotiation and education can no more make a difference than negotiation or education can make a difference in the essence of a tiger. If tigers threaten us, all tigers are targets—old and young, near and far, in striped form or albino.

In general it is not useful to ask people directly, Do you think group X has an essence? But there are several useful indicators of essentialist thinking.

One such indicator is too-easy generalization, such as the hostility toward Arabs and Muslims in the United States that followed the attacks by nineteen Arabs and Muslims on September 11, 2001. It should

---

8. Della Porta, D. (1995). *Social movements, political violence, and the state: A comparative analysis of Italy and Germany*. Cambridge, UK: Cambridge University Press, p. 174.

surprise us that the actions of a few are so easily generalized to hostility against the many. Categorical hostility should be particularly surprising given that polling in the months after 9/11 revealed that most Arab Muslims judged the 9/11 attacks immoral—a violation of the Koran's strictures against attacking civilians. Suppose nineteen members of the French Greens Party (*Les Verts*) were to mount an attack on Wall Street. We doubt that the reaction in the United States would be nearly as large as the reaction to the 9/11 attacks (although the brief vogue of "freedom fries" in the United States when France declined to join the war in Iraq indicates that *some* anti-French reaction is likely). Our thought experiment suggests that essentializing a group—"they're all like that"—is easier when considering less familiar groups.

A second indicator of essentialist thinking is fear of contamination. Even the idea of contamination requires a high level of cognitive development. Neither dogs nor primates show contamination effects; humans begin to show these effects only in late childhood. Before the age of four or five, children will object to a cockroach floating in their orange juice but gladly drink the juice if the roach is removed. Older children will continue to refuse the orange juice even if the roach is removed and out of sight: contamination implies the transfer of an invisible essence that makes the juice undrinkable. Contamination is more than sensitivity to germs; most adults will refuse juice in which a "guaranteed sterilized" cockroach has been dipped.

Anthropologists report that, around the world, humans understand animal species to have essences: something hidden inside rats, bluebirds, and tigers that makes them different from one another. The essence idea is called by different names in different cultures: "blood" or "spirit" or "soul" or "nature" or even "genome." For our purposes, the key point is that humans too can be seen to have essences. Not just individuals but families, clans, tribes, ethnic groups, and nations can be seen as having different essences, as evidenced by concerns about mixing good and bad families, clans, tribes, ethnic groups, and races. Hitler's fear that the German *volk* would be contaminated by Jews culminated in the Holocaust. Less threatening forms of essentialist thinking are visible in special rights for groups defined by race or ethnicity, including the right of return accorded by Germany to those who can show German descent and by Israel to those who can show Jewish descent.

It would be at least slightly reassuring to conclude that essentialist thinking occurs only for groups (family, clan, ethnicity, race) defined by descent, groups that can be described as "blood relations."

Unfortunately, it appears that groups defined by class and culture can also be essentialized. Stalin eliminated the Kulaks (wealthy peasants) because they were a class threat to the purity of "the new Soviet man." Most of the 1.5 million Cambodians killed by the Khmer Rouge were ethnic "blood-descent" Cambodians, but Pol Pot killed them in fear that "Cambodians with Vietnamese minds" would contaminate the "authentic" Khmer culture. It may be easier to essentialize blood-relation groups than cultural or class groups, but perhaps only slightly easier.

Sprinzak describes this kind of categorical derogation of class and culture among members of the 1970s U.S. terrorist group the Weather Underground:

> Individuals who are identified with the "rotten" and "soon to be de-stroyed" social and political order are depersonalized and dehumanized. They are derogated into the ranks of the worst enemies or subhuman species. Dehumanization makes it possible for the radicals to disengage morally and to commit atrocities without a second thought . . .[9]

Weather Underground first lady Bernardine Dohrn was address-ing the December 1969 Weather War Council when she referred to the Manson family's murder of actress Sharon Tate—eight months pregnant—as follows: "Dig it! First they killed those pigs and then they put a fork in pig Tate's belly. Wild!" Referring to the LaBiancas, a couple stabbed to death by the Manson family the day after Tate's murder, she went on: "Offing those rich pigs with their own forks and knives, and then eating a meal in the same room, far out! The Weathermen dig Charles Manson!"[10] Of course neither Tate nor the LaBiancas were pigs by descent; they were "pigs" as members of the capitalist class.

Finally, a third indicator of essentialist thinking, already evident, is language. Reference to the enemy as "gooks" or "slopes" or "towel heads" already implies a commonality of bad essence: "they're all the same." The implication of bad essence is even stronger when the enemy is identified as an animal life form such as lice, roaches, dogs, or

9. Sprinzak, E. (1991). The process of delegitimation: Toward a linkage theory of political terrorism. In C. McCauley (Ed.), *Terrorism and public policy*. London: Frank Cass, p. 56.
10. Bugliosi, V., with Gentry, C. (1994). *Helter skelter: The true story of the Manson murders*. New York: Norton, p. 296.

pigs. An animal name implies an animal essence, and an animal essence is lower than human essence. Humans have experience butchering and eating some animals and trying to exterminate other animals; referring to a human group with an animal name is the first step toward treating others as animals.

Another kind of language is more abstract: the enemy is *evil*. To say that enemies "are evil-doers" is not essentializing because the focus is on bad behavior. But to say that the enemy "is evil" implies a single bad essence; the focus is no longer on behavior but on a deep-core character or spirit or nature that can only produce bad behavior. What is sometimes called a Manichaean worldview divides the world between good and evil, and the result is two essences.

The distinction between bad behavior and bad essence comes into play in a conspicuous way in the penalty phase of a murder trial. The defendant has already been found guilty, and now the issue is whether the penalty will be death or imprisonment, usually life imprisonment. The defense attempts to bring forth mitigating factors, which can include any positive relationship or good behavior in the defendant's life history. The prosecution seeking the death penalty argues that there are no mitigating factors, that the defendant is "bad to the bone": has always been bad, irredeemably bad, the kind of bad from which no good can come. In short the prosecution argues *for* bad essence—the defendant is evil—whereas the defense argues *against* bad essence, that there is some mitigating good in the defendant despite horrifically bad behavior. The evil defendant must be executed; the merely bad one may profit from time in prison.

Of course it is not news that thinking evil of others can support and encourage harsh treatment of others. Concern about "hate speech" is one expression of this idea, and concern about "dehumanizing" the enemy is another. But "bad essence" goes beyond these concerns to specify the mechanism of dehumanization in a way that links hate speech with two other signs of hate: too-easy generalization of individual acts to group characteristics. and fear of contamination.

Essentializing Terrorists and Their Enemies

Looking back now at the conflict between the students and the czar, we see there were examples of negative essence on both sides and at every level: individual, family, and group. Kravchinsky said of his target, General Mezentsev, "[His] is a worldview of a tiger that attacks his victim from the jungle to carry it to his cubs."[11] The students come to see the czar's whole family as bad seed: "Death to the czar's bloodline!" The government was seen by students as a predatory monster. Tolstoy notes that neither students nor government could see the other as human.

It is interesting to note that government officials and student radicals were often from the same eminent families, which makes descent-based essentializing more difficult. Minister Pobedonoscev's reference to Jews and Poles is an effort to give an ethnic essence to the student enemy, but this line is strained and far-fetched. Rather, the opposing bad essences in this conflict were cultural. The czar's view of the students is that they shared a bad character; they were ungrateful. There is no implication in this view that the students were born ungrateful; their bad character was achieved rather than inherited.

Modern instances of hatred and bad essence are available in Della Porta's interviews with Red Brigades and Red Army Faction (RAF) militants.[12] These instances conform to a suggestion by Nick Haslam that there are at least two ways of seeing an individual or a group as not human: we can see them as animals ("dogs," "vermin") or we can see them as bloodless automata ("wheels," "tools"). Animals are lower forms of life; automata are not life forms at all. In the five quotations that follow, the first denies the humanity of an individual, the next two assert an animalistic group essence ("pigs"), and the last two assert a machine-like group essence.

- "Even today, I do not feel any general scruple concerning a murder because I cannot see some creatures—such as, for instance, Richard Nixon—as human beings."
- RAF leader Ulrike Meinhof wrote: "We say that policemen are pigs, that guy in uniform is a pig; he is not a human being. And we behave toward him accordingly."
- The most frequently quoted German terrorist slogans were those that emphasized the "fight of the human beings against the pigs in order to free humankind" and proclaimed that "humanity toward the enemy of human kind is inhuman."
- . . . from the very beginning of Italian terrorism, the militants defined the victims of their attacks as "wheels of the capitalist machine."

---

11. Available at http://narovol.narod.ru/. Accessed May 3, 2010.
12. Quotations in this and the following paragraph from Della Porta, chap. 7.

- [On picking a target for murder] "Then you don't care anymore which responsibilities that person has; you ascribe everything to him ... he is only a small part of the machine that is going to destroy all of us."

Perhaps most surprising in Della Porta's materials is an indication that terrorists can essentialize themselves no less than their enemies. Militants can see themselves as parts of a machine, a war machine. Thus,

> Ideology offered images of the "self" that, internalized by the militants, complemented the idea of "depersonalizing the enemy" with the image of the "freedom fighter" as "cold executioner" who must fulfill his duty. Italian and German militants alike described how this "bureaucratic" perception of their role eliminated moral scruples in their everyday life. A German interviewee explained, "Most of the fear you feel disappears in the phase of the planning and repetition of the exercise until perfection.... then you become nothing more than a working gear."

More commonly, radicals essentialize themselves as supermen, a virtuous vanguard, a chosen people, embattled heroes, and freedom fighters.

> The elitism common to the self-definition of German and Italian militants accomplished an important function: it made isolation appear to be a positive self-imposed quality.... As a German interviewee explained, one's comrades became the only ones who possess the "truth": "It was wonderful to belong to [a group of people] who had a complete understanding of the world and who had really started to work hard instead of sitting and complaining"; it was exhilarating to be one of "these extremely intelligent comrades with an iron will."[13]

Logically, it should be possible to essentialize *them* without essentializing *us*. Psychologically, however, it may be very difficult to see their bad essence without counterposing our own good essence. Neo-Nazi Ben Klassen makes the contrast about as strong as it can be: "What is good for the White Race is the highest virtue; what is bad for the White Race is the ultimate sin."[14] Klassen also provides

---

13. Della Porta, p. 173.
14. Klassen, B. (1981). *The white man's bible*. Otto, NC: Creativity Book Publishers, pp. 5–6. Available at http://www.archive.org/details/WhiteMansBible.

an explicit example of fear of contamination of a white essence that includes both race and culture.

> The need for hard and decisive action by the total forces of the White Race is great indeed, and it is extremely urgent. We have no more time to lose. Aroused, organized and united we are ten times more powerful than all the Jews and other mud races combined. Divided and disorganized as we now are, we are heading for certain destruction and total oblivion. The Jews are feverishly accelerating their program of mongrelizing The White Race here in America, and everywhere else in the White Man's domain. They are importing (at the initiative of the United States government) Vietnamese, Haitians, Cubans, Mexicans and other mud races by the hundreds of thousands and by the millions. No civilization, no race can stand such an onslaught for long. Unless we take urgent and decisive action we will soon be reduced to a mongrelized mass of miserables as in Haiti, or in India.

It is easy to laugh at this florid example of essentializing. But we can do so only because Klassen makes explicit what other essentialist rhetoric leaves implicit. Around the world, ethnic minorities fearing assimilation are a source of political conflict and radicalization. This fear is common because the idea of essence is a kind of cognitive default. Its clear value in making sense of the animal world is captured in the story of the ugly ducking who turns out to be a beautiful swan, but this value makes the idea of essence all too available for making sense of the human world. The result is group conflict that can too easily move to impersonal violence.

If the idea that the enemy has a bad essence is as accessible as we are suggesting, then it is worth remarking that Osama bin Laden did not use this idea in relation to Americans. He used videos—some with English subtitles—to try to reach U.S. citizens over the heads of the U.S. government. He argued that attacks on U.S. civilians are justified because the United States is a democracy, that citizens vote for and pay taxes to their government, and that therefore citizens are responsible for the harm the United States does to Muslims. It is not necessary to agree with this argument to see that it is an assertion of moral culpability, not an assertion of an American bad essence.

There are perhaps two ways to understand why bin Laden did not essentialize Americans. The histories of the student radicals of the 1970s—Red Brigades, RAF, Weather Underground—indicate that the more marginalized they became politically, the more they retreated to seeing themselves as heroes and their enemies as "pigs." These histories suggest that, wherever he was hiding out when he tried to appeal to the U.S. public, bin Laden did not feel marginalized. Another possibility is that his internationalist and proselytizing view of his religion made it difficult for bin Laden to see any group as permanently alienated from Islam. Even bin Laden could not hope to convert a bad essence.

Looking Further

Chirot, C., & McCauley, C. (2006). *Why not kill them all? The logic and prevention of mass political murder*. Princeton, NJ: Princeton University Press. Chapter 2, The psychological foundations of genocidal killing.

Haslam, N. (2006). Dehumanization: An integrative review. *Personality and Social Psychology Review* 10(3): 252–264.

Medin, D. L., & Atran, S. (2004). The native mind: Biological categorization and reasoning in development and across cultures. *Psychological Review* 111(4): 960–983.

Royzman, E. E., McCauley, C., & Rozin, P. (2005). From Plato to Putnam: Four ways of thinking about hate. In R. J. Sternberg (Ed.), *The psychology of hate*. Washington, DC: APA Books, pp. 3–35.

CHAPTER THIRTEEN

Martyrdom

A successfully constructed martyr can radicalize sympathizers for the martyr's cause.

Meaning in Martyrdom

An idea—be it democracy, free market economy, or communism—can be more or less successful depending on the cultural soil on which it falls. In some cases the society's history and social norms discredit the idea, making it seem ridiculous, dangerous, or empty, and it dies without developing a significant following. In other cases a society ready for a new framing, a new solution to the old problems, will readily embrace the idea, allowing it to grow and evolve. There are also cases where a particular idea is so successful that it keeps reoccurring in a variety of forms and media, time and again, seemingly part of some endless cycle. The last is the case of the idea of martyrdom in Russia.

The tortures and deaths that the Russian people suffered throughout their history at the hands of Tartars, Turks, Germans, and other invaders are rivaled only by the tortures and deaths they suffered at the hands of their own rulers. Ivan the Terrible, Peter the Great, and Nicholas I, in their efforts to unify and rule a vast land with many diverse ethnic and religious groups, all imposed a relentless dictatorship where unprovoked top-down cruelty was the norm.

When Vassili Blazhenny Temple on what is now Red Square was built for Ivan the Terrible and he saw how magnificent the building was, he had the two architects blinded lest they build anything in the future that could complete with the temple. Peter the Great personally tortured countless people, including his own sister, on suspicions of treason; he murdered his own (and only) son because Alexi was not interested in governing and wanted to live a simple life in a remote village. Cutting off noses and tongues, branding faces, and public floggings were used as punishment for minor offenses to remind people not to challenge their rulers. Landowners conveyed the reign of cruelty down to the serfs, whose existence was defined by suffering.

In a land where so many suffer so much, where there is little rule or reason behind the suffering, finding meaning in their pain is all that keeps people going. For those who are suffering, martyrdom provides this meaning. Maybe not here and now, but someday, the pain and sacrifice will be appreciated. Maybe suffering serves some higher purpose, bringing one closer to God. In the Russian Orthodox tradition, the most important holiday of the year is Easter. The forty days of Lenten fast and penance that precede Easter provide a daily reminder of the suffering and sacrifice of Christ, which culminates in the celebration of his rising. There is hope for those suffering now: they will be blessed later. The Christian message of martyrdom fell on a very fertile soil in Russia.

The first Russian Orthodox saints were two eleventh-century brothers, Boris and Gleb, heirs to the throne of Kievan Russia, sons of Volodimir the Baptist. They were warned that a rival, their half-brother Svyatopolk (later named Svyatopolk the Accursed), was plotting to kill them; but they refused to fight him or flee their tents and met their death in prayers. They were canonized for their nonresistance to violence and started a Russian Orthodox Christian tradition of martyr-saints.

A vast Russian political landscape provided occasions for martyrdom. A famous Soviet stand-up comic had a sketch about food shortages of the 1980s: the representative of a remote village telephones the Kremlin to say, "We have no food anyway; give us a cause and a slogan, so we know what we are hungry for." In the nineteenth century the cause that gathered most martyrs under its banners was *Narod* ("the people"—peasants and poor workers).

Martyrs for the Russian People

The first martyrs for the peasants' cause emerged a generation before People's Will. They were the elite, the cream of the Russian nobility who decided they could not put up with the practice of slavery in all its horror and could no longer rest all hope for change in a monarch's benevolence. They organized a rebellion with some army units on their side, hoping to force Nicholas I, the heir of Czar Alexander I, to refuse the throne and make Russia a constitutional republic. These men became known as Decembrists because their uprising took place on December 14, 1825.

The government responded to their demands with cannon fire. The crowd turned against the rebels as soon as the first shots were fired, and the army units that had supported the rebels fled the square. The uprising failed; the organizers were captured, tried, hanged or sentenced to hard labor in Siberia, and stripped of their noble status and possessions. The condemned men walked for many months in shackles from St. Petersburg to Siberia, enduring cold, diseases, and hunger. When their wives followed them to their Siberian exile, the women too were stripped of status and possessions. Throughout the thirty-year rule of Nicholas I the Decembrists' relatives petitioned that their sentences be softened, to no avail. Their case became the inspiration for novels, poems, and political movements.

A Martyr on Martyrdom

Almost forty years later, Nikolai Chernyshevsky, the talented son of a provincial priest, was a beneficiary of the educational reform and the newly liberal press established by Alexander II. Having received an elite education at St. Petersburg University, Chernyshevsky traveled abroad, learned multiple languages, published philosophical essays, and eventually became chief editor of a prominent intellectual journal, *The Contemporary* (*Sovremennik*). His numerous essays and his PhD thesis reflected his utilitarian socialist views.

In a series of articles in his journal Chernyshevsky addressed an anonymous person, presumably the monarch Alexander II, offering an extensive critique of the reforms, including in particular liberation of serfs. These essays caused security services to pay special attention to their author, and when in 1861 Chernyshevsky organized a discussion group to address the inadequacies of the reforms and how to avoid a potential peasant revolt, he was arrested on suspicion of treason. Without any legal proceeding, he was placed in the Peter and Paul Fortress in St. Petersburg.

Two years went by before Chernyshevsky was tried and sentenced (despite lack of evidence against him) to seven years of hard labor and a subsequent twelve years of Siberian exile. During his two years in prison Chernyshevsky wrote a novel that was to become the most powerful instrument of mass radicalization of his and many future generations of young Russians. He titled the novel *What's to Be Done? (Chto Delat?)*.

Smuggled out of prison, the novel was published by *The Contemporary* and swiftly banned by the government. Issues still in circulation were copied by hand, and foreign editions, published by radical émigré circles, soon began to pour over the border despite the ban. Popular songs were written (and promptly banned) about the novel and its author. Student discussion groups began by talking about this book and ended by resolving to become activists or terrorists. There was not a single member of People's Will or, indeed, of the many activist or radical organizations of that time who had not read *What's to Be Done?* There was not a single one who had not tried, in some way, to emulate its characters. Almost every Russian case described in the preceding chapters of this book in some way referenced *What's to Be Done?* What was so powerful about this book, besides the appeal of the forbidden that the government conferred by officially banning it?

What's to Be Done? had at least two characteristics that were bound to make it a sensation with the young generation of Russians in 1865. First, it was a scandalous novel, not because of its subject matter—it talked about falling in love, getting married, living a married life, and building one's skills and career—but because of the way these everyday events were described. Chernyshevsky interspersed his narrative with a conversation with (or lecture to) the reader. In these first-person monologues, he is alternatingly condescending, ridiculing, and demeaning; the author directly and indirectly accuses the reader of dimwittedness, closed-mindedness, and inability to appreciate real art and "real, special people," such as his character Rachmetov. He mockingly questions readers' understanding of his (writer's) meanings and intentions. He calls his female readers stupid and his male readers lustful.

But this disrespect of readers is nothing compared to the author's disrespect of traditional Russian society. In the novel, the traditional family is dominated either by a despotic father or by a cold, calculating mother; individuals' true nature and will are routinely sacrificed for the benefit of money and social status. Morality, religion, and art have no place in characters' actions and motivations.

Chernyshevsky's answer to this anti-utopia is equally shocking. The rare "special" people who realize and defy the inadequacies of such a life should abandon all convention and instead be guided by their own intuition, no matter how self-serving. Thus, the main heroine, Vera Nikolaevna, escapes her parents' house to marry her brother's tutor instead of the suitor the parents preferred for her. The newlyweds call each other exclusively "my friend," live in separate rooms for fear of offending each other with their underdressed morning or evening appearance, and do not share anything in each others' lives that they do not wish. They choose to work for a living, although they could live more lavishly (this does not prevent their keeping a servant and a cook). Vera Nikolaevna opens a tailor workshop, which becomes a commune, with all members and their relatives sharing several rooms, buying necessities in bulk, dividing profits equally, and giving the sick or disabled easy duties. Notably, Vera Nikolaevna, hard worker that she is, nevertheless allows herself luxuries like taking two afternoon naps and drinking cream daily. When she falls in love with Kirsanov, a friend of her husband Lopuhov, her husband fakes suicide and leaves town to enable the two lovers to live free of the stigma that comes with a divorce or affair. It is left unclear why they would care about others' opinion in this case when they were oblivious or defiant of it in all other cases.

Continuing to shock the reader, Vera Nikolaevna reads serious literature and studies medicine to avoid being too involved in her feelings—apparently a common problem for women. The book ends on a happy note, with Vera Nikolaevna married to Kirsanov and her ex-husband, formerly known as Lopuhov, married to her friend, all living together in a commune of their own, amidst a growing number of tailor workshops that they help organize.

The blatant denial of all conventions and rules, from the voice of the writer to the marital arrangements of the characters, appealed to the rebellious spirit of the 1860s. Nihilism, rejection of the old, was in full swing; the aptly named novel gave young nihilists a prescription for action that they could accept. That was one of the two reasons the book became so successful.

The second reason, as Chernyshevsky would put it, "should be obvious to you, our reader: can you guess it?" A book written by an unfairly imprisoned intellectual about other intellectuals who willingly subjected themselves to hardships—a book by a martyr about martyrs—could not fail to inspire young intellectuals in Russia in the 1860s. Chernyshevsky's suffering in prison and in exile, which he refused to appeal when the authorities suggested he do so (he believed he did nothing wrong and so had no grounds to ask for mercy), made him the perfect herald for the message of martyrdom. His characters become credible advocates for their cause when they knowingly and voluntarily chose to suffer for it. A beautiful woman who refuses to marry into riches so that she can be independent, a promising medical student who refuses to take on a lucrative practice in order to advance science, a young family who decide to work when they don't have to—these were sacrifices that, Chernyshevsky believed, were the first step in the right direction, although not a big step. These were what he called "ordinary people."

The novel's real inspiration is a figure who comes into the plot only tangentially and briefly. Rachmetov, the "special person," dedicates himself to alleviating the suffering of simple people. To gain physical strength, he takes on hard physical labor and eats a lot of undercooked (and expensive) meat. He saves money and eats little else, except at dinner invitations from others, and only such foods as simple people occasionally eat—to share their hard lives. Yes to apples, but no to peaches; yes to oranges when in St. Petersburg, but no to oranges in other cities.

This diet and exercise had the desired effect, enabling him, at one point, to stop a fast-moving horse-drawn carriage by grabbing it with his bare hands (a feat later repeated, on a bet, by Andrei Zhelyabov in front of admiring friends; see chapter 2). Rachmetov does not drink, smoke, or touch women, and at one point sleeps on a bed of nails—to discipline himself and to keep his focus on the goal. His very presence is a reminder to others that there is more they can do to serve the people.

But if that is not enough, he does not shy away from pointing to others' flaws. He reprimands Vera Nikolaevna for not dismissing her servant in time for bed and for thinking of leaving her tailoring workshop without asking the workers' opinion first. The "special person" also keeps a servant, of whom we hear little besides Rachmetov's order to her to buy only the highest-quality meat. Presumably, he treats her better than any other person of his station would treat a servant. He disappears from the novel soon after appearing, and of his future we only learn that it was probably he who, some years later, came to a poor German philosopher to give him five-sixths of a sizable fortune so that the philosopher could publish his works. Dear reader, does the name Nietzsche come to mind?

The numerous amusing inconsistencies in the novel's message did not register with the young student audience. The main characters insist on selfishness when it comes to the feelings of "nonspecial" people, yet they carefully protect each others' feelings—to the point of faking suicide so that nothing, not even a rumor, will mar the lovers' union. They preach by word and action, working for a living instead of relaxing into the vain consumption of the noble classes, yet they retain the luxuries of daily naps, expensive diets, and servants—all foreign to the simple people for whom they claim to sacrifice. They condemn the elaborate entertainment of the rich, yet the novel ends with the main characters taking several horse-drawn sleds into the Russian winter to a wonderland cottage, where they enjoy playing the piano, singing, dancing, and playing games—very like the privileged existence they profess to shun and in stark contrast to the colorless, hungry, miserable existence of the peasants and workers.

In short, any critical or experienced reader should have found the novel artless and tacky (the latter point was readily admitted by the author himself). A peasant would not understand it; a factory worker would laugh at it; a mature person would sneer at it. But falling on the freshly opened, rebellious, mostly well-off ears of Russian university students in the 1860s, the novel was thunderous. The students were a perfect audience: adolescents ready to break with the past and the conventional, eager for a new authority to guide them. The novel, written by a martyr of the regime they despised, delivered and read in secrecy under the threat of imprisonment, told them exactly "what's to be done."

Special-person Rachmetov was the great inspirational figure not only for Chernyshevsky's contemporaries but also for many Russian revolutionaries in years to follow. Lenin admitted to reading the novel five times in one summer, and he later wrote a famous political essay by the same name. According to the Communist Party's official biography, Lenin attempted to emulate Rachmetov in his personal habits by lifting weights, eating little, sleeping four hours per night, and denying himself romantic relationships (although recent documents indicate that he spent heavily on prostitutes).

As Russian students took Chernyshevsky's message to heart, they began concerning themselves with social issues, learning trades, organizing gender-segregated communes, limiting their diets to vegetarianism (unlike Rachmetov, they usually could not afford to switch to prime-cut meats but sought an ideological diet). Although some were content with the level of sacrifice of "ordinary people," others went further. They "went into the people."

What's to Be Done? gained a new meaning for those who tried martyrdom on for size. According to Alexander Michailov, one of the founders of the Executive Committee of People's Will, "a revolutionary is a doomed person." For him and for his followers that meant being ready to die at any moment. At the beginning of their terrorist activity the Executive Committee did not plan for terrorists to die—only their targets; later they realized the tactical advantages of having a ready-to-die assassin. They began to plan terrorist acts so that, in case of capture, terrorists had a way of quickly killing themselves.

During the work on an underground tunnel as a part of a plan to blow up the czar's train (Sonia Perovskaya's first terrorist act), all diggers carried poison with them in case of a cave-in or discovery. Sonia, who kept watch in the house above the dig, carried a gun, ready to shoot into a container with explosive liquid to blow up the house at any sign of an impending arrest. During their executions, some of them screamed at the crowd "We are doing it for you." When Michailov himself was arrested, he mused in quiet content at the news of his death sentence but was later crushed to find out that the sentence was changed to life in prison. Rotting in a prison cell did not constitute the caliber of martyrdom these star-struck young people envisioned for themselves. A quiet death away from the public eye would do nothing for their cause, nothing for their ambitions. They wanted to go out with a bang.

Doing "What's to Be Done"

If Chernyshevsky had written a memoir of his own suffering in the life-threatening dankness of Peter and Paul Fortress, he might have been seen by readers as weak and self-seeking. His suffering could have been compared with the suffering of others, including those who had been tried and executed, whereas he was only awaiting trial. The results in terms of establishing himself as witness and model would be doubtful.

Instead he demonstrated his political strength and zeal in an act of creativity. He violated the first rule of writing—write about what you know—to write about fictional martyrdom. His pure devotion to the cause can be judged by the fact that he did not write about himself—he wrote about the cause. The triumph of his martyrdom was that the oppression of his cell did not stifle his literary impulse; indeed he invented a new novelistic form in which he could lecture his audience, not in relation to his own sacrifice but in relation to the sacrifices of his characters.

Chernyshevsky's main characters appear at first a cipher: their inconsistencies about which sacrifices are required of them are laughable to modern eyes. "Special-person" Rachmetov attains greater consistency at the cost of remaining mostly offstage. But what both main and special characters convey is a scale of sacrifice. Well-to-do students can sacrifice in learning a trade, organizing communes, and accepting a new personal and political morality. They should work all the harder for recognizing that they have not attained real martyrdom. Rachmetov is the real martyr, the standard to strive for, a rich man who—except for fancy meats and a servant—becomes a peasant. A loner, he tests himself with physical privation, does without the support of commune and community, affection, or connection. Rachmetov is the model of "going into the people." Commune students should admire him, support him, and occasionally send a few of their best to emulate him.

The result was a two-tier scale of martyrdom, in which most students do the most that they can do by living the commune life. A few heroic souls can join and mobilize the peasants. This scale quickly moved from the pages of a novel to the norms of a social movement. In the transition, Chernyshevsky became a martyr's martyr. His own moldering in prison and exile were turned to witnessing for a new Russia, and his characters, even more than he, became the models for new Russians.

The Psychology of Martyrdom

The root meaning of *martyr* is "witness," and there is something particularly powerful about a witness ready to sacrifice even life to give testimony. The sacrifice does not have to be immediate death; in many ways the sacrifice may be greater if the martyr gives up individual ambitions in order to work and suffer day after day over years for the cause. This was the situation of most People's Will members, who were ready to die if necessary but who did not volunteer for suicide missions.

There are three questions that can be raised about martyrdom. How are individuals moved to self-sacrifice? What makes an individual act of self-sacrifice more or less likely to be seen as martyrdom? Once accepted as a martyr, how does the martyr's example rally terrorist sympathizers and discourage terrorist targets?

The history of People's Will suggests that the first question engages some important circularity: one martyr is likely to encourage others. Part of the power of *What's to Be Done?* was the perceived martyrdom of its author. The book and its author had, as we have seen, an enormous impact on Russian students, not only on their readiness for sacrifice but even on the forms and directions of sacrifice. Communes were *in*, old morality was *out*, learning a trade and "going into the people" were the future.

In short, the martyr is not only witness but model. Martyrdom is a mechanism of radicalization when others are moved to greater sacrifice for the martyr's cause; some may then be moved to become martyrs themselves. Of course not all martyrs emerge as followers of martyrs. Most of the mechanisms already presented in this book can contribute to individual readiness for martyrdom, including personal and political grievance, love, a slippery slope, the dynamics of group competition, and group isolation.

Individual extremes of self-sacrifice cannot be very mysterious to Americans when so many U.S. Medal of Honor winners have died in the heroism for which the medal was awarded. More mysterious are the questions about what makes a particular death accepted as martyrdom and about the political impact of martyrs.

The Making of a Martyr

Self-sacrifice is not self-evident; it has to be constructed in the public eye. The perception of self-sacrifice depends on seeing a costly or even fatal act as motivated by devotion to the cause. An individual under compulsion cannot choose, and anything that undermines the attribution of choice is likely to undermine the perception of self-sacrifice. A self-harming act may be attributed to the influence of drugs, for instance, or the delirium of extreme emotion. Even if the costly act is perceived as freely chosen, other motivations besides devotion to the cause may be entertained. Perhaps the choice was motivated by desire for personal status or glory or for status or money for family members. Or perhaps the choice was motivated by fear or pain or fatigue that made a painful choice better than the alternatives. In general, attribution of any kind of selfish motivation will undermine the attribution of self-sacrifice for a cause that defines martyrdom.

Both Islamic and Christian authorities have emphasized purity of motive as the key to martyrdom.

Third-century Christians thirsting for martyrdom had to be restrained by bishops from volunteering themselves to Roman authorities. Acknowledging yourself a Christian when asked by authorities was approved. Trying to take your fate in your own hands by volunteering for death was rejected. Martyrdom is a sure way to heaven, but God determines the martyrs; for the bishops, anything else was pride and vainglory.

Centuries later St. Thomas More provided a powerful example of the Christian martyr. He would not sign the Oath of Succession that acknowledged the claim of Henry VIII to supremacy of the Church of England; but he did not deny the claim. Instead he used his considerable abilities to argue that, legally, his silence should be taken as assent. Executed despite his best efforts, he died "the King's good servant— but God's first."

The same focus on motivation is evident in Islam, even the extremist version of Islam that justifies martyrdom-murder. Found in the personal belongings of several of the 9/11 attackers were copies of a handwritten document, a kind of manual for the attack. The author of the document is not known with certainty, although it has sometimes been attributed to Mohammed Atta ("Atta's Manual") as the presumed leader of the 9/11 operation.

Perhaps the most surprising aspect of the manual is that it is does not incite hatred of the enemy. There is no list of outrages to justify the mission. There is no mention of infidels in Saudi Arabia or children dying in Iraq or U.S. support for Israel. On the contrary, the manual argues explicitly against individual motivation based in personal feelings: "Do not act out of a desire for vengeance for yourself. Let your action instead be for the sake of God."

Atta's Manual reinforces this injunction with the example of Ali ibn Abi Talib, as described in Muslim sacred writings from the seventh century. Ali was engaged in combat with an infidel who spat on him. Rather than strike the infidel in anger, Ali held his sword until he could master himself and strike for Allah rather than for himself. The importance of this example is increased by the paraphrase that follows in the manual: "He might have said it differently. When he became sure of his intention, he struck and killed him." Here the focus on intention resonates with the concerns of third-century bishops about the intentions of Christian martyrs, although the 9/11 attackers were martyr-murderers rather than martyrs. Indeed the concern with intention in

Atta's Manual suggests that a selfless intention can be powerful enough, for some observers, to give the gloss of martyrdom to murder.

The impact of martyrdom depends, of course, not on the historical fact of the martyr's motive but on the publically accepted version of the martyr's sacrifice. Like the tree that falls in a forest with no one to hear it, martyrdom without witnesses is not witnessing. National groups, no less than religious groups, try to provide continuing celebration of their martyrs. The United States has Memorial Day and the roll call of Medal of Honor winners; France has memorials to World War I and World War II in every town and village; Great Britain commemorates Armistice Day and Fields of Remembrance.

Radical and terrorist groups also have rituals recalling and rekindling their martyrs. The Liberation Tigers of Tamil Eelam would yearly celebrate three days of Martyrs' Day activities, with special honors for the parents of dead heroes. Palestinian suicide bombers against Israel are remembered with portraits, graffiti, shrines, and rallies such as are often held in Martyrs' Square in Gaza; Palestinian web sites offer videos made by suicide terrorists before their attacks.

There is reason to believe that keeping the memory of martyrs alive can have powerful political effects. Mahatma Gandhi's hunger strike against British rule in India is probably the best-known political success of martyrdom, although his was not a fast to the death. *Ten Men Dead* recounts the history of Irish Republican Army and Irish National Liberation Army prisoners who died in a hunger strike to protest British efforts to treat political prisoners as common criminals. The hunger strikers died over a period of seventy-three days. Several were elected to the Irish or British parliament, and many observers believe that the hunger strikes resuscitated a moribund Republican cause.

The Mobilizing Power of Martyrdom in Lincoln's Gettysburg Address

The political psychology of martyrdom is yet to be written, but the question is clear enough. Once a particular sacrifice is accepted as martyrdom within a group, how does it lead to mobilization for a cause and increased sacrifice from group members? Talented leaders practice answers to this question, even if they do not theorize about it, and their practice can suggest how martyrdom encourages new sacrifices. Here we turn to Lincoln's Gettysburg Address, one of the strongest political evocations of martyrdom ever written. Lincoln first establishes the cause Union soldiers died for, then turns to the obligations of the living.

> Four score and seven years ago our fathers brought forth on this continent a new nation, conceived in Liberty, and dedicated to the proposition that all men are created equal.
>
> Now we are engaged in a great civil war, testing whether that nation, or any nation, so conceived and so dedicated, can long endure. We are met on a great battle-field of that war. We have come to dedicate a portion of that field, as a final resting place for those who here gave their lives that that nation might live. It is altogether fitting and proper that we should do this.
>
> But, in a larger sense, we can not dedicate ... we can not consecrate ... we can not hallow this ground. The brave men, living and dead, who struggled here, have consecrated it, far above our poor power to add or detract. The world will little note, nor long remember what we say here, but it can never forget what they did here. It is for us the living, rather, to be dedicated here to the unfinished work which they who fought here have thus far so nobly advanced. It is rather for us to be here dedicated to the great task remaining before us—that from these honored dead we take increased devotion to that cause for which they gave the last full measure of devotion—that we here highly resolve that these dead shall not have died in vain—that this nation, under God, shall have a new birth of freedom—and that government of the people, by the people, for the people, shall not perish from the earth.[1]

The address begins with the martyrs' cause: nation and nationalism. The Civil War was fought to determine whether the United States was indeed one nation for one people or whether it was a voluntary association of the peoples of the several states. Lincoln begins by assuming the Union answer to this question: that Americans are one nation: "Four score and seven years ago our fathers brought forth on this continent a new nation." As with most nations, there is a natural homeland, "this continent," and Lincoln implies that neither nation nor homeland can be divided. This is nationalism, the

---

1. Lincoln, A. The Gettysburg address. Gettysburg, Pennsylvania, November 19, 1863. Available at http://www.abrahamlincolnonline.org/lincoln/speeches/gettysburg.htm.

idea that every nation should have a state—one state for the homeland of one people. Lincoln goes on to specify the political essence of the new nation: liberty and equality.

Next is his assertion that the nation is in danger: "Now we are engaged in a great civil war, testing whether that nation, or any nation, so conceived and so dedicated, can long endure." This threat is reiterated at the close of the address: "that government of the people, by the people, for the people, shall not perish from the Earth." Indeed at the time he gave the address, Lincoln was facing a rising tide of war weariness and the prospect that he would lose the coming election and that peace terms with the Confederacy would be forthcoming.

In the context of this threat to the nation, Lincoln advances the meaning of the sacrifice, the definition of martyrdom. "We have come to dedicate a portion of that field, as a final resting place for those who here gave their lives that that nation might live." Whatever the individual motives that brought these men as soldiers to Gettysburg, here they are joined in the attribution of a common devotion to the nation. They did not give their lives for soldiers' pay, for their status among fellow soldiers from the same town, or even to attain a personal "red badge of courage." Rather, they gave their lives for a secular religion of national unity that could only be achieved by sacrifice and martyrdom. It is their martyrdom that now consecrates and hallows the place of sacrifice—Gettysburg, site of the bloodiest battle of the Civil War.

With both cause and martyrs established, Lincoln moves on to political mobilization. First, he presents a kind of social comparison in which a new scale of sacrifice is established. Union supporters who saw themselves as committed to the martyrs' cause—the nation's cause—must now see themselves as falling short in comparison with the martyrs' example. The martyrs gave "the last full measure of devotion." Martyrdom raises the bar for those aspiring to do the most for the cause, perhaps inducing shame or guilt for individuals who see their own sacrifices as falling short of the standard established by the martyrs.

Second, Lincoln advances a "sunk-costs" motivation: "that we here highly resolve that these dead shall not have died in vain." If the cause for which these young martyrs gave their lives does not succeed, these lives were wasted. If civil war does not produce one nation that triumphs over those who would divide it, then tens of thousands have given their lives for nothing. If you love those who died, you must finish their work.

Third, Lincoln evokes a pricing model that is usually applied to more mundane choices. One guarantee that a Mercedes is a better automobile than an Opel, for instance, is that many are willing to pay more for a Mercedes. All kinds of goods are subject to this kind of evaluation, including rock concert tickets, baseball players' salaries, and Wall Street bonuses. The price that others pay is an index of value that cannot be ignored, particularly when the purchase is something as intangible as beauty or immortality. The martyr prices the cause as worth more than life and becomes both witness and model for this evaluation.

In the film *The Maltese Falcon*, Gutman is surprised to find that detective Sam Spade does not know the story of the black bird they are both seeking: "You mean you don't know what it is?" Sam says he knows what it looks like, but, more important, "I know the value in life you people put on it . . ."

Fourth and finally, Lincoln offers the prospect that sacrifice can bring immortality. The dead are not dead: "brave," "noble," and "honored," they live on in the memory of the nation. Perhaps even stronger would be a promise of immortality in another, better world, the kind of promise offered by major religions. As a secular religion, the nation cannot offer this form of immortality but can perhaps recruit some of the emotional and motivational value of religion by adopting quasi-religious rituals of consecrating and hallowing.

Rituals of remembrance are important because living on in the memory of the nation must be demonstrated in the here and now in order to encourage new sacrifice. A nation—or any cause—that does not reverence its past martyrs is unlikely to produce future martyrs.

The Political Power of Suicide Terrorism

Many have noticed that suicide attacks have become more frequent in the past two decades. The usual explanation is that they are effective: they inflict damage where more conventional attacks could not succeed. Israelis face this threat from Palestinians, U.S. forces face this threat in Iraq and Afghanistan, and until recently Sinhalese in Sri Lanka faced this threat from the Tamil Tigers.

The difficulty of countering suicide attacks has led to seeing suicide terrorists as "smart bombs"—a low-tech answer to the high-tech weapons of modern states. Powerful Western states have cruise missiles and radar-guided bombs, and terrorist groups in their weakness have suicide terrorism. The "smart bombs" metaphor has some truth to it, but the political power of suicide bombers goes far beyond the damage that smart bombs can accomplish. Three aspects of this power are mobilizing by sacrifice, outbidding, and eliciting emotional reactions that support jujitsu politics.

Mobilizing by sacrifice has been described in our analysis of the Gettysburg Address. Martyrs establish a new scale of sacrifice against which others must measure themselves; their sacrifice cannot be allowed to have been for nothing; their sacrifice measures the value of their cause as greater than life itself; and their memory among the living is a promise of immortality for new martyrs. In these ways martyrs encourage and even require increased sacrifices from the living. In these same ways suicide bombers seen as martyrs encourage and even require new sacrifices from those who reverence the bombers' cause. Of course suicide bombers are not just martyrs but martyr-murderers, but recent history suggests that martyrdom in the course of political murder can still have the mobilizing power of self-sacrifice for some audiences.

The phenomenon of *outbidding* that Mia Bloom has made salient is another aspect of the power of martyrdom (chapter 9). A group or organization that produces martyrs makes a claim for public recognition as doing the utmost for the cause its martyrs die for. This claim is particularly important when there are multiple groups competing to represent the same cause. As the Popular Front for the Liberation of Palestine found out, when other groups are deploying martyrs (Hamas, Fatah) and there is mass support for this tactic, political survival can depend on joining the competition of martyrdoms.

Still another aspect of martyrdom is its capacity for *eliciting emotional reactions*. For jihadist terrorists and their sympathizers, martyrdom attacks provide a kind of cognitive liberation: no matter the awesome power of the government of the United States or the government of Israel, a dedicated warrior can still inflict damage that restores the honor of those humiliated by enemy power. For the targets of suicide attacks, there is discouragement—a forboding that these people will never quit, they can outlast us. Perhaps most important are victim reactions that include fear and anger, emotions that can build walls against whole categories of people when any one of them could be a suicide bomber. As described in chapter 11 in relation to jujitsu politics, walls both psychological and physical can be just what terrorists are hoping for.

It is important to notice that the political effects of suicide terror-ism do not depend greatly on success as measured by damage to the enemy. If all suicide attacks are thwarted, then the political power of such attacks might be attenuated. But in principle, individuals who try but fail to give their lives in a martyrdom operation can never-theless have mobilizing power, outbidding power, and jujitsu power. Politically, Richard Reid, the "Shoe Bomber," was not a failure, and the extent to which he imposed new costs on air travel is undeniable. Neither was Umar Farouk Abdulmutallab, the "Underwear Bomber," a failure; his failed explosives nevertheless succeeded in producing in-creased scrutiny and visa problems for travelers from Abdulmutallab's native Nigeria.

To sum up, suicide terrorism has political effects that go beyond the damage inflicted—far beyond the value of "smart bombs." The political power of suicide terrorism means that this tactic is likely to endure unless and until the base of terrorist sympathizers and supporters turns against it.

A Muslim Martyr: Sayyid Qutb

A precocious student in his small village in Upper Egypt, Qutb had memorized the Koran by the age of ten. He went to Cairo for a Western-style education and graduated to become a teacher in 1933, the year his father died. After several years of provincial teaching posts, he obtained a teaching post in Cairo and brought his family—mother, brother, two sisters—to live with him. In 1939 his career in the civil service brought him to a post as supervisor in the Ministry of Education.

While teaching, he was writing both novels and literary and social criticism. Some of his more political essays brought an order for his arrest from King Farouk, but powerful friends arranged a two-year scholarship to study the U.S. educational system. He sailed from Alexandria to New York City in 1948, as Egypt and its Arab allies were losing their war against the new state of Israel.

In person Qutb was anything but charismatic. His health was deli-cate, including lung problems, heart problems, and recurring painful sciatica. He was polite and well spoken, with an odd combination of shyness and pride. Although one of his novels describes a failed rela-tionship with a woman, he never married and complained to his read-ers that he could not find a suitable woman. His vivid descriptions of the sexual allure of American women, however, suggest that he was far from insensible to the attractions that he condemned.

Politically Qutb was a typical Egyptian middle-class nationalist, opposed to the dissolute King Farouk and the British colonial power that supported him and opposed as well to the Communist Party and its atheism. His view of Western countries was ambivalent. His Western education in Cairo was reflected in a love of French literature, his ever-growing record collection of classical music, and his preference for dark three-piece suits even in the heat of Egyptian summers. He saw the British and French as tarred by colonialism but, like many others after World War II, saw the United States as the promise of a different form of modernity, an immigrant nation liberated from the old divisions of race and culture.

There is no telling what Qutb might have made of the United States if he had seen it without the context of the 1948 war that founded the state of Israel. For him, the promise of American exceptionalism was betrayed when the United States joined Britain and France in support of the new Israeli state carved from lands occupied by Arabs. His two years in the United States left him disgusted with what he saw as the spiritual vacuum of American obsessions with money and sex. Himself a man of color, he saw American racism as the truth behind a façade of equality and opportunity. He wrote about these things during and after his visit, making him perhaps a kernel of truth in the stereotype of Muslims who "hate us for our values."

On his return to Egypt, Qutb joined the Muslim Brotherhood, gravitating toward the leadership role left open when the Brotherhood's founder, Hassan al-Banna, was assassinated. In 1952 King Farouk was overthrown by the nationalist Free Officers Movement headed by Gamal Abdel Nasser. The Brotherhood supported the coup, but relations with the Free Officers soon soured as it became clear that Nasser had no intention of implementing Islamic law. Nasser put Qutb in prison for three months in 1954, then allowed him to become editor-in-chief of the Brothers' weekly *Al-Ikhwan al-Muslimin*.

After the attempted assassination of Nasser in 1954, the Egyptian government acted to crush the Muslim Brotherhood, imprisoning Qutb and many other actual or suspected members of the Brotherhood. Years of close confinement and torture were followed by years of greater leniency in which he could write and get his work out of the prison. He produced a multivolume commentary on the Koran and a political manifesto titled *Milestones*. Together these works argued that the only legitimate Islamic text is the Koran and the only legitimate form of government for Muslims is the original community of the Prophet and his companions. True Muslims, he wrote, must struggle against Muslim leaders infected with Western ideas of secular democracy no less than against Western powers trying to control Muslim countries.

Released from prison in 1964 at the urging of the prime minister of Iraq, Qutb refused the safety of a government post in Iraq because he believed that Egypt still needed him. Eight months later he was again arrested and accused of plotting to overthrow the government. The case against him was largely based on quotations from *Milestones*. Qutb defended his statements in court and was sentenced to death with six other members of the Muslim Brotherhood. "Thank God," he is quoted as saying, "I performed jihad for fifteen years until I earned this martyrdom."[2]

Demonstrations against the death sentence in the streets of Cairo soon indicated to Nasser that Qutb might be more dangerous dead than alive. Nasser sent Anwar al-Sadat to make an offer: if Qutb would appeal for clemency, he would be freed and could even become minister of education. Qutb refused. Qutb's sister was brought to his cell to beg him to write the appeal because the Islamic movement needed him. Qutb refused again: "My words will be stronger if they kill me."

On August 29, 1966, Sayyid Qutb was executed by hanging. His body was not released for fear the burial place might become a shrine. Nevertheless the power that Nasser feared and Qutb anticipated was soon evident. After Qutb's execution, his *Milestones* became the inspiration of an Islamic revival that continues today to seek political reform in a radical version of Islam. Qutb's torture and martyrdom were vividly conveyed to Ayman al-Zawahiri by his uncle, Mahfouz, who was Qutb's lawyer. Qutb's younger brother Muhammad left Egypt for Saudi Arabia, where Osama bin Laden attended Muhammad's public lectures at King Abdel-Aziz University.

Looking Further

Cook, D. B. (2002). Suicide attacks or "martyrdom operations" in contemporary jihad literature. *Nova Religio* 6(1): 7–44.

---

2. Wright, L. (2006). *The looming tower: Al-Qaeda and the road to 9/11.* New York: Knopf. Chapter 1, The martyr. Available at http://brock911.wikia.com/wiki/The_Looming_Tower_full_text.

Hafez, M. M. (2006). *Manufacturing human bombs: The making of Palestinian suicide bombers*. Washington, DC: United States Institute of Peace Press.

Hafez, M. M. (2007). *Suicide bombers in Iraq: The strategy and ideology of martyrdom*. Washington, DC: United States Institute of Peace Press.

Hassan, N. (2001). An arsenal of believers. *New Yorker*, November 19, 36–41.

McCauley, C. (2002). Understanding the 9/11 perpetrators: Crazy, lost in hate, or martyred? In N. Matuszak (Ed.), *History behind the headlines: The origins of ethnic conflicts worldwide*, Vol. 5. New York: Gale Publishing Group, pp. 274–286. Available at http://www.ideologiesofwar.com/docs/cm_understanding.htm.

McCauley, C. (2005). The politics of terrorism. Review of Robert Pape, *Dying to win*, and of Mia Bloom, *Dying to kill. Middle East Journal* 59(4): 663–666.

McCauley, C. (2007). Review of Mohammed Hafez, *Manufacturing human bombs: The making of Palestinian suicide bombers*, of Mohammed Hafez, *Suicide bombers in Iraq: The strategy and ideology of martyrdom*, and of David Cook & Olivia Allison, *Understanding and addressing suicide attacks: The faith and politics of martyrdom operations. Middle East Journal* 62(1): 179–182.

Mneimneh, H., and Makiya, K. (2002). Manual for a "raid." *New York Review of Books*, January 17.

Wright, L. (2006). *The looming tower: al-Qaeda and the road to 9/11*. New York: Knopf. Chapter 1, The martyr.

SECTION 4

Wrapping Up

In our introductory chapter, we took issue with some popular ideas about where terrorism comes from: that terrorists are crazy, evil, or somehow very different from people like ourselves. Chapter by chapter we have identified mechanisms of radicalization that are based in normal psychology—mechanisms that can and do move people like ourselves and may even have moved us personally. In this final section we consider the mechanisms together, in their similarities and differences, and their potential for better ways of coping with political violence.

First, how do different mechanisms combine in one person? To answer this question, chapter 14 examines the trajectory of radicalization for one prominent terrorist, Osama bin Laden.

Second, can individual-level mechanisms of radicalization account for lone-wolf terrorists like Major Nidal Hasan? Lone actors have become a salient terrorist threat, and chapter 15 offers two possible profiles of lone-wolf terrorists.

Third, what is the relation of radical beliefs and radical action? Chapter 16 presents a two-pyramids model of radicalization that recognizes that this relation is weak.

Fourth, looking back over all sixteen chapters, what themes emerge? In chapter 17 we see how mechanisms of radicalization can also support peaceful movements. We see the importance of emotion in these mechanisms, especially the emotion of anger. Most generally, we see the mechanisms as part of the action and reaction of intergroup conflict, in which both terrorists and their targets are radicalized.

SECTION 4

Wrapping Up

CHAPTER FOURTEEN

Osama bin Laden

IN HIDING AFTER the attacks of September 11, 2001, Osama bin Laden remained a giant of inspiration to jihadis and a djinn of terrorist innovation to his enemies. But the public persona is not a reliable introduction to the real person. Even accounts of his height differed widely, with some witnesses reporting Osama to be six feet eight inches tall and others claiming he was only about six feet. Little known outside of Saudi Arabia until his attacks on U.S. embassies in 1998, Osama grabbed the attention of the Muslim world as a man so threatening to the United States as to bring U.S. cruise missiles against him in two Muslim countries, Sudan and Afghanistan. In Europe and North America, however, Osama did not become larger than life until after the attacks of 9/11. In both Muslim and Western countries, the sudden transformation in the public figure was only vaguely and belatedly related to the smaller, slower changes that took place in the real person.

Many have sought to find a great man hidden in his boyhood. Simpler versions of this quest sometimes sound like the old homunculus theory of biological transmission, in which a complete miniature individual was thought to be contained in the ovum that began a new life. More sophisticated versions seek childhood traits of character or interest that can explain adult success. There are some memorable examples of adult success predicted by youthful abilities: six-year-old John Stuart Mill walking in the park with his father, practicing his Greek, is the picture of young genius. So is Nobel physicist Richard Feynman playing his way through college math texts during high school.

Reinforcing familiar examples of precocious individuals is the testimony of common experience. Whatever doting relatives may say, a newborn looks much more like other newborns than like the infant's parents. As the child grows older, similarities of appearance, character, and ability emerge until, as an adult, the individual is easily recognizable as a family member. Our experience of the trajectory from birth to adulthood supports a view of human development in which childhood potential unfolds into adult performance. The poet Wordsworth captured the unfolding model in a notable oxymoron—"The Child is father of the Man"—and the same model is represented in the myths, legends, and stories of many lands. In Western cultures the unfolding model is popularized in the story of the ugly duckling: only slightly different from other ducklings at hatching but triumphantly different as an adult swan.

Of course human development is more than the unfolding of native potential or inborn essence (see chapter 12); children can be helped or hurt by the opportunities, challenges, and traumas they experience. Still, the unfolding model has considerable support in everyday experience. The danger is that this model can be too easily extended to adults and can obscure the importance of situations and events in the continuing development that occurs between the ages of eighteen and eighty.

The life of Osama bin Laden offers a case study of the power of situations and events. Osama is a disappointment for those who would find the man in the boy: neither his unusual height nor his unusual piety can explain Osama's political stature. A shy youth became a world-famous leader of terrorism and insurrection. Osama's history is unique but shows, at crucial transition points, the power of mechanisms of radicalization described in previous chapters. Some of the mechanisms are at the individual level, others at the level of group dynamics. Taken together, these mechanisms offer a story of normal psychology in progressively more extreme circumstances.

Except where indicated, our history relies on Michael Scheuer's *Imperial Hubris: Why the West Is Losing the War on Terror* (2004) and *Through our Enemies' Eyes: Osama Bin Laden, Radical Islam, and the Future of America* (2006).

Early Years

Osama's father, Muhammad bin Laden, was born poor in Yemen, moved to Saudi Arabia for construction work, and became the Saudi royal family's favorite building contractor. Muhammad began by building roads and expanded his company to include remodeling everything from the king's 747 to the Grand Mosque of Mecca. He was illiterate but had a head for figures and a talent for placing dynamite. He lived modestly and talked with his workers as if he were one of them. A good Muslim—he would use his private aircraft to pray in Mecca, Medina, and Jerusalem in the same day—Muhammad followed the Koran in having only four wives at a time. But he married and divorced and remarried to produce a total of twenty wives and over fifty children. Osama was born in 1957 or 1958, the only son of Muhammad's tenth wife.

For most of his early years, Osama and his mother lived as part of his father's manifold and child-filled household in Jeddah, then a sleepy town on the Red Sea. The child did not see much of his father, who traveled often on business and became a kind of visiting dignitary at home. When Osama was four or five, his father divorced his mother and awarded her in marriage to one of his business associates. Mother and son moved a few blocks to another house in Jeddah, where Osama was joined over the years by three half-brothers and a half-sister born to his mother and stepfather.

Osama was about ten years old when Muhammad bin Laden, by then one of the richest men in Saudi Arabia, died in a plane crash in 1967.

Osama attended al-Thagr school in Jeddah, founded to educate Saudi princes and other elite youths but granting admission also to poor and middle-class boys who scored high on entrance exams. At school Osama was an average student, notable only for his height and his shyness. In high school he is described as tall and gangly, still smooth-faced when classmates began sporting facial hair. It seems likely that his height and slower development contributed to his shyness.

His average performance at school should not be overinterpreted as indicating average intelligence; he was an average performer in the best preparatory school in Saudi Arabia. It was a secular school based on the English model, priding itself on its science curriculum and requiring all students to wear Western-style slacks and shirts.

At about the age of fourteen, Osama joined an Islamic study group that met after hours at al-Thagr. The group appears to have been inspired by the ideas of the Muslim Brotherhood, who believed that only government according to the Koran—Sharia government—could save Arab countries from misrule and Western domination. The Brotherhood's message was reinforced when Israel humiliated Egypt, Syria, and Jordan in the 1967 war and Gamel Abdel Nasser's pan-Arab socialism was discredited. For many Arabs, political Islam was the only remaining alternative; this turn defined the *Sahwa*, the Islamic Awakening.

Friends and family describe a religious and political awakening in Osama after he joined the study group. He stopped watching television except for news—no movies, no music, no card playing, no photographs, no shorts or short sleeves, no Western dress outside of school, no sexual jokes, no looking at women's faces except sisters and mother; also, no liquor, no smoking, no gambling. All these are *harem*—forbidden—for conservative Muslims. He began fasting two days a week, as the Prophet did. He tried to move his mother and stepfamily away from television and popular music and toward more conservative Islamic practice.

At the same time his concern for the political plight of Arabs grew. According to his mother, "He was frustrated about the situation in Palestine in particular, and the Arab and Muslim world in general. He wanted Muslims to unite and fight to liberate Palestine."[1] In general he followed the Muslim Brotherhood in judging that Arab political problems could only be solved if the new generation were better and stronger Muslims.

At this time Osama opposed what he saw as an American culture of indulgence and pornography, soft drinks and soft living. But he was not politically opposed to the United States. The extended bin Laden family and its construction business were dependent on the Saudi royal family, who were allied with the United States. Osama probably knew that his father's pilots were often American and that Aramco (Arabian American Oil Company) had given his father a year's leave to start his own company so that Muhammad could come back to Aramco if the new company did not succeed. Politically Osama was focused not on the United States but on the need for Islamic reformation of Arab politics.

Osama was about seventeen, still attending al-Thagr, when he married a cousin from his mother's village in Syria. Two years later in 1976, he began his studies at King Abdul Aziz University in Jeddah. He was supposed to be studying economics and management, but he seems to have spent more time in religious activities, including charitable work, than at his books.

After a few years of university studies, Osama sought a job working in his father's construction company. There seems to have been a family

---

1. Scheuer, M. (2011). *Osama bin Laden*. New York: Oxford University Press, p. 40.

understanding that only sons who worked for the company would stand to inherit it. He was given charge of a project. Emulating his father, he worked night and day and spent a lot of time driving a bulldozer. By this time, few Saudis, let alone rich Saudis, were getting dirty in construction; guest workers from other countries had replaced them.

Personality

There are only a few reports of what Osama was like outside of politics and religion, and these do not indicate anything exceptional. From early years he loved horses and riding fast. He liked watching TV, especially Westerns, the horse drama *Fury*, and Bruce Lee karate films. He is reported to have gone mountain climbing in Turkey and on safari in Africa. He had a white Chrysler that he drove at high speeds before wrecking it in a culvert. He liked to drive a Jeep at speed over the top of a hill with no idea what was beyond. He loved playing soccer; as forward he could use his height to head the ball into the goal. Years later, when Osama was in Pakistan and Afghanistan, he was still finding opportunities to play soccer and volleyball.

These activities suggest a risk taker and a sensation seeker in the physical world. But in the social world Osama was quiet, courteous, and unassertive. In class his work was neat, precise, and conscientious; he would answer direct questions but did not volunteer answers or otherwise compete with his classmates to look clever. Many have reported his unusual politeness and good manners. He was seldom angry, and the few reports of his anger seem to be associated with violation of Islamic norms, as when others around him would listen to a woman singing romantic songs or look at a pornographic magazine. Over many years, observers have agreed that he was gentle and even indulgent with his family. No one ever saw him shout at his children or strike them, and his wives were said to love him for his gentle manners.

A neighborhood friend, Khaled Batarfi, describes a confrontation between Osama and an opposing soccer player, who was trying to push Osama around. Osama was still remonstrating peacefully when Khaled moved in to push the other boy away. Khaled says that in those days he was the tough guy and Osama the peaceful one. Nevertheless Khaled describes Osama as a natural leader:

> ... he leads by example and by hints more than direct orders. He just sets an example and expects you to follow, and somehow you follow

even if you are not 100 percent convinced. I remember I was driving my car going to play soccer and I saw him standing near his door, so I had to stop because he saw me. So the problem was I was wearing shorts [which is not strictly Islamic]. So I was trying to avoid him seeing me, and then when I had to stop, I had to get out and kiss him. So he saw me and was very embarrassed, talking small talk while I was thinking, what I'm going to say if he said, "So why are you wearing shorts?" Finally at the end he just looked at my legs and said, "Good-bye." And from that day on I didn't wear shorts. So he has this charisma.[2]

In this story is the beginning of a significant ambiguity in descriptions of Osama's leadership potential. Khaled recognizes Osama as a natural leader. But Osama is not the captain of the neighborhood soccer club; Khaled, several years younger than Osama, is captain. Osama is quiet, his voice high and soft, he listens more than he speaks and tends to look at the ground when speaking. His handshake is soft. He seldom smiles or laughs. His status with his peers depends on his family name and, more importantly, on his religious devotion and self-denial. He lives simply, wearing plain clothing and eating plain food. He has the temptations of being rich but does not give in to them.

Beginning with the work of John French and Bertram Raven (1959), psychologists have recognized different sources of power: reward power, punishment power, expert power, legitimate power (from position in a hierarchy), and referent power (from personal liking). In his teen years, Osama had some reward power from family money, no punishment power, no legitimate power, and no expert power except perhaps with regard to religious knowledge. He did, however, have referent power to the extent that peers liked and respected him. More specifically, he had what might be called moral power: he was superior to his peers in denying himself more creature comforts and in his devotion to prayer and fasting. He was closer to the Muslim ideal than most of his friends, and they guarded their mouths around him as if he were an imam.

Supporting Jihad from Pakistan

Just as he began to gain recognition in the family construction company, bin Laden was distracted from business. In December 1979 the

---

2. Bergen, P. L. (2006). *The Osama bin Laden I know: An oral history of al Quaeda's leader*. New York: Free Press, p. 14.

Soviets sent troops into Afghanistan to support the Communist government against an insurrection of traditional Islamic warriors, who were resisting imposition of economic and social modernization modeled after the Soviet Union. For bin Laden this was godless communism invading a Muslim country. Dr. Abdullah Azzam, a Palestinian cleric renowned for the power of his speeches and his writing, began encouraging jihad against the Soviets. Bin Laden was deeply impressed with Azzam and took up his challenge.

Beginning in early 1980 bin Laden made multiple trips to Afghanistan. He made contact with Afghan leaders fighting the Russians, ascertained their needs, brought money from Saudi and other Arab donors, and joined Azzam in organizing and supporting movement of Arab volunteers to join the jihad.

In 1982 bin Laden expanded his activities. Seeing the effects Russian bombing had on *mujahideen* positions, he concluded that the resources of his family's construction business should be brought to bear. With his brothers' support, he imported heavy construction equipment to dig trenches and to bore tunnels into mountain rock to provide increased protection against Russian attacks. He built mountain roads to support these positions.

Around 1984 bin Laden further expanded his activities. He began to build training camps that served both Afghan and Arab volunteers for jihad. In Peshawar, Pakistan, bin Laden joined Azzam in founding the Services Bureau to support the young Arabs from many countries who came to wage jihad against the Russians in Afghanistan. The Saudi government and most other Muslim governments at the time also supported the call for jihad against the Russians. So did the United States.

Most U.S. support to Afghan jihadists went through Pakistan; the Saudis, however, preferred to channel support through fellow Arabs such as Azzam and bin Laden. The Services Bureau became a kind of nongovernmental organization (NGO) that provided housing, stipends, transportation, and even vacations to Arab volunteers for jihad. By this time bin Laden was living most of the year in Pakistan, with a growing entourage of wives and children with him in Peshawar. For a time Azzam and bin Laden were like father and son, with the charismatic older man eclipsing the younger one. But after a few years in Peshawar, they began to have different goals.

Azzam's goal was to bring Arabs from around the world to support the Afghans' battle against the Russians. Azzam believed that it had to be the Afghans' battle because a few thousand foreign volunteers could not change the military outcome. But dispersed with Afghan fighters, the Arab volunteers could bring a leavening of political and religious sophistication to the Afghans and could by their letters, videos, and public-relations tours help rally additional support for jihad from Arabs around the world. But bin Laden began to feel that supporting the jihad of others was not enough.

Fighting Russians

Azzam preached persuasively about the glories of martyrdom, and bin Laden himself has suggested that he began to feel guilty sending others to martyrdom while remaining in safety himself. This sentiment was reinforced by his interactions with the veterans of two Egyptian terrorist groups who had taken refuge in Pakistan: Egyptian Islamic Jihad (EIJ) and Gamaat Islamiyah or Islamic Group (IG). The leader of EIJ was Dr. Ayman al-Zawahiri, who became bin Laden's personal physician during the years in Pakistan. Personal connection with hardened terrorists thus encouraged his doing more, risking more.

In the summer of 1986 bin Laden led construction work in Khowst, in eastern Afghanistan, and may have been wounded while driving a bulldozer under fire. The battles around Khowst were the first in which an all-Arab unit entered combat against the Russians, and bin Laden saw the high casualty rates resulting from lack of military training. Typically, Arab recruits wanted only minimal training in their rush to the battlefield.

Bin Laden's answer to the problem was to establish separate training camps for non-Afghan fighters, including not just Arabs but Muslim volunteers from lands as disparate as Sudan, Philippines, Kashmir, and Chechnya. In October 1986 he established a base camp called *Masadah*, the Lion's Lair, near Jalalabad in Afghanistan. He had no military experience, but he did have the services of two of Zawahiri's lieutenants— Abu Ubaydah and Abu Hafs—who had been police officers in Egypt. He led his little group to establish a camp near a Russian outpost, to maximize the chances of combat and martyrdom. Testifying to their close relationship, Azzam came to visit the camp.

bin Laden and his men withstood Russian shells and napalm, survived several blundering attempts to mount attacks against the Russians, and finally beat off an attack by Russian troops in May 1987. Dramatic reports of the fighting in the Arab press made bin Laden a heroic figure, with a reputation for courage and leadership to match his piety. After this, friends report that bin Laden became more confident and more assertive; when back in Saudi Arabia, he was more likely to speak up in the mosque. Bin Laden was not the only one feeling new strength and confidence. When Russian forces began withdrawing from Afghanistan in 1988, the whole world took note.

The Russian defeat in Afghanistan had an enormous impact on the Muslim world. The faith and courage of jihadis had routed a superpower in just ten years. Nevermind that the West had supported the liberation, nevermind that Afghans had never lost the confidence of their successes against Alexander the Great and Queen Victoria, nevermind that the combat role of international Muslim volunteers was minor—for non-Afghan *mujahideen*, especially for the Arab Afghans, hundreds of years of Muslim losses to Western power had been reversed. The Russian departure from Afghanistan in 1989, following on the success of the 1979 Islamic Revolution in Iran, produced a cognitive liberation in which anything and everything now seemed possible for Muslims.

al Qaeda and Renewed Combat in Afghanistan

The first result of this new confidence was a new organization for foreign jihadis. In 1988 bin Laden and Azzam agreed to create a force that could take the momentum of jihad from Afghanistan to fighting infidels in other Muslim countries, including the Communist governments of South Yemen, Chechnya, and central Asia. In particular Azzam wanted the Arabs he had sent out to various Afghan factions to come together and avoid fighting one another in the civil war that was shaping up as the Russians withdrew. The base of this new force—al Qaeda—would be the best of foreign jihadis in Afghanistan. Recruiting could be selective because many more Arabs were coming to Afghanistan after the Russians began to retreat.

As Saudi and U.S. funds to fight the Soviets were discontinued, bin Laden's family money loomed larger. He was elected emir of al Qaeda. When Azzam was killed by a roadside bomb—by perpetrators still uncertain today—bin Laden's leadership of al Qaeda was reinforced.

Another result of the new confidence was disastrous. The various Afghan jihadi factions made a frontal assault on the Communist government forces in Jalalabad, on the Afghan side of the Khyber Pass. Bin Laden brought his Arabs to the assault and, like the rest of the jihadis, suffered heavy losses. The Communist government held on for several years, and, when it finally collapsed, the various jihadi leaders and their forces indeed fell into civil war over who would control Afghanistan. In dismay at jihadis fighting jihadis, bin Laden returned to Saudi Arabia and rejoined his father's company.

A War Hero Returns

At home, bin Laden was a celebrity, and he tried to put his new status to work. He made fiery speeches demanding that Saudis boycott U.S. products in response to U.S. support for bringing a million Russian Jews to Israel. The Saudi government, closely allied with the United States, was not amused. He volunteered his Arab Afghans to liberate South Yemen—including his father's home village—from its Communist government. The Saudi government was not interested. He predicted that Saddam Hussein and his apostate Baathist party would invade Kuwait and Saudi Arabia, and, when Iraq indeed invaded Kuwait in 1990, bin Laden volunteered his al Qaeda forces to evict them. The Saudi government instead invited U.S. assistance; beginning August 7, 1990, half a million U.S. troops moved into Saudi Arabia.

To bin Laden, U.S. forces in Saudi Arabia were infidel invaders just as the Russians had been infidel invaders of Afghanistan. He insisted that King Fahd was wrong to invite the Americans and that the official Saudi religious scholars who legitimated the American presence were self-serving hypocrites. Rather than attacking the king and the religious establishment directly, however, he spoke and wrote against the presence of U.S. troops in the sacred land of Mecca and Medina.

This seems to be the first step in bin Laden's turn from the near enemy of corrupt Muslim leaders to the far enemy of Western allies of these leaders. His attacks on Americans were rhetorical rather than violent, and his immediate goal was to undermine support for the Saudi regime. Nevertheless, bin Laden here initiated a political attack on Americans, whereas before he had attacked only American culture. Getting U.S. troops out of the Holy Land of Mecca and Medina was a political issue in a way that boycotting Coca-Cola was not. The Saudis understood that they were the target of bin Laden's anti-American rhetoric, first restricting him to Jeddah and then, after U.S. troops arrived, placing him under house arrest.

Not only was this a turn toward the far enemy, it was an example of "jujitsu politics." The goal of attacking the U.S. presence in Saudi Arabia was not, or not only, to move U.S. troops out of the country. The goal was to elicit a response from King Fahd and his religious scholars that would undermine their own political support. Bin Laden expected that the authorities would rise to defend their invitation of U.S. troops into Saudi Arabia and that, in arguing for the continued presence of U.S. troops, they would do for bin Laden what he could not do by direct attacks on them: king and scholars would lose legitimacy, and bin Laden would gain.

Peacemaking in Afghanistan and Exile in Sudan

In response to bin Laden's attacks on Americans, the Saudis had lifted his passport. In 1991 bin Laden's brothers negotiated a one-trip extension of his passport, and he arrived in Afghanistan just as the Communist government was collapsing. He busied himself immediately in trying to mediate a peace among the various jihadist factions and their leaders. His efforts for reconciliation were not successful, but he did develop a reputation among Afghan leaders as a fair-minded negotiator concerned that the fruits of victory over the Russians not be lost.

It is important to notice that bin Laden had not at this time embraced open warfare on civilians. Paulo Jose de Almeida Santos, a Portuguese convert to Islam and al Qaeda, reports that bin Laden, back in Peshawar, was asked about killing civilians. Bin Laden's opinion was that adult Israelis, male or female, could be killed because they served in the Israeli Defense Force but that only American government forces could be attacked because most Americans are politically apathetic and do not vote.

Discouraged by his peacemaking failures and in fear of assassination by Saudi intelligence, bin Laden gathered one to two hundred al Qaeda men and their families and in 1992 moved them from Afghanistan to Sudan, where the National Islamic Front had taken power in 1989 and was welcoming Muslims without a visa. Al-Zawahiri and many of his fellow Egyptians from EIJ also moved to Sudan, and bin Laden later paid for hundreds of Arab Afghans to move from Pakistan to Khartoum, including members of IG who had joined in the fight against the Russians in Afghanistan.

In Sudan bin Laden built roads for the government and took payment in land. He became one of the largest landowners in the country, employing al Qaeda members in his many enterprises with "refresher" military training on the side. Still focused on Western influence in Arab countries, he was not involved in the Sudanese jihad against Christian and animist tribespeople in Southern Sudan. Competing with his interest in his burgeoning new businesses was his anger at the continued presence of U.S. troops in Saudi Arabia, months after Iraq had been expelled from Kuwait.

Politically bin Laden was relatively quiet in Sudan. In 1992, he sent $40,000 to Algeria with a message that rebel leaders should not compromise with the government that stole the election from the Islamic Front. Later he distanced himself from the violence that cost 100,000 lives in Algeria. In 1993 Ramzi Yousef used bomb-making skills learned in Afghanistan to attack the World Trade Center in New York City, but there is no evidence that bin Laden had anything to do with this attack. Also in 1993 U.S. military forces withdrew from Somalia after the loss of Black Hawk helicopters. Bin Laden seems to have sent dozens or even hundreds of al Qaeda people to Somalia when hostilities broke out, but their impact is not clear. They may have been military trainers, teaching Somalis to shoot at the vulnerable tail-rotor of U.S. helicopters; or they may have participated in actual combat against the Americans. Either way, bin Laden later took credit for the U.S. defeat in Somalia and often referred to it as an indication of American cowardice and unwillingness to take casualties.

According to a number of reports, bin Laden was homesick for Saudi Arabia, and several Saudi emissaries, including his mother, came to Sudan to propose a deal: if he would say that King Fahd was a good Muslim and give up radical talk and jihad, bin Laden could return to Saudi Arabia. He refused, and in April 1994 the Saudi government announced that it was revoking his citizenship, lifting his passport, and freezing his Saudi assets. Under pressure from the government, his family officially cut him off from his share of income from the construction company. Whether some of his brothers continued to send him money is debated.

After losing his Saudi citizenship and his income from the family business, bin Laden had less to lose. In late 1994 and in 1995 he published attacks on Bin Baz, leader of the official clergy in Saudi Arabia, and on King Fahd. Bin Baz he described as a hypocrite and apostate for supporting the invitation of Americans into Saudi Arabia and for authorizing reconciliation with Israel. He indicted King Fahd for corruption, mismanagement, and apostasy; he called on King Fahd to resign. This was the kind of direct assault on the legitimacy of Saudi authorities that he had previously avoided when speaking against U.S. forces in Saudi Arabia.

If bin Laden felt for a time the attractions of peace and commerce in Sudan, al-Zawahiri did not. With his sometime Egyptian rivals of IG, Zawahiri joined in an attempt to assassinate Egypt's president, Hosni Mubarak, in June 1995. There is no evidence that bin Laden participated in this plan. The attempt failed, and Zawahiri and the Sudanese government were implicated. In November 1995, Zawahiri's EIJ group bombed the Egyptian embassy in Islamabad, Pakistan. Bin Laden had not approved the operation, nor had Sudan. In 1996 Zawahiri executed two boys blackmailed by Egyptian intelligence into spying against EIJ. With this third strike, they were out: Zawahiri and his EIJ people were expelled from Sudan.

Several months later pressure from Saudi Arabia, Egypt, and the United States led Sudan to expel bin Laden also. His construction equipment was confiscated, and he had to sell his farms and other businesses in a hurry. Estimates of his investment in Sudan run into tens of millions of dollars, but he left with only tens of thousands. He and many of his al Qaeda people found their way back to Afghanistan, where the Taliban welcomed them in recognition of their contributions against the Soviets. This was bin Laden's nadir: twice exiled and twice impoverished.

Exile in Afghanistan

From Afghanistan bin Laden fought back with the strength remaining to him: words. In August 1996 he issued a "Declaration of War against the Americans Occupying the Land of the Two Holy Places." In it he addresses himself to Muslims around the world and asks help for jihad against Americans in the Arabian Peninsula, for overthrow of the apostate government of Saudi Arabia, and (again) for a boycott of American products in the Muslim world. Notably, he does not call for attacks on American civilians. His call for jihad is successful in bringing new volunteers to al Qaeda—from Pakistan, Indonesia, North Africa, and even Europe and North America. As with many other kinds of Internet commerce, bin Laden was able to turn fame into money and people power.

In 1998 bin Laden explicitly claimed the right to attack American civilians. He joined with representatives of EIJ (Egyptians represented by Zawahiri), IG (Egyptians), and the Jihad Movement (Bangladesh) to announce a "World Islamic Front" that should try to kill Americans anywhere in the world they could be reached. The results of this new resolve were not long in coming.

Al Qaeda suicide bombers set off trucks full of explosives against U.S. embassies in Kenya and Tanzania on August 7, 1998. In Dar es Salaam the toll was eleven killed and eighty-five wounded; none of the casualties was American. In Nairobi 213 were killed and thousands injured, including twelve Americans dead. The timing of the embassy attacks was significant; they occurred on the anniversary of the arrival of U.S. troops in Saudi Arabia on August 7, 1990.

Wright suggests that the timing was significant also in relation to ongoing negotiations between the United States and the Taliban. The Americans were offering a deal: U.S. recognition of the Taliban government and big petrodollars in exchange for Taliban support of an oil and gas pipeline across Afghanistan from the Caspian Sea to Pakistan's ports on the Arabian Sea. For bin Laden, normalization of relations between the United States and the Taliban would threaten al Qaeda's refuge in Afghanistan. As late as August 2001, the United States was still offering the Taliban a choice between a carpet of gold and carpet-bombing.

Cullison and Higgins (also Wright, p. 268) report another and more personal threat. Saudi Arabia's chief of intelligence, Prince Turki al Faisal, visited Afghanistan in 1990 to ask the Taliban leader, Mullah Omar, to hand over bin Laden for trial in Saudi Arabia for treason. Irritated with bin Laden's grandstanding press conferences, Mullah Omar agreed in principle but asked for a religious commission to formulate a justification for expulsion.

These threats to bin Laden and al Qaeda were eliminated on August 20, 1998, when seventy-five U.S. missiles descended on al Qaeda camps in Afghanistan. President Clinton ordered the missiles in retaliation for the attack on U.S. embassies, but the collateral damage was Afghan outrage over a foreign attack on Afghan soil. The pipeline deal and the deal to hand bin Laden over to the Saudis were both blown off the table. Cullison and Higgins summarize the result of President Clinton's Operation Infinite Reach: "The retaliation had fateful consequences. It turned Mr. Bin Laden into a cult figure among Islamic radicals, made Afghanistan a rallying point for defiance of America, and shut off Taliban discussion of expelling the militants. It also helped convince Mr. Bin Laden that goading America to anger could help his cause, not hurt it."[3]

With a similar view of bin Laden's profit in goading America, Wright (p. 272) suggests that the embassy attacks were only the first attempt to draw the United States into Afghanistan, the "graveyard of empires." The second attempt was the attack on the *USS Cole* on October 12, 2000. Two suicide bombers maneuvered a small boat against the side of the *Cole*, tied up at an Aden dock in Yemen, and detonated a bomb that killed seventeen sailors and injured thirty-nine more. Wright reports that, in Afghanistan, bin Laden prepared for another U.S. attack in retaliation for the *Cole* attack and was disappointed when none was forthcoming.

Finally, the attacks of September 11, 2001, did bring U.S. forces into Afghanistan. In anticipation, bin Laden arranged a suicide bombing to kill the leader of the only remaining Afghan resistance to the Taliban. Sheik Ahmed Shah Massoud, leader of the Northern Alliance, was assassinated just two days before the 9/11 attacks. For al Qaeda, the assassination served two useful purposes. First it eliminated a charismatic leader who might lead Afghans against the Taliban if, as expected, U.S. forces responded to 9/11 by sending troops to Afghanistan. Second it was a gift to the Taliban whose hospitality would certainly be tested by U.S. reaction to 9/11.

In retrospect, it is surprising that bin Laden did not publically claim the 9/11 attacks until October 2004, well after the United States had moved into Iraq in 2003. Perhaps he was concerned about possible Muslim condemnation of killing U.S. civilians as indeed polls showed after 9/11 that most Muslims around the world thought the attack on civilians in the World Trade Center was immoral according to the Koran. But he may also have been concerned about the reaction of his Taliban hosts in Afghanistan, a concern suggested by his initial disavowals of the embassy attacks in Nairobi and Dar es Salaam.

For Muslims, the last step and the most extreme extension of al Qaeda targeting was the May 2003 attack in Riyadh. Three vehicle bombs inside three housing compounds for Westerners killed fourteen, including nine Americans, and wounded hundreds. The bombing campaign that followed killed mostly Saudis and foreign workers and appears to have undermined support for al Qaeda in

---

3. Cullison, A., & Higgins, A. (2002). A once-stormy terror alliance was solidified by cruise missiles. *Wall Street Journal*, August 2. Available at http://www.wsj.com/articles/SB1028236160532452080.

Saudi Arabia as well as eliciting a crackdown on militants by Saudi security forces.

Mechanisms of Radicalization

Looking back at the long sequence of change and development in Osama bin Laden's life, there are two notable characteristics of his trajectory. First, bin Laden changed in response to the events around him; these events and his reactions to them must figure in any attempt to understand his personal and political development. Second, his development was slow and gradual, taking place over decades. With these characteristics in mind, we are in a position to examine the forces that moved a shy and pious youth to terrorist icon.

Personal Grievance

It is commonplace to trace political radicalization back to a personal grievance, but bin Laden's political transformation did not begin with personal grievance; he did not experience any kind of victimization or harm to himself or his loved ones.

Group Grievance

Instead bin Laden's politics began with a group grievance: his feelings for the sufferings of Palestinian Muslims he considered victimized by Israel. These feelings echoed his father's; his identification with Palestinians was linked with personal grief when his father died in the same year that Egypt and Syria had been humiliated by the Israelis in the 1967 war. At al-Thagr, his initial political concerns were with reforming Arab politics. His transition from construction work to supporting jihad in Pakistan was again based in a group grievance: Russian troops in Afghanistan. This grievance was not his alone; most of the Arab world experienced some degree of outrage, and in Saudi Arabia this outrage was reinforced by the royal family and religious authorities who encouraged jihad against the Russians.

Love

For Osama bin Laden group grievance was turned to action by his admiration for Dr. Abdullah Azzam, a charismatic recruiter for jihad against the Russians. Bin Laden may have met Azzam as a teacher at al-Thagr or as a guest in his father's house. In Pakistan, his admiration for Azzam became a close personal connection in which bin Laden seems to have felt something like a son's love for the older man. Love for one already more radicalized is an important mechanism of radicalization.

Risk and Status

Another individual-level motive for radicalization is thrill and adventure seeking. The kind of individual who likes riding fast horses, driving fast cars, and topping blind crests at high speed is likely to feel the attraction of physical challenge and risk taking. As already noted, bin Laden from an early age showed a taste for physical risk taking even if his social risk taking was slower to develop. Jihad against the Russians called out to bin Laden and to many young Muslims: What kind of man could stand back from the greatest challenge of his generation?

Slippery Slope

Arching over all the previous mechanisms is the power of the slippery slope—a slow progression of increased radicalization in which each step becomes a preparation and justification for the next step. In bin Laden's case, the slippery slope was tilted toward radicalization.

In Afghanistan he moved from organizing money for jihad to organizing equipment for jihad to combat engineering on jihadi battlefields to training and leading a jihadi force in combat. Returned to Saudi Arabia he slowly escalated from fiery speeches for jihad against Communists in Yemen to urging boycott against U.S. products to opposing U.S. troops in Saudi Arabia in an indirect attack on Saudi authorities. In exile in Sudan he went further in challenging Saudi government policies; in a second exile in Afghanistan, after losing Saudi citizenship and properties, he called first for overthrow of the "apostate" government of Saudi Arabia and jihad against Americans in the Arabian Peninsula, then for attacks on U.S. people and property wherever they could be found. In targeting Americans he justified at first U.S. government targets and hit embassies and a warship; then he justified attacks on civilians and organized the attacks of 9/11. The same slow escalation of radicalization is evident in opposing first the Russians, then Communist Afghans, then the Saudi king and clerics, and lastly the "far enemy" of Americans and American allies.

Unfreezing

In addition to personal grievance there is another individual-level mechanism that does not appear in bin Laden's trajectory of radicalization. He was nowhere impelled to radicalization by fear as can happen in places like Iraq and Colombia, where an individual can be safer joining a group with guns than walking the street alone. Nor was he at any point unfrozen from his values by deep personal loss, as can happen when an individual loses a spouse or friend or job and is suddenly left searching for new sources of connection and meaning. Bin Laden was never left searching in this way; he was never without comrades, wives, and children close at hand.

Group Polarization

In Pakistan, bin Laden's transition from NGO work to jihad in Afghanistan was facilitated by the dynamics of two different groups. One was the Services Bureau that supported young Arabs for war against the Russians. Those recruiting and supporting martyrs for Islam could not escape martyrs' values, which gave highest status to those who risked their lives in battle. Bin Laden and some of his comrades from the Services Bureau participated in group polarization as they moved from encouraging and supporting the risk taking of others to themselves becoming risk takers in combat.

Bin Laden also became involved with two groups of Egyptian terrorists—EIJ led by Zawahiri and IG—who had taken refuge in Pakistan. The Egyptians were already steeped in violence, including not only the terrorist violence they perpetrated in Egypt but the violence of imprisonment and torture they had experienced in Egyptian prisons. Values of risk, action, and revenge were paramount among these hardened men, and bin Laden's interaction with Egyptians in Pakistan was another experience of group dynamics pressing him toward jihad himself.

Group Isolation

Both the Services Bureau Arabs and the Egyptian refugee terrorists were foreigners in Pakistan. The landscape, the climate, the food—all were foreign to them. The Arabs lived in Peshawar as a small minority, cut off from their homelands by thousands of miles and isolated further from the local population by a language barrier. They brought a different culture to Peshawar, including levels of formal education higher than those possessed by most residents of a frontier town. The Arabs were living in a new world, different not only from the indigenous population of Peshawar but also from the Arabic world they came from. The high-intensity, no-alternative group life of the Arabs in Peshawar gave their groups extra power over group members—power over values and actions similar to that of small cult groups or small groups of soldiers in combat. The extreme cohesion of a small group cut off from other contacts provides a multiplier mechanism for the extremity shift dynamics already described.

Bin Laden's shift from supporting jihad to fighting jihad was therefore multiply determined. Competition for status among Arabs in Pakistan favored those doing the most for jihad; higher status went to those taking more risks by going to fight Russians. The group shift to increased risk taking was amplified by the isolation of Arab groups in a foreign land. Into this pressure cooker of group dynamics, introduce a young man with a taste for risk taking, and bin Laden's transition to jihad can hardly be surprising.

The same two groups and the same group dynamics can help explain bin Laden's increasing radicalization after being expelled from Sudan. His situation in Afghanistan as the Taliban took power was even more isolated than his earlier experience in Pakistan. He was able to bring only a few hundred of his al Qaeda men with him to Afghanistan, where al-Zawahiri and his EIJ Egyptians were the most organized group of Arabs in the country. Making common cause with al-Zawahiri and his group, bin Laden expanded his definition of acceptable targets to include first U.S. troops in the Arabian Peninsula and then, in the infamous 1998 video, joined with Zawahiri in calling for killing of Americans anywhere they could be reached.

Intergroup Competition

As described in chapter 9, conflict between groups has two kinds of effects. First, it produces hostility toward the competitor. Second, it changes in-group dynamics: group cohesion increases, and with high cohesion comes idealization of in-group norms and values, increased punishment for deviation from in-group norms and values, and increased respect for group leaders. These changes prepare the group for unity and sacrifice against a competitor.

Group reactions to external threat are so reliable that they can be used as a political strategy. The first time bin Laden realized the power of jujitsu may have been when the fumbling attacks of his Arab contingent finally elicited the Russian attack that he became famous for beating back. Later he hoped by his verbal attacks on U.S. troops in Saudi Arabia to provoke a defense of these troops by King Fahd and the Saudi religious establishment—setting them at odds with most Saudis. Still later he aimed to provoke the United States to send troops into Afghanistan: first by attacking U.S. embassies, then by attacking a U.S. warship, then by authorizing the attacks in New York and Washington on 9/11. Even the first attack on Americans demonstrated the value of jujitsu politics: the embassy attacks elicited the cruise missiles that made Osama bin Laden a hero in parts of the Muslim world and saved him from being expelled from Afghanistan.

In a letter dated July 9, 2005, Zawahiri tried to teach Abu Musab al-Zarqawi how to avoid misuse of the jujitsu strategy in Iraq: stop the video beheadings, Zawahiri advised, and stop bombing Shi'ite holy places, lest we lose the broad mobilization of Muslims that U.S. troops in Iraq should bring.

The November 2008 attacks on Mumbai are another testimony to the power of jujitsu; these attacks took Pakistani troops from chasing jihadis to guarding the border against India's threatened response. The 2015 terrorist attacks in Paris and San Bernardino are the most recent tests of jujitsu politics; the attacks will have succeeded to the extent that European and U.S. Muslims feel increased government surveillance and increased public hostility (see chapter 15).

Person Versus Persona

In *The Looming Tower*, Wright focuses on the special importance of Osama bin Laden's connection with Ayman al-Zawahiri. "The dynamic of the two men's relationship made Zawahiri and bin Laden into people they would never have been individually; moreover, the organization they would create, al Qaeda, would be a vector of these two forces, one Egyptian and one Saudi. Each would have to compromise in order to accommodate the goals of the other; as a result, al Qaeda would take a unique path, that of global jihad."[4] The relation between bin Laden and Zawahiri was complicated by the fact that Zawahiri became bin Laden's personal physician; the authority of the physician could not be absent from discussion of political issues and directions.

---

4. Wright, L. (2006). *The looming tower*. New York: Vintage. p. 146.

In his trajectory of political radicalization, Osama bin Laden's many small steps to radical terrorism had taken twenty years, from 1979 to 1998, with each step bringing new experiences, new reactions from others, and new justifications for the next step.

A privileged start is often thought to produce a sense of entitlement that undermines motivation for work and the capacity to learn from failure. Instead Osama's reputation for personal piety and self-denial in lifestyle—including the risks of combat—became moral power against Russians, those he called apostate Muslims, and Westerners. As his feelings, beliefs, and behavior became more extreme, Osama became a different person. The shy youth became a construction supervisor, then an organizer for jihad against the Russians, then a combat leader, then a war hero, then a fiery political voice in Saudi Arabia, then the leader of al Qaeda in exile in Sudan and Afghanistan, and finally a media star headlining for a worldwide social movement responding to the perception of a war on Islam.

Like his political transformation, Osama bin Laden's personal transformation is a long trajectory in which the end cannot be found in the beginning. According to Prince Turki, former head of Saudi intelligence, "I saw radical changes in his personality as he changed from a calm, peaceful and gentle man interested in helping Muslims into a person who believed that he would be able to amass and command an army to liberate Kuwait. It revealed his arrogance."[5] Bin Laden may have been arrogant, but he was not crazy. The motives and mechanisms identified in his radicalization are familiar from research in normal psychology—often based on experiments with American and European university students—and neither his planning nor his social skills show any sign of the incompetence that comes with frank psychopathology.

Osama bin Laden became not just the unfolding of the young Osama—not an ugly duckling becoming a hawk—but a radically different person, a man formed over decades in a complex interplay of political conflict and personal development. No political profile of the young man who carried Saudi support to the Afghan jihad against Russians could have predicted the older man's support for bombing targets in Saudi Arabia. No character profile of the shy young man who joined his father's construction company could have predicted

5. Bergen, P. L. (2006). *The Osama bin Laden I Know: An oral history of al Qaeda's leader.* New York: Simon and Schuster, p. 112.

the charismatic leader. A social psychological perspective turns attention away from personality traits to interaction between person and situation, in Osama bin Laden's case a sequence of escalating conflict situations.

In contrast to the slow and interactive evolution of his politics and personality, the public persona of Osama bin Laden remains a monolith of certitude that encourages simple explanations. The temptation is to imagine an unfolding of innate qualities that are consistent with the myth. The boy must be father to the man. This temptation leads to a satisfying caricature of a notorious enemy, but it cannot do justice to the development of an individual.

One of the consequences of the caricature is that, when youthful description and adult persona are inconsistent, we may feel compelled to choose between the two. Prince Bindar bin Sultan met Osama bin Laden in the 1980s: "He wouldn't impress me as somebody who would be a leader for anything. Actually, at that time, I thought he couldn't lead eight ducks across the street."[6] According to his brother-in-law Mohammed Jamal Khalifa, "I am very surprised to hear about what Osama is doing now because it is not in his personality. He doesn't have the capacity to organize something as simple as a 15-minute trip. Even at prayer time he would say: 'You lead the prayers.'"[7]

The unfolding model points to one of two possibilities for making sense of these reports. Either they are inaccurate representations of the young Osama, or today's bin Laden is only a figurehead and mouthpiece for others, perhaps for the notably intelligent Zawahiri. Understanding the mechanisms of radicalization through which bin Laden has passed offers a third interpretation: the dynamics of conflict slowly built a giant where before there was only a boy.

---

6. Frontline. (2001). Interview: Bandar bin Sultan. Available at http://www.pbs.org/wgbh/pages/frontline/shows/terrorism/interviews/bandar.html.

7. Scheuer, M. (2004). *Imperial hubris: Why the west is losing the war on terror*. Dulles, VA: Potomac Books. Chapter 4. Available at https://books.google.com/books?id=Mmtxqal MXY8C&pg=PT124&lpg=PT124&dq=Mohammed+Jamal+Khalifa,+%E2%80%9CI+am+very+surprised+to+hear+about+what+Osama+is+doing+now+%22&source=bl&ots=8nWbuDheBr&sig=YruDL09wxB0s1Nmo6SmaioeuDw4&hl=en&sa=X&ved=0ahUKEwjEkJP_-s3MAhWM7CYKHemXA4QQ6AEIIDAB#v=onepage&q=Mohammed%20Jamal%20Khalifah%2C%20%E2%80%9CI%20am%20very%20surprised%20to%20hear%20about%20what%20Osama%20is%20doing%20now%20%22&f=false.

Looking Further

al-Zawahiri, A. (2001). *Knights under the Prophet's banner*. Serialized in *Al-Sharq al Awsat* (London), December 10, 2001. Available at https://azelin.files.wordpress. com/2010/11/6759609-knights-under-the-prophet-banner.pdf.

Batarfi, K. (2001). Report: Mom says bin Laden innocent. Associated Press, December 23.

Bergen, P. L. (2006). *The Osama bin Laden I know: An oral history of al Qaeda's leader*. New York: Free Press.

Brisard, J.-C. (2002). Al-Qaida monitored U.S. negotiations with Taliban over oil pipeline. Salon.com, June 5. Available at http://www.salon.com/2002/06/05/memo_11/.

CBS News (2004). "Bin Laden claims responsibility for 9/11." Available at http://www.cbc.ca/world/story/2004/10/29/binladen_message041029.html. Accessed December 23, 2008.

Cullison, A., & Higgins, A. (2002). A once-stormy terror alliance was solidified by cruise missiles. *Wall Street Journal*, August 2. Available at http://www.wsj.com/articles/SB1028236160532452080.

French, J. R. P., & Raven, B. (1959). The bases of social power. In D. Cartwright (Ed.), *Studies in social power*. Ann Arbor, MI: University of Michigan Press.

Gutman, R. (2008). *How we missed the story: Osama bin Laden, the Taliban, and the hijacking of Afghanistan*. Washington, DC: US Institute of Peace Press. Available at http://books.google.com/books?id=A9eqvc-Ru3cC. Accessed December 4, 2008.

Perera, A. (2002). *Suicide cadres still evoke fear.* Available at http://www.ipsnews.net/2003/07/politics-sri-lanka-suicide-cadres-still-evoke-fear/. Accessed December 23, 2008.

Pew Global Attitudes Project. (2005). Support for terror wanes among Muslim publics. Available at http://pewglobal.org/files/pdf/248.pdf. Accessed August 23, 2010.

Scheuer, M. (2004). *Imperial hubris: Why the West is losing the war on terror*. Dulles, VA: Potomac Books.

Scheuer, M. (2006). *Through our enemies' eyes: Osama bin Laden, radical Islam, and the future of America*. Revised ed. Dulles, VA: Potomac Books.

United States Department of State. (2006). Country reports on terrorism. Chapter 1, Strategic assessment. Available at http://www.state.gov/documents/organization/83383.pdf.

Whitlock, C. (2004). Al-Qaeda shifts its strategy in Saudi Arabia: Focus placed on U.S. and other Western targets in bid to bolster network, officials say. *Washington Post*, December 19, A28. Available at http://www.washingtonpost.com/wp-dyn/articles/A10780-2004Dec18.html. Accessed December 4, 2008.

Wright, L. (2006). *The looming tower*. New York: Vintage.

CHAPTER FIFTEEN

The Challenge of
Lone-Wolf Terrorists

O N NOVEMBER 5, 2009, Major Nidal Malik Hasan opened fire
on his fellow soldiers at Fort Hood, leaving thirteen dead and
thirty-two wounded. On March 2, 2011, two U.S. soldiers
died after a lone gunman, Arif Uka, opened fire on them at Frankfurt
airport. On July 22, 2011, Anders Breivik killed seventy-seven in and
around Oslo. Although lone-wolf terrorists are rare, they can do disproportionate damage: although a very small proportion (6 percent) of
U.S. terrorists, they have been responsible for one-fourth of the terrorism incidents in the United States.[1]

In 2011 President Obama expressed growing concern about the
threat of these kinds of attacks. "The risk that we're especially concerned over right now is the lone wolf terrorist, somebody with a single
weapon being able to carry out wide-scale massacres of the sort that
we saw in Norway recently," he said. "You know, when you've got one
person who is deranged or driven by a hateful ideology, they can do a
lot of damage, and it's a lot harder to trace those lone wolf operators."[2]

---

1. Hewitt, C. (2003). *Understanding terrorism in America: From the Klan to al Qaeda.*
   New York: Routledge, Chapter 5, The terrorists.
2. CNN Security Blogs. (2011). Obama: Biggest terror fear is the lone wolf (Wolf
   Blitzer interview with President Obama). Available at http://security.blogs.cnn.
   com/2011/08/16/obama-biggest-terror-fear-is-the-lone-wolf/.

In his testimony to the Committee on Homeland Security in 2015, New York Police Department Commissioner William Bratton stated that "in many respects, we currently face a greater likelihood of attack than we have seen in years." This threat is associated with the rise of Islamic State (IS or ISIS or ISIL). Since 2011 Islamic State has developed as a competitor to al Qaeda and has put more resources than al Qaeda ever did toward encouraging lone-wolf attackers around the world to do as much damage as they can with whatever means they have at hand. According to Commissioner Bratton, "This threat is decentralized and much harder to detect than threats orchestrated by Al-Qaeda. ISIL's alarmingly effective messaging—as refined as anything found on Madison Avenue or in Hollywood—reaches marginalized, solitary actors. These are terrorists who largely operate outside the kind of command-and-control systems, or cells, that we have learned to penetrate and dismantle."[3]

The social network that made al Qaeda strong was also its weakness: security officials could trace communications and money transfers within the network, with each node in the network a new opportunity for counterterrorism. Lone-wolf attackers have none of the organizational, interpersonal, and financial support that the 9/11 hijackers received from al Qaeda; but this seeming weakness is also their strength because it makes it harder to catch them before they attack.

The term *lone wolf* was popularized in the 1990s by U.S. white supremacists Tom Metzger and Alex Curtis, who encouraged followers to act alone when committing violence in order to avoid the government agents who had been successfully infiltrating right-wing groups.[4] Solo political violence has also been referred to as *lone-actor terrorism*, *leaderless resistance*, and *freelance terrorism*.

Lone-wolf terrorists plan and carry out an attack without assistance from others. They usually see themselves as representing some larger group or cause and may have some experience in the fringes of a group, organization, or social movement related to this cause. Their grievance is thus shared by many, although their attack is carried out alone. In a later section of this chapter we will raise the possibility that closely related pairs of terrorists may share some characteristics of lone actors.

---

3. Bekiempis, V. (2015). Terorism after 9/11: Dealing with lone wolves. *Newsweek*, September 13. Available at http://www.newsweek.com/september-11-lone-wolf-terrorist-terrorism-nypd-isis-isil-371216.

4. Bakker, E., & de Graaf, B. (2011). Preventing lone wolf terrorism: Some CT approaches addressed. *Perspectives on Terrorism* 5(5–6): 43–50.

In this chapter we will pursue three directions in understanding lone-wolf terrorists. First, we will examine mechanisms of radicalization to action that apply to lone actors. Second, analyzing results from research on school attackers and assassins—predominantly lone actors—we will suggest two possible psychological profiles of lone-wolf terrorists. Finally, we will highlight the importance of means and opportunity and the power of emotion for understanding how individuals are moved to lone-wolf attacks.

Mechanisms of Radicalization in Lone-Wolf Attackers

Of the twelve mechanisms of radicalization identified in earlier chapters, one holds special promise for understanding lone-wolf terrorists. Group grievance was what radicalized Vera Zazulich to plan and carry out an assassination attempt against General Trepov. Zazulich's identification with prisoners mistreated by General Trepov made her risk everything, including her life, to—as she saw it—bring justice against a cruel and unjust government official (see chapter 3). Likewise, Clayton Waagner was moved by political grievance when he began his crusade against abortion providers, whom he saw as inflicting suffering and death on countless unborn infants. Sending threatening letters with what looked like anthrax, Waagner believed he was doing God's work. Both Zazulich and Waagner acted alone. Both took significant risk and paid a high price for their actions. Both took radical action in support of people they did not personally know.

Getting Past the Free-Rider Problem: The Power of Emotion

Lone-actor terrorists are risking life and liberty for their cause. Why would any individual take this kind of risk? More generally, why would anyone choose to sacrifice for a cause?

The usual answer to this question is that group and organizational pressures move us to do what we would not choose to do if we considered only our personal welfare.[5] As described in chapter 8, small-group dynamics can provide rewards of love and status for those who take

---

5. Moskalenko, S., & McCauley, C. (2011). The psychology of lone-wolf terrorism. *Counseling Psychology Quarterly* 24(2): 115–126.

risks and make sacrifices for the group and punishments of discon-nection and contempt for those who do not. Organizations similarly provide rewards for those—fire fighters, police, soldiers—who take risks for organizational goals and punishments for those who shirk their duty.

The psychological puzzle presented by the lone-wolf terrorist is that the individual takes risks and makes sacrifices as a free choice, not subject to social pressures. The lone wolf does not feel the power of group dynamics and group pressures and does not have institutional support. The puzzle then is why an individual would freely choose vio-lence for a cause, knowing that the choice will be costly in terms of self-interest.

A rational choice perspective highlights the puzzle. If sacrifice for a group benefits all members of the group, self-interest dictates letting others pay the costs of advancing the group and share in the benefits they win. This *free-rider problem* applies in spades to the lone-wolf ter-rorist, who takes great risk and often pays great costs for moving alone to violent action.

One way past the free-rider problem is the power of emotion. In analyzing the case histories of Zazulich and Waagner, we suggested that sympathy and empathy can be important in moving an individual to terrorist action, especially for individuals particularly sensitive to the suffering of others. Zazulich was not present on the prison yard when the abuse of the prisoner took place; Waagner had not witnessed abortion or seen aborted fetuses. Their radicalization was the result of their imagination of others' suffering.

Group grievance powered by unusual sensitivity to the suffering of others seems to have played a role in our next case, the radicalization of Major Nidal Malik Hasan. Several other mechanisms of radicalization to action can also be observed in this case.

Major Nidal Hasan

Born into a family of Palestinian immigrants in the United States, Hasan was raised Muslim. He enlisted into the U.S. Army immedi-ately after high school and served while attending college. After get-ting a medical degree, Hasan completed his residency and internship at Walter Reed Army Medical Center and went on to receive a mas-ter's degree in public health in 2009. That same year he was promoted to major. On November 5, 2009, Hasan entered the Soldier Readiness

Center of Fort Hood (Texas), shouted "Allahu Akbar," and began shooting, killing thirteen people and wounding over thirty others. He was subdued by other soldiers, tried and convicted, and sentenced to death.

Group Grievance

Hasan's self-identification as a Muslim put him at odds with other army personnel. He found online inspiration in the teachings of Anwar al-Awlaki, an American-born preacher calling for jihad in response to Western violence against Muslims. Soon the two were exchanging e-mails. They discussed, among other things, the suffering of Muslims in Iraq and Afghanistan. Hasan was scheduled to be deployed in Afghanistan in late November of 2009, and he felt deeply conflicted about participating in a war against his fellow Muslims. In his e-mail exchanges with Awlaki, Hasan inquired whether killing innocents was allowed in jihad and how to transfer money without alerting U.S. authorities. He found more than inspiration online: he found encouragement and instruction.

Thus, like Zazulich and Waagner, Hasan was moved to radical action by empathizing with the suffering of others—a political grievance. And there are reports indicating that Hasan was deeply sensitive to the suffering of others. He mourned a pet bird for months after it died. During medical training, he fainted in attendance at a childbirth, which led him to choose psychiatry as a medical specialty. Ironically, treating U.S. soldiers afflicted with post-traumatic stress disorder (PTSD) after bloody battles in Muslim countries may have added to his concern for Muslims on the other side of these battles, who did not have modern medicine to fall back on.

Personal Grievance

On the army base, Hasan felt persecuted for his faith. Hasan's cousin and aunt claimed that Hasan sought to pay the army back for his education and get out of the military and that he even hired an attorney to help him. They also claimed that Hasan sought a discharge because of harassment he experienced related to his Muslim faith. The army did not confirm these claims. According to police records, in August of 2009 Hasan's car was vandalized with a key, and a soldier had been charged. Hasan's neighbor said the soldier vandalized the car because of Hasan's faith. It seems likely therefore that Hasan's radicalization was influenced by personal grievance: feeling alienated and persecuted as a Muslim.

Unfreezing

In addition to political and personal grievances, Hasan's history shows the power of *disconnection*—loss or weakening of social ties and a change in way of life. Hasan turned to the Koran after the death of his parents, seems to have had no close relationships after he was transferred to Fort Hood, and was about to be transferred to Afghanistan. His cousin recalled that Hasan was terrified of his impending deployment that would take him far away. With social ties weak or gone and with his life out of control, Hasan was moved to action. Indeed, it seems likely he would not have moved to action except that a choice was forced upon him by his scheduled deployment: to join U.S. forces fighting Muslims in Afghanistan or to resist deployment. Later in this chapter, and in the next chapter, we will return to the idea that radical opinions can persist for long periods without radical action; the turn to action requires separate explanation.

Possible Profiles of Lone-Wolf Terrorists

Because there are many possible mechanisms of radicalization, it is generally not possible to determine a useful terrorist profile. Many mechanisms, and many combinations of these mechanisms, produce many trajectories to terrorism and many "profiles."

But lone-wolf terrorists may be easier to profile. Group-level mechanisms are not relevant for lone wolves, who are moved to violent action by individual-level mechanisms (including group/political grievance!). Even among the individual mechanisms, several are irrelevant. Lone-wolf terrorists are not joining a militant group, so love for a member of the group is not a factor. Lone-wolf terrorists are not slowly increasing their commitment to radical action; indeed, most lone-wolf terrorists have no previous history of radical action. So slippery slope is not a factor. It appears that the relevant individual-level mechanisms for lone-wolf radicalization are personal grievance, group/political grievance, risk and status seeking, and unfreezing.

Additionally helpful is the fact already mentioned in relation to lone-wolf Ted Kaczynski (the Unabomber)—lone-wolf terrorists are more likely to suffer from psychopathology than group-based terrorists.

The previously cited study by Hewitt identified twenty-seven lone-actor U.S. terrorists between 1955 and 2001 and found that the rate of psychological disturbance was higher (six of twenty-seven) among the lone actors than among other U.S. terrorists. Hewitt's result suggests that psychopathology may be a useful indicator of potential for lone-wolf terrorism.

Taking a different approach to the problem, we sought to develop hypotheses about the characteristics of lone-wolf terrorists by looking for the common characteristics of two kinds of predominantly lone-actor violent offenders: assassins and school attackers. Our study used existing U.S. government–sponsored reports to examine these two kinds of offenders.[6]

The logic of comparing school attackers with assassins is that these two groups of offenders are like lone-wolf terrorists in perpetrating planful violence fueled by grievance (whereas most criminal violence in the United States is impulsive or motivated by greed). To the extent that assassins and school attackers share common characteristics, these characteristics may be risk factors for lone-wolf terrorists as well. The obvious demographic differences between the two groups (teenagers vs. adults) are actually a strength of the comparison: any commonalities uncovered are the more striking and unlikely to be a reflection of life status or demographic factors.

The school attackers report focused on thirty-seven incidents of targeted school attacks between 1974 and 2000; thirty of the total of forty-one attackers acted alone (73 percent). The assassins report focused on seventy-four assassination incidents between 1949 and 1996 in which eighty-three people had either attacked (46 percent) or tried to attack (54 percent intercepted in the vicinity of the target with a weapon) a prominent person in the United States. Of the eighty-three assassins, sixty-three (76 percent) acted alone.

As a study of lone-actor violence, the comparison had an unavoidable limitation: most, but not all, of the assassins and school attackers were lone actors. Thus, the study compared two groups of predominantly lone actors, but the comparison was made coarser by the inclusion of a minority of group actors whose characteristics cannot be separated from the characteristics of lone actors.

---

6. McCauley, C., Moskalenko, S., & Van Son, B. (2013). Characteristics of lone-wolf violent offenders: A comparison of school attackers and assassins. *Perspectives on Terrorism* 7(1): 4–24.

We identified four common characteristics of assassins and school attackers: grievance, depression, unfreezing, and weapons experience outside the military.

We coded grievance in school attackers and assassins from reports of having been persecuted, bullied, threatened, attacked, or injured (school attackers) and any grievance at the time of the principal incident (assassins). The prevalence of grievance was high for both school attackers (81 percent) and assassins (67 percent), and this result echoes findings from the histories of Zazulich, Waagner, and Hasan that showed political grievance in each case.

Depression, including despair or suicidal ideation, was coded for the great majority of school attackers (78 percent), and nearly half of assassins (44 percent) had this history.

Unfreezing, a situational crisis of personal disconnection and maladjustment, was coded from reports of having experienced or perceived major loss (for school attackers) and of having experienced accident or illness, loss of relationship, or failure or loss of status (for assassins). Loss of connection and status leaves an individual with less to lose in radical action, including violence. Almost all school attackers (98 percent) were coded for unfreezing, and "almost half" (the best summary figure available) of assassins showed unfreezing. Again, this finding is in agreement with our case study of Hasan whose unfreezing contributed to his radicalization.

Finally, experience with weapons was coded for both assassins and school attackers (with experience during military service excluded for assassins). Over half of assassins and school attackers showed a history of weapons use outside the military (71 percent and 63 percent, respectively). This characteristic points to the importance of means and opportunity as well as motivation for understanding lone-wolf terrorists.

Other studies of lone-wolf terrorists reinforce attention to all four characteristics that we identified in school attackers and assassins. Spaaij examined eighty-eight cases of lone-wolf terrorists aggregated across fifteen Western countries and found that lone wolves are likely to suffer from some form of psychological disturbance and tend to be loners with few friends.[7] Gill, Horgan, and Deckert put together an international collection of 119 mostly lone-actor terrorists (including isolated dyads and some individuals with loose group connections); no single profile was identified, but many of the lone actors seemed to be

---

7. Spaaij, R. (2012). *Understanding lone wolf terrorism: Global patterns, motivations and prevention.* New York: Springer.

socially isolated.[8] Gruenewald, Chermak, and Freilich compared lethal attacks by lone-actor and group-actor U.S. far-right extremists.[9] The results indicated that the lone actors were younger and more likely to have a military background, suffer mental illness, and experience disconnection by separation, divorce, or death of a partner.

Taken together, these results point to a *disconnected-disordered* profile: individuals with a grievance and weapons experience who are socially disconnected and stressed with psychological disorder. These are loners with little to lose, pushed to action to escape personal problems and to gain status in notoriety.

But at least two of our case histories do not fit this description: Zazulich and Waagner had social skills, solid social connections, and no sign of mental disorder. Rather, these individuals fit a *caring-compelled* profile: they felt strongly the suffering of others and a personal responsibility to reduce or revenge this suffering. We suspect that the caring-compelled profile is less common than the disconnected-disordered profile—not least because self-sacrifice for others is less common than self-interest—but this hypothesis will have to be tested as we learn more about lone-actor violence.

Major Hasan's case is more complex. He brought two weapons to his attack, one a sophisticated "cop-killer" pistol for which he purchased a laser sight—indicating experience with weapons beyond whatever slight weapons training the U.S. Army provides for physician-psychiatrists. So far as we can ascertain, Hasan showed anxiety about being deployed to Afghanistan but no signs of depression. Thus, Hasan had three of the four characteristics common to assassins and school attackers: unfreezing, grievance, and weapons experience. In addition, as already noted, Hasan was particularly sensitive to the suffering of others, a characteristic of the caring-compelled profile. Hasan's case thus alerts us to the possibility of overlap in the two profiles: a lone wolf may be both disconnected and caring-compelled.

The next case study challenges the boundaries of lone-wolf terrorism: a self-radicalized terrorist who reached for a militant group as

8. Gill, P., Horgan, J., & Deckert, P. (2014). Bombing alone: Tracing the motivations and antecedent behaviors of lone-actor terrorists. *Journal of Forensic Science*, 58(2): 425–435.

9. Gruenewald, J., Chermak, S., & Freilich, J. D. (2013). Distinguishing "loner" attacks from other domestic extremist violence: A comparison of far-right homicide incident and offender characteristics. *Criminology and Public Policy* 12(1): 65–91.

another might reach for a firearm. This case will again point to the importance of means and opportunity for understanding lone-wolf terrorists.

Momin Khawaja: A Case of Self-Radicalization[10]

Mohammad Momin Khawaja is in a Canadian prison for developing a radio-igniter for a fertilizer bomb planned by British jihadists. His first step toward radical action was flying to Pakistan to try to join the Taliban after the U.S. invasion of Afghanistan in 2001. He was too late and returned home to Canada, later taking a trip to London where he became involved in the bomb plot. But what is notable in this case is that Khawaja determined to go to Afghanistan on his own, without being a member of any radical or terrorist group. His individual decision to join the fight in Afghanistan made him, in psychological terms, a lone-wolf terrorist.

Khawaja had a well-paid job as an information technology consultant, he lived at home in a loving family, he had no signs of mental disorder, and he had no weapons experience.

What he did have was a collection of jihad videos that showed Muslims being victimized by Western powers and fighting back. He asked others to watch these videos, from which it is reasonable to infer that he thought they were persuasive. These videos are designed to elicit emotions: outrage at victims' suffering, shame at doing nothing while others are fighting back, pride at seeing Muslims successfully attacking Western forces.

Of course many Muslims have watched jihad videos without joining jihad. Khawaja, like Zazulich and Waagner, appears to have been unusual in his capacity for empathy, to the point where the suffering of others made him feel a personal responsibility to join their fight. The capacity for empathy or sympathy is generally seen as quintessentially human and eminently humane. Here we have a hint that there can be a dark side to caring greatly about others. Individuals can kill for love, including love for victims.

---

10. McCauley, C., & Quiggin, T. (2015). Momin Khawaja: Mechanisms of radicalization. Draft report for CSTAB 2.5 grant from Department of Homeland Security through the National Coalition for Study of Terrorists and Responses to Terrorism (START). Available at https://www.researchgate.net/publication/303264208_Radicalization_of_Momin_Khawaja_draft_not_final_report.

The next section looks at family love as a source of cohesion that can make two terrorists as difficult to detect as one.

Family Pair Terrorists

Our discussion of lone-wolf terrorism would not be complete without mentioning a new phenomenon that has yet to be conceptualized by researchers or profiled by security services: *family pairs*. In several recent terrorist attacks the perpetrators were two members of a family unit. The Tsarnaev brothers, Tamerlan and Dzhokhar, attacked the Boston Marathon with home-made pressure-cooker bombs; the Kouachi brothers, Cherif and Sayid, attacked the office of Paris magazine *Charlie Hebdo* with Kalashnikov automatic rifles; the Abdesalam brothers, Brahim and Salah, carried out terrorist attacks in Paris, one brother blowing himself up at a café, while the other escaped in the car used to deliver terrorists to their target locations. Most recently, husband and wife Syed Farook and Tashfeen Malik attacked California's San Bernardino Regional Office of Public Health with military-style automatic weapons. We will look at this case more closely.

San Bernardino

On December 2, 2015, Syed Rizwan Farook, a U.S. citizen of Pakistani descent, attended a Christmas party that was held by his employer, the San Bernardino Department of Public Health. He left early, and when he returned, he was accompanied by his wife, Tashfeen Malik, a recent immigrant to the United States from Pakistan. They had a six-month-old daughter they left at home with Farook's mother.

Farook and Malik entered the party dressed in ski masks and black tactical gear, including vests loaded with rounds of ammunition and explosives. Using assault rifles, the husband and wife opened fire on the party gathering. They fired between sixty-five and seventy rounds in the course of about four minutes and left before police arrived, leaving behind three pipe bombs that failed to detonate. A total of fourteen people were killed in the attack, and twenty-two others were injured.

Attendees at the party recognized Farook in one of the shooters, and they gave the police his name, which led to the discovery of a rented SUV in which the terrorists drove off. A chase and a shoot-out ensued, in which both terrorists were killed and two police officers were injured. An initial investigation uncovered a pledge of allegiance to Islamic State, left on the day of the attack on Malik's Facebook page.

A key question in this case is about timing: When were Farook and Malik first radicalized to violent action?

Farook's childhood friend Enrique Marquez told investigators that he bought the two automatic rifles used in the attack and gave them to Farook in 2011 and 2012. Marquez said that he and Farook were considering an attack in 2012 but gave up their plans when the FBI arrested a group in nearby Riverside, California, who had been planning to join al Qaeda in Afghanistan. Thus, Farook was moving to violent action before he met Malik, and before Islamic State declared itself the new caliphate in 2014.

It seems Malik also was seeking violent action before the couple connected. In 2012 Malik sent an e-mail in Urdu to friends in Pakistan expressing her desire to join in jihad. She seems to have met Farook on an Internet dating site, meeting him in person for the first time in Saudi Arabia when Farook made the Hajj pilgrimage to Mecca in 2013. In 2014 Malik traveled to the United States on a K-1 fiancée visa, and the couple were married. In e-mail messages before their marriage, Farook and Malik talked of martyrdom and jihad, suggesting that readiness to join in jihad was part of what brought them together.

In sum, Farook and Malik were both ready to participate in jihad against the West before they met and before Islamic State rose to prominence in 2014. Together they strengthened their commitment to action, a commitment strong enough to leave their daughter an orphan.

From this timeline, it is clear that, whatever symbolic value was represented by pledging allegiance to Islamic State as the couple moved to their attack, Islamic State cannot be the source of the couple's radicalization to violent action. It cannot be the brutal interpretation of Islam advanced by Islamic State that moved them. It cannot be the new caliphate claimed by Islamic State that inspired them. In short, the San Bernardino attack cannot be attributed to Islamic State; before Islamic State existed, Malik and Farook were seeking jihad and Farook was preparing weapons for jihad.

Family Pairs and Lone Wolves

Neither Malik nor Farook was part of any larger group or organization. Each was self-radicalized to seek jihad even before they met. In their close relation as husband and wife, and as parents of a child, they seem to have felt as one and acted as one. Although not lone wolves in the sense that they did not act alone, they also differ significantly from a traditional terrorist group, especially where it comes to identifying them and tracking their actions. An oncoming threat from the Tsarnaev brothers or the Kouachi brothers would likewise be difficult to detect.

Unlike a terrorist cell of unrelated individuals, siblings and spouses living together do not raise the suspicions of neighbors or security forces. Financial transactions between family members are seen as routine, whereas they could be red flags for security officials when made between unrelated persons. There is little chance of one member of the pair betraying the other one's trust and cooperating with the authorities or of an outsider infiltrating their two-person cell. Detecting and preventing a terrorist attack are thus more difficult for family pair terrorists than for other kinds of terrorist groups. In other words, from a security standpoint, family pair terrorists look a lot like lone wolves.

Similarly, the psychology of radicalization in a family pair is likely closer to that of a lone wolf than to that of a traditional terrorist group member. Family members—brothers or spouses—are likely to share personal grievances (one brother's experience of discrimination is felt keenly by the other brother). They are likely to share attitudes about political grievances. They are likely to have gone through the same life transitions that can result in unfreezing (moving to a new country or losing family members). They can train together to use weapons (as Farook and Malik did) or to build bombs (as the Tsarnaevs did). Finally, in a pair one person may dominate, as Tamerlan Tsarnaev dominated his brother Dzhokhar, so that the weaker individual is more an extension of the stronger than an equal partner. (We thank Lisa McCauley for this suggestion.)

In short, family pair terrorists can be more like lone-wolf terrorists than a traditional terrorist group, in both the psychological origins of their radicalization and their potential for evading security services. With governments becoming more efficient at identifying terrorist networks, terrorists have undergone an evolution of their own. Family pair terrorists create a social structure that has most of the lone wolf's camouflage yet allows for some of the specialization and social support found in traditional terrorist groups and cells. As more information about family pair terrorists becomes available, it may be possible to develop a psychology of radicalization to violent action that is specific to this new social form.

This chapter began by recognizing the special challenge of understanding the radicalization of lone-wolf terrorists. The rewards and punishments wielded by groups and organizations cannot explain the risk taking and sacrifice by individuals who work alone to plan, prepare, and carry out a violent attack. We focused therefore on individual-level mechanisms of radicalization, and now we want to look back at the chapter to recognize the extent to which lone-wolf cases have expanded our view of these mechanisms.

Statistical compilation of the characteristics of lone-wolf terrorists agreed with statistical compilation of the characteristics of school attackers and assassins in pointing to a possible profile of lone-actor mass violence: individuals with a grievance, weak social connections (unfreezing), mental health issues (especially depression), status seeking (notoriety), and weapons experience. Whether because of personality or mental health issues, many lone-wolf terrorists are loners; unfreezing opens some normal individuals to joining a terrorist group, but lone-wolf terrorists may often have no strong ties to lose. *Disconnected* seems thus a more useful term than *unfreezing* for understanding lone-wolf terrorists. From this point we will refer to the mechanism of *unfreezing/disconnection*.

Relatedly, we see disconnection and depression as closely linked.[11] Disconnection makes an individual depressed; depression, by interfering with normal social relations, can make an individual disconnected. The combination of disconnection and depression is painful, painful enough to push individuals to any kind of action that promises an end or at least a distraction from the pain.

This recognition gives new weight to a mechanism of radicalization alluded to only briefly in chapter 6, where Barannikov was described as desperate to escape the boredom of military service and the boredom of distributing political texts. Boredom, family and romantic problems, financial problems, threat of torture or prison, humiliation—any of these, like the pain of disconnection and depression, can come to seem intolerable. Given a grievance, an individual seeking escape can turn to violent action with a sense of "nothing to lose." Where most individual-level mechanisms of radicalization are "pull" factors

---

11. Coyne, J. C., & Downey, G. (1991). Social factors and psychopathology: Stress, social support, and coping processes. *Annual Review of Psychology* 42: 401–425.

(personal and group grievance, love, risk and status seeking), escape is a "push" factor that includes not only disconnection and depression but any kind of painful life experience.

Turning now to the caring-compelled profile, consideration of lone-wolf cases led us to focus on emotions associated with empathy and sympathy. Identification with family members is everywhere; identification with a sports team or an ethnicity is nearly as common. If caring about others is common, then feeling anger, sadness, shame, or pride depending on what happens to these others is likewise common.

Our suggestion for the caring-compelled profile is that some individuals feel emotion-by-identification so strongly that the emotion impels action. Especially we point to anger and outrage in response to the suffering of others as having in some individuals the capacity to submerge considerations of risk and self-interest; the action tendency of the emotion of anger is of course retaliation.

The power of emotion as a mechanism of radicalization thus arises for both profiles. For the disconnected-disordered, the emotion is self-centered and painful and attack is a form of escape. For the caring-compelled, the emotion is other-centered and the attack is a form of self-sacrifice—related to the altruistic suicide described by sociologist Emile Durkheim.[12] The next chapter gives further attention to the power of emotion, this time examining the emotions of the targets of terrorist attack.

Looking Further

Bakker, E., & de Graaf, B. (2011). Preventing lone wolf terrorism: Some CT approaches addressed. *Perspectives on Terrorism* 5(5–6): 43–50.

Gill, P., Horgan, J., & Deckert, P. (2014). Bombing alone: Tracing the motivations and antecedent behaviors of lone-actor terrorists. *Journal of Forensic Science* 58(2): 425–435.

Gruenewald, J., Chermak, S., & Freilich, J. D. (2013). Distinguishing "loner" attacks from other domestic extremist violence: A comparison of far-right homicide incident and offender characteristics. *Criminology and Public Policy* 12(1): 65–91.

McCauley, C., & Moskalenko, S. (2014). Toward a profile of lone wolf terrorists: What moves an individual from radical opinion to radical action? *Terrorism and Political Violence* 26(1): 69–85.

Spaaij, R. (2012). *Understanding lone wolf terrorism: Global patterns, motivations and prevention*. New York: Springer.

12. Durkheim, E. (1897) [1951]. *Suicide: A study in sociology*. New York: Free Press.

CHAPTER SIXTEEN

Radicalization of Opinion and Action

The Two-Pyramids Model

I N EARLIER CHAPTERS we distinguished mechanisms of radicalization at three levels: individual, group, and mass mechanisms. In this chapter we focus on an important distinction between the first two levels and the third level: mechanisms of radicalization at the individual and group levels produce radicalization of action, whereas those at the mass level produce predominantly radicalization of opinion. In our introduction to section 3, *Mass Radicalization*, we noted that "Understanding mass psychology means understanding what moves a mass public to support for political and social action around a particular identity." Now in this chapter we go further in distinguishing radicalization of opinion for the many from radicalization of action for the few.

We begin with a case history of radicalization that demonstrates the importance of the gap between opinion and action, then present a two-pyramids model of radicalization that recognizes this gap, and conclude the chapter by drawing out implications of this model.

Internet Warrior Abu-Mulal al-Balawi

Humam Khalil Abu-Mulal al-Balawi, recruited by Jordanian intelligence as a double agent to gather information on high-profile Taliban and al Qaeda leaders, blew himself up on December 30, 2009, in Khost Province of Afghanistan. He killed seven CIA agents and one Jordanian agent. We distinguish two phases in al-Balawi's trajectory to violence: radicalization of opinion during his life in Jordan working as a physician from 2002 to 2009 and radicalization of action in Pakistan between March and December 2009. In our interpretation, his radicalization in action depended on the means and opportunity offered by Jordanian intelligence and the CIA. This section of the chapter draws on a case history by Turcan and McCauley, especially on interviews with al-Balawi's wife Defne Bayrak conducted by Turcan; sources for all the quotations used in this section are detailed in the published paper.[1]

Early Life and Education

Al-Balawi was born in Kuwait on December 25, 1977, to a middle-class family of ten children. He came from a Bedouin clan from Tabuk (Saudi Arabia), which has branches in Jordan and Palestine. His Palestinian family came to Kuwait in 1948 after the foundation of Israel, and his family lived there until Iraq's invasion of Kuwait in 1990. After the invasion, the family moved to the city of Zarqua, Jordan; his father, a middle-class professional, still owns two pharmacies in Zarqua. Unlike al-Balawi's family, most Palestinians around Zarqua live in refugee camps with bitter memories of their former properties now controlled by Israel.

Al-Balawi graduated with honors from a high school in Amman. His hope was to go to medical school and become a pediatrician. In 1995, mainly owing to his outstanding grades, al-Balawi was awarded a fellowship from the Jordanian government; and he went to Ankara, the capital city of Turkey, to learn Turkish. After a year of language lessons, he moved to Istanbul in 1996, where he was accepted as a medical student in the Medical Faculty of Istanbul University. In 2001, in an Internet chat room, he met Defne Bayrak, a Turkish student in the

---

1. Turcan, M., & McCauley, C. (2010). Boomerang: Opinion versus action in the radicalization of Abu-Mulal al-Balawi. *Dynamics of Asymmetric Conflict* 3: 14–31.

Faculty of Communication of the same university. When they married later the same year, al-Balawi was in his last year of medical school. Their match was for love, rather than arranged by their families, and cut across differences of language and nationality.

After graduating from Istanbul University and becoming a physician in 2002, al-Balawi moved back to Zarqua with his wife. Bayrak says that al-Balawi deeply wanted to go back to his people—to help fellow Palestinians. After moving back to Jordan, he worked in local hospitals run by the Muslim Brotherhood charity, including a clinic in Hittin, a Palestinian refugee camp on the outskirts of Zarqua where thousands of Palestinians live in an extremely deprived and isolated environment.

Radicalization of Opinion in Jordan

Bayrak contends that the American-led invasion of Iraq in 2003 ignited a transformation of her husband's beliefs. She says that at the end of 2004, for the first time, he began to talk to her about his strong belief in the need for violent jihad against Western occupiers in Muslim lands such as Iraq, Afghanistan, and Gaza. However, she explicitly asserts that he had not connected with any jihadist organization or group. "He followed all of them, but from a distance," she says. She insists that "He was constantly reading and writing by himself and had not participated in a radical group activity."

It appears that al-Balawi's jihadist postings on the Internet began with U.S. troops entering Iraq in 2003, but his radicalization accelerated after the Israeli attack on Gaza in late 2008 (Operation Cast Lead). Bayrak says that he began spending three to four hours on the Internet every day after the Gaza attack, and she adds that his interest in the Internet continued at this level until his departure to Pakistan in March 2009. Al-Balawi posted under the name *Abu Dujana*, a famous Muslim warrior and companion of the Prophet Mohammed. His posts glorified those who fight and those who die in jihad against Western forces in Iraq and Afghanistan.

The radicalization that began with the invasion of Iraq had an important limitation: al-Balawi did not agree with the version of radical Islam that calls for attacks on civilians. He participated in a version of Salafi Islam that heeded the Koran's injunctions against such attacks. He supported attacks on invaders of Muslim lands—on the Israeli Defense Forces in Gaza and the West Bank and on Western troops in Afghanistan and Iraq—but did not support attacks on European or

U.S. civilians. This distinction would prove important when he moved to radicalization in action.

It may have been during the period of the Israeli incursion into Gaza that al-Balawi first attracted the attention of Jordan's General Intelligence Directorate (GID). Ali bin Zaid, a young cousin of King Abdullah, who was to be the Jordanian agent killed by al-Balawi with seven CIA agents in the suicide attack, was among the analysts who kept a close watch on jihadist Internet forums. Jordanian officials said that al-Balawi was interrogated by officers from the GID in March 2009 because of suspicions about his activities in the online world. He had been released because the inquiry found "nothing relevant." Bayrak says that it was very surprising for her to see her husband three days after his being taken into custody because it took months for others to be released by Jordanian intelligence. She said that when she asked him how he could be released so quickly, he answered, very softly, "by the help of Allah."

> Before the arrest, he had been talking about going back to Turkey or to the USA for medical specialist education. After being released, however, he suddenly changed his mind and started talking about going to Pakistan for surgeon education. I still do not know why he suddenly changed his mind and decided to go to Pakistan. I did not want to let him go and tried to change his mind, but he did not listen to me.

Radicalization of Action in Pakistan

In March 2009 al-Balawi flew to Dubai and then to Pakistan, where, maybe for the first time in his life, he made face-to-face contacts with hard-core militants. During this period he was in touch with Bayrak by Internet and called her in late August 2009 (roughly five months after his departure) and asked her to leave Jordan and to go to Turkey with their daughters. He also wired $4000 to her from Peshawar—a wire delivery unlikely to have gone through without the knowledge and approval of Jordanian intelligence. At the end of September, Bayrak left Jordan with her daughters and went back to Istanbul. Bayrak says that she communicated with her husband via the Internet for the last time ten days before his attack at Khost on December 30.

> He said he was in Peshawar, working in a local hospital there to help people. He seemed very normal and we talked about everyday things. But he was lamenting the deaths of children from the air

attacks of the Americans. At the beginning of December 2009, just three weeks before the attack, he said that he was extremely sorry to see the deaths of hundreds of children caused by the air attacks in the last two months. This was the second time I sensed his mood of agony since the Israeli attack on Gaza in the winter of 2008. He said to me that he was extremely affected by the deaths of the children and lamented that he could do nothing to prevent this. The last thing he mentioned to me was his plan to come back to Turkey. He did not mention his plan of an attack, nor did I sense that something abnormal was going on.

Radicalization to Violence: Opinion Versus Action

Beginning in late 2004 al-Balawi was telling his wife that violent jihad was necessary against Western occupiers in Muslim lands, pointing especially to Afghanistan and Iraq. At this point, in his Internet postings, he was justifying violence. In 2008, like other Palestinians, he was outraged by the Israeli attack on Gaza; as Abu Dujana, he expressed his outrage on the Internet in ever more fiery calls for jihad. At this time, according to Bayrak, he also began to talk about going himself to jihad.

> Increasingly, he started to talk about his desire to go to some of the battlefields where jihads were being fought in late 2008. He was very adamant about going to Iraq or Afghanistan and was looking for an opportunity to do this. It was impossible for anybody to go to these states without being monitored by Jordanian intelligence. If he was able to go Pakistan, I think that it was because he had completely deceived Jordanian intelligence and the CIA and used them as a means to pursue jihad. He may have agreed to work for them and take money, but this was a part of his deception plan. He did not say anything to me about his plans before his departure, but he was very happy to go to Pakistan. His morale was high.

Thus, after four years of radical postings as Abu Dujana, al-Balawi began talking of a personal obligation for jihad against Western forces in Muslim lands after the Israeli invasion of Gaza in 2008. And then, it is very important to note, he did nothing. He continued posting his fiery opinions, but he did not connect with any militant group and did not try to go to Iraq or Pakistan to fight. He did not even engage in what small levels of political activism were available in Jordan. He posted and he doctored.

This is an interesting case: someone at the peak of opinion radicalization who did nothing to move toward political violence. From late 2008 until March 2009 al-Balawi was talking personal jihad but made no move toward doing jihad.

These four months underline the importance of distinguishing radicalization of opinion from radicalization of action. In the cases of Vera Zazulich and Clayton Waagner, the interval between experiencing a personal moral obligation to take up violence and the beginning of violent action is not clear but appears to have been brief. Looking at these cases, one might think that violent action is the inevitable next step after reaching the peak of opinion radicalization. But al-Balawi's four months of talking jihad while doing nothing shows that there is an important gap between even the most radical idea and radical action. We believe that it was the opportunity, or the pressure, brought by Jordanian intelligence that moved al-Balawi across the gap.

Bayrak asserts that al-Balawi had already decided to conduct an attack when he was in Jordan and had used CIA and Jordanian intelligence to get to Afghanistan to achieve this objective. On the contrary, we suggest that he decided to conduct his attack after he arrived in Afghanistan and Pakistan. When Jordanian intelligence provided him with a free ticket and visa to Pakistan, he could not have been planning an attack because he knew nothing and no one in Pakistan. Without any idea of means or opportunity, he could not, in Jordan, choose to attack anyone or anything in Pakistan or Afghanistan. But Jordanian intelligence offered him the sort of challenge he had said he wanted.

An interview with al-Balawi's father indicates the importance of the opportunity offered by Jordanian intelligence. "Had they left him, he would have stayed behind his computer forever—he would only be expressing his opinion, only talking."

Talking violence is easier than doing violence, especially for a man with a wife and daughters who love him—especially for a man with no history or experience of violence, not even experience with non-violent activism. But for a man who has been preaching violence to others, there would be something hypocritical about refusing a ticket to the battlefield. The internal pressure toward consistency of words and action—which Zazulich called *conscience* and Waagner called the *voice of God*—is evident in one of the videos al-Balawi made before his suicide attack at Khost. The title of his post was "When Will My Words Drink My Blood?—I Am Now Fit for Publication."

Oh, you who write about jihad and urge people to it, beware of falling into the same trap that I fell into. What I fear most is that [when I die] I will meet a man who died as a martyr under the effect of my words, whereas I shall die in bed. This is a nightmare which makes me sleepless and racks my nerves. I'm afraid that on the day of resurrection, standing before a mountain of sins, I shall be asked to account for each and every one of them, and it shall be a long account, and I will be covered with sweat, while they [martyrs] will be moving about the halls of paradise in everlasting pleasure. One of them will say to the other: "What do you say about him who used to be called Abu Dajana Al-Khorasani, who used to urge people to go to jihad?" And the other one will answer: "But he died in bed, a contemptible death, having stayed away from jihad. I wish for him that he had benefited by his own words. He was like a candle that burned itself to give light to the others." I'm afraid to be branded as a liar, and that my words will be the evidence for my conviction. ... My words are going to die if I don't save them with my blood, and my emotions will be extinguished if I don't kindle them with my death.

One more link with Zazulich and Waagner is al-Balawi's strong identification with those he saw as victims. The medical student who hoped to be a pediatrician became the surgeon who identified with the young victims he worked on. Bayrak reports the special pain al-Balawi felt for the suffering of Palestinian children, and his last communication with his wife expressed the pain he felt for the suffering of the children he saw die in Pakistan. "My husband stated to me that he had personally witnessed the deaths of more than 300 children from April to November 2009 on the border of Pakistan and Afghanistan." To those who killed children, in a camp with no civilians, he carried a bomb he could not have made himself.

Al-Balawi's history highlights the gap between radical opinion and radical action. More than that, it shows that motive for violence is not enough; opportunity and means of violence are required to get across the gap. For al-Balawi, Jordanian intelligence provided the opportunity, and the militants he met for the first time in Pakistan provided the means. His move to violent action, like that of Momin Khawaja, tests the distinction between lone-wolf violence and group violence: al-Balawi developed radical opinions without group support but developed violent action by connecting with a violent group. In this trajectory, Balawi was self-radicalized but not a lone wolf.

The Two-Pyramids Model of Radicalization

Al-Balawi's case history points to the importance of distinguishing radicalization of opinion (beliefs and feelings) from radicalization in action. In this section we present a model of radicalization built on this distinction, focusing on examples of opinion and action relating to al Qaeda–inspired terrorism.[2]

Radicalization in the Opinion Pyramid

The narrative frame of global jihad has four major parts: Islam is under attack by Western crusaders led by the United States; jihadis, whom the West refers to as "terrorists," are defending against this attack; the actions they take in defense of Islam are proportional, just, and religiously justified; and, therefore, it is the duty of good Muslims to support these actions.

This narrative is conveniently represented in terms of a pyramid of opinion radicalization (Figure 16.1) in which the base includes Muslims who currently do not accept any of the global jihad narrative. A level above the base are those who agree with the first part of the jihadist frame: that the West is waging a war on Islam (sympathizers). Next higher in the pyramid are Muslims who believe that jihadis are acting in defense of Islam and that their actions are morally and religiously justified (justifiers—al-Balawi 2004–2008). Finally, at the apex of the opinion pyramid are Muslims who believe there is an individual duty to participate in defending Islam against the West (personal moral obligation—al-Balawi after the Israeli invasion of Gaza in 2008).

There is a complexity here: Islam distinguishes between defense mandated by legitimate authority, a group responsibility, and defense that is an individual obligation for every good Muslim. Osama bin Laden argued that the current threat to Islam justifies an individual obligation to take up arms, an obligation not dependent on having state or religious authorization for jihad. We identify belief in the individual

---

2. Leuprecht, C., Hataley, T. Moskalenko, S., & McCauley, C. (2010). Containing the narrative: Strategy and tactics in countering the storyline of global jihad. *Journal of Policing, Intelligence, and Counter Terrorism* 5: 42–57. Leuprecht, C., Hataley, T., McCauley, C., & Moskalenko, S. (2010). Narratives and counter-narratives for global jihad: Opinion versus action. In E.J.A.M. Kessels (Ed.), *Countering extremist narratives*. The Hague: National Coordinator for Counterterrorism, pp. 58–70.

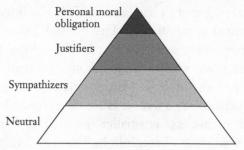

FIGURE 16.1 Opinion Radicalization Pyramid.

moral obligation to use violence as the highest, most radicalized level of the opinion pyramid.

ICM telephone polls of U.K. Muslims have asked the following question: "President Bush and Tony Blair have said the war against terrorism is not a war against Islam. Do you agree or disagree?" In November 2004, 80 percent of a national sample of 500 Muslims disagreed, that is, endorsed the idea that the war on terrorism is a war against Islam. In other words, about 80 percent of U.K. Muslims agreed with the sympathizer level of the global jihad narrative.[3]

A July 2005 ICM poll of U.K. Muslims asked a more extreme question: "Do you think any further attacks by British suicide bombers in the U.K. are justified or unjustified?" This poll was conducted after the July 7, 2005, bombings in the London underground, and 5 percent of a national sample of 500 Muslims said that further attacks were justified. In other words, about 5 percent of U.K. Muslims agreed with the second and third parts of the global jihad narrative.[4]

Thus, polling research can put numbers on at least the first three levels of the opinion pyramid: no war on Islam 20 percent (neutral), war on Islam but violence not justified 75 percent (sympathizers), violence justified 5 percent (justifiers). We have not found any polls asking Muslims about an individual obligation for jihad. If this question were asked and if honest answers could be obtained, we are confident that the number agreeing would be less than 5 percent and probably less than 1 percent.

---

3. Guardian/ICM Poll. (2004). Muslim poll—November 2004. Available at http://image.guardian.co.uk/sys-files/Guardian/documents/2004/11/30/Muslims-Nov041.pdf. Accessed December 1, 2012.

4. Guardian/ICM Poll. (2005). Muslim poll—July 2005. Available at http://image.guardian.co.uk/sys-files/Politics/documents/2005/07/26/Muslim-Poll.pdf. Accessed December 1, 2012.

It is worth noting that in the case of U.K. Muslims in 2004–2005, the pyramid model is misshapen. The neutral base of the pyramid, those who do not accept even the first level of global jihad—that the West is engaged at war against Islam—is smaller than the next higher level. Only 20 percent of U.K. Muslims do not see a war on Islam, whereas 80 percent do see a war on Islam. Descriptively, then, the base of the pyramid in this case is smaller than the first level of opinion radicalization, producing what might be called a Christmas tree model of radicalization.

A 2007 Pew poll of U.S. Muslims produced results similar to the U.K. polls. The Pew poll included an item similar to the "suicide bombers" item used by ICM in polling U.K. Muslims: "Some people think that suicide bombing and other forms of violence against civilian targets are justified in order to defend Islam from its enemies. Other people believe that, no matter what the reason, this kind of violence is never justified. Do you personally feel that this kind of violence is often justified to defend Islam, sometimes justified, rarely justified, or never justified?" In 2007 and again in 2011, about 8 percent of U.S. Muslims said that this kind of violence is often or sometimes justified.[5]

In general, the opinion pyramid represents the front line in the "war of ideas" between terrorists and the government. Polling data from a particular population at a particular time provide a snapshot of how the war is going, as shown in the percentages associated with the different levels of radicalization in the opinion pyramid. Tracking polls, with repeated measurements over time, can provide a trajectory of success or failure in the war of ideas as polling data show shifts in the percentages of poll respondents with more and less radical opinions.[6]

---

5. Pew Research Center. (2007). Muslim Americans: Middle class and mostly mainstream. Available at http://www.pewresearch.org/2007/05/22/muslim-americans-middle-class-and-mostly-mainstream/. Accessed May 10, 2016. Pew Research Center. (2011). Muslim Americans: No signs of growth in alienation or support for extremism. Available at http://www.people-press.org/2011/08/30/muslim-americans-no-signs-of-growth-in-alienation-or-support-for-extremism. Accessed May 23, 2013.

6. McCauley, C., & Stellar, J. (2009). U.S. Muslims after 9/11: Poll trends 2001–2007. *Perspectives on Terrorism* 3(3): 35–47. Available at http://www.terrorismanalysts.com/pt/index.php?option=com_rokzine&view=article&id=86&Itemid=54. Accessed December 1, 2012.

For decades psychologists have studied the relation between beliefs and feelings (cognition and attitude) and action (behavior).[7] There is no simple generalization to be made about this relation. Under some circumstances beliefs and feelings are good predictors of action (in a voting booth, for instance), and in other circumstances beliefs and feelings are weak predictors of action (when strong social norms run counter to an individual's attitude, for instance). When action consistent with beliefs and feelings is costly (such as committing oneself to terrorism), the gap between belief and action is likely to be large.

The gap between belief and action is evident in the contrast between polling data and security reports in the United Kingdom, where 5 percent of adult Muslims saw suicide attacks as justified but only several hundreds of terrorism-related arrests have been made since 9/11. Five percent of Muslims projects to about 50,000 of the roughly 1 million adult Muslims in the United Kingdom, indicating that only about one in a hundred U.K. Muslims who justify suicide terrorism have moved to violent action.

A similar ratio appears in the United States. According to Pew polls in 2007 and 2011, 8 percent or about 80,000 of about 1 million adult U.S. Muslims find suicide attacks justified *often* or *sometimes*. In contrast, only hundreds of terrorism-related arrests have been made in the United States since 9/11.[8]

The gap between opinion and action is also evident in case histories of terrorists. At least four individual-level mechanisms of radicalization do not depend on radical ideas. Some individuals join a terrorist group in order to seek revenge for a personal injury by government or its representatives (*personal grievance*). Some join because a person they care about—friend, relative, romantic partner—is a member of the group and asks for help (*love*). Some join in search of excitement, status, or money (*thrill and status seeking*). Some join in search of social ties (*disconnection*). To these we might add, from chapter 14, that some join to *escape* threat and pain in personal life. These five mechanisms

---

7. Sabini, J. (1995). *Social psychology* (2nd ed.). New York: Norton. Chapter 17, Attitudes and Behavior.

8. Anti-Defamation League. (2015). 2015 sees dramatic spike in Islamic extremism arrests. Available at http://www.adl.org/combating-hate/domestic-extremism-terrorism/c/2015-terror-arrests-30-april.html?referrer=https://www.google.com/#.Vngx1_krLIU. Accessed December 21, 2015.

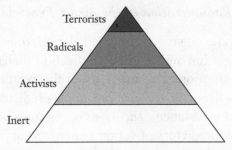

FIGURE 16.2 Action Radicalization Pyramid.

can bring previously apolitical individuals to join a militant group, that is, can bring individuals without radical ideas to radical action.

Thus, the gap between radical opinion and radical action has two aspects. The great majority with radical ideas do not take radical action. And some join in radical action without prior radical ideas (though they will likely learn radical ideas after joining).

The gap between radicalization of opinion and radicalization of action indicates the need for another pyramid model, the pyramid of action (Figure 16.2). Here the base includes all Muslims who are politically inert, whatever their beliefs or feelings. The next higher level represents Muslim activists, engaged in legal and nonviolent political action. Hizb ut-Tahrir members, for instance, are legal activists in both the United Kingdom and the United States (Hizb had its first national meeting in the United States in Chicago in July 2009), even though Hizb, like al Qaeda, aims to reestablish a supranational caliphate. Higher yet are radicals, engaged in illegal political action that may include violence. Finally, at the apex of the action pyramid are the terrorists, radicals who target civilians with lethal violence.

The borders between the levels of the action pyramid represent the most important distinctions in radicalization of action: from doing nothing to doing something, from legal political action to illegal political action, and from illegal political action to killing civilians. It is important to be clear, however, that the action pyramid is not a stage theory in which an individual must progress through each succeeding level in a linear fashion to become a terrorist. Most activists never become radicals, and it is not necessary to be an activist to become a radical (e.g., radicalization by personal grievance, love, thrill and status seeking, unfreezing/disconnection, and escape).

We turn now to drawing out some implications of the two-pyramids model for understanding and responding to terrorist attacks.

Implications of the Two-Pyramids Model

We consider first research implications of the two-pyramids model, then implications for security officials charged with preventing and responding to terrorist attacks.

Research Implications

Liberated from a supposed common grounding in radical ideas, *research on radicalization to terrorist violence can focus on different behavioral trajectories.* There seem to be at least five trajectories of radicalization to terrorist action. (1) An individual can move to political violence alone, without group or organizational support (lone wolf, discussed in the previous chapter). (2) An individual can move to violence by joining an already violent group (chapters 2–7). (3) An individual can move to violence by volunteering as a suicide bomber for an already violent group (al-Balawi's attack on the CIA at Khost). (4) A small and isolated group can move to initiate or to escalate political violence (chapters 8 and 10). (5) A small group within a larger activist movement can move to violence as part of intergroup competition (Weatherman from Students for a Democratic Society, chapter 9).

Case histories suggest that the psychologies associated with these five trajectories may be different; it is even possible that there are different personality and demographic profiles associated with these trajectories. More confidently we can predict that group-level mechanisms of radicalization to action will be stronger for the last two trajectories, which focus on group dynamics and intergroup conflict.

Mechanisms of radicalization to action may help connect terrorism research with social movement theory. Working from a social movement theory perspective, Munson interviewed members of nonviolent antiabortion organizations in four U.S. cities; one-quarter of the activists had been more sympathetic to the pro-choice position when they first became involved in pro-life activities and another one-quarter had been ambivalent.[9] That is, about half did not join in antiabortion activism because of preexisting beliefs, though most learned antiabortion ideology after joining. Rather than preexisting ideology, life histories suggested that disconnection and the accidents of social networks were crucial in

---

9. Munson, Z. (2008). *The making of pro-life activists: How social movement mobilization works*. Chicago: University of Chicago Press.

moving individuals to join in antiabortion activism. Munson's results suggest that mechanisms of radicalization to terrorist action are also mechanisms that move individuals to join a nonviolent social movement or activist organization.

Moving now to focus on the opinion radicalization pyramid, we *need more and more focused polling research.* Why do some Muslims see a war on Islam, while others do not? Why do some justify suicide bombing in defense of Islam, while others do not? With regard to these opinions, how do U.S. Muslims differ from Muslims in predominantly Muslim countries? How do these opinions differ for Muslims coming to the United States from different origin countries? As we write this chapter in late 2015, there is no answer to the question of why some Muslims justify violence in defense of Islam and some do not.

It is not only Muslim opinions that are of interest. *Understanding jujitsu politics requires understanding how terrorist targets react to terrorist attacks.* In this action-and-reaction view of terrorism, U.S. public opinion relating to terrorism is a crucial part of the conflict. Are Americans aware of terrorist grievances? Are any of these grievances seen as justified? Do Americans sympathize with or justify the kinds of hostility toward U.S. Muslims that the FBI counts as hate crimes? We return to this issue in the next and concluding chapter.

Finally we need to know how changes in the opinion pyramid affect the action pyramid and vice versa. Suppose we had an intervention that could cut the percentage of U.S. Muslims who justify suicide bombing in defense of Islam from 8 percent to 1 percent—next week! It is plausible to suppose that reducing radicalization in the opinion pyramid would reduce radicalization in the action pyramid, but currently we have no systematic evidence or theory for this kind of connection. Similarly, we have only a few examples of how change in the action pyramid— beginning to target civilians, for instance—might decrease or increase radicalization in the opinion pyramid.[10]

Similar issues can be raised with regard to the opinion and action pyramids for those attacked by terrorists: How does change in U.S. public opinion affect U.S. counterterrorism policies and vice versa?

---

10. Dugan, L., Huang, J. Y., LaFree, G., & McCauley, C. (2009). Sudden desistance from terrorism: The Armenian Secret Army for the Liberation of Armenia and the Justice Commandos of the Armenian Genocide. *Dynamics of Asymmetric Conflict* 1(3): 231–249. Wheatley, J., & McCauley, C. (2009). Losing your audience: Desistance from terrorism in Egypt after Luxor. *Dynamics of Asymmetric Conflict* 1(3): 250–268.

Security Implications

There is no "conveyor belt" from extreme beliefs to extreme action. It is plausible that radical beliefs produce radical action, but research indicates that the connection is weak. The implication of an inevitable trajectory from bad ideas to bad behavior—the conveyor belt—is contradicted by the fact that the great majority of those with extreme ideas do nothing to act on these ideas.

Groups with radical ideas who argue against violence may be allies in fighting terrorism. Hizb-ut-Tahrir, for instance, wants the same international caliphate that al Qaeda and Islamic State are seeking, but Hizb teaches that it is not time for violence in Western countries. Notably Hizb has denied the authority of Islamic State's caliphate to order attacks on Western civilians.[11]

Give more attention to the practical, situational requirements for crossing the gap between radical opinion and radical action. Criminologists give attention to means and opportunity for crime, whereas terrorism researchers—we include ourselves here—tend to focus on motives. The case of al-Balawi illustrates the importance of giving more attention to situational factors.[12] Al-Balawi was talking about a personal moral obligation to participate in jihad for months before Jordanian intelligence gave him means and opportunity to act on his radical opinions.

The case of al-Balawi indicates that security officials should avoid forcing an action choice on someone at the peak of opinion radicalization. The same implication emerges from the case of Major Hasan, whose scheduled assignment to Afghanistan amounted to a deadline for choosing between the U.S. Army and his concern for Muslim suffering. This seemingly simple advice may apply also in domestic sting operations in which a U.S. Muslim is caught in some illegal act and asked by security officials to choose between paying the penalty and becoming an informant trolling for extremist Muslims. The hall of mirrors such an informant can enter is vividly represented in the film (T)ERROR.[13]

---

11. Qataishaat, Mamdooh Abu Sawa. (2014). Official media statement regarding ISIS's declaration in Iraq. Head of the Media Office of Hizb ut Tahrir, Wilayah of Jordan, July 2. Available at http://islamicsystem.blogspot.com/2014/07/official-media-statement-regarding.html. Accessed December 11, 2015.

12. Currie, P. M., & Taylor, M. (Eds.) (2012).*Terrorism and affordance.* New Directions in Terrorism Studies. New York: Continuum.

13. Aaronson, T. (2015). The FBI informant who mounted a sting operation against the FBI. *The Intercept,* April 15. Available at https://theintercept.com/2015/04/15/fbi-informant-stung-fbi/. Accessed December 30, 2015.

But the issue is broader than the dangers of pressing an action choice on someone not yet acting. Much has been made of the fact that Major Hasan had exchanged e-mails with Islamist firebrand al-Awlaki, although apparently the content of these e-mails did not raise warning flags for U.S. security officers.[14] An emphasis on means and opportunity might have found out that Major Hasan, a psychiatrist with no military need for experience with weapons, had recently bought and (presumably) practiced with firearms. This step toward acquiring the means of violence might be more diagnostic than any assessment of perceived grievance.

Given that radical opinions are common and radical action is rare, attention to means and opportunity for radical action may be particularly useful in narrowing the risk pool for lone-wolf and small-group terrorism. Security officials aiming to forestall terrorist attacks might better troll through shooting ranges than mosques.

Fewer enemies is better. Targeting radical or extremist ideas is another kind of success for jujitsu politics. As noted earlier, individuals with radical ideas are 100 times more common than individuals involved in radical action; targeting ideas rather than actions multiplies the enemy by a factor of a hundred.

In February 2015 the White House convened a three-day Summit on Countering Violent Extremism (CVE). Since the summit, CVE has become the predominant U.S. framing of response to terrorist threats. As an indication of the salience of this framing, we note that our Google search for "countering violent extremism (CVE)" in December 2015 produced 371,000 hits.

But what is CVE? The U.S. Department of Homeland Security defines violent extremists as "individuals who support or commit ideologically-motivated violence to further political ends."[15] This definition assumes that terrorist violence is ideologically motivated—emotional reactions are off the table. As Khouri points out, a motive as simple as revenge for perceived Western humiliation of Muslims is

---

14. Ross, B., & Schwartz, R. (2009). Major Hasan's e-mail: "I can't wait to join you" in afterlife. ABC News, November 19. Available at http://abcnews. go.com/Blotter/major-hasans-mail-wait-join-afterlife/story?id=9130339#. ULpaGqzVrXQ. Accessed December 1, 2012.

15. Department of Homeland Security. (2016). Countering violent extremism. Available at https://www.dhs.gov/sites/default/files/publications/Countering%20 Violent%20Extremism-508-1.pdf. Accessed May 10, 2016.

not conceivable under this definition.[16] The Department of Homeland Security definition also makes it easy to conflate radical opinion and radical action. If "support" is construed as opinion—justifying suicide bombing in defense of Islam, for instance—then the CVE target includes 50,000 U.S. Muslims.

In short, the words and concepts used by the U.S. government to describe extremists and to frame the government response to extremist threat—language now dominant in the U.S. government—can work against separating radicalization of opinion from radicalization of action. A modest suggestion to strengthen this separation is so simple that it may be practical: to rename countering violent extremism (CVE) and refer to this effort as countering extremist violence (CEV).

Looking Further

Currie, P. M., & Taylor, M. (Eds.) (2012). *Terrorism and affordance*. New Directions in Terrorism Studies. New York: Continuum.

Leuprecht, C., Hataley, T., McCauley, C., & Moskalenko, S. (2010). Narratives and counter-narratives for global jihad: Opinion versus action. In E.J.A.M. Kessels (Ed.), *Countering extremist narratives*. The Hague: National Coordinator for Counterterrorism, pp. 58–70.

McCauley, C. (2012). Testing theories of radicalization in polls of U.S. Muslims. *Analyses of Social Issues and Public Policy* 12(1): 296–311.

McCauley, C. (2013). Ideas versus actions in relation to polls of U.S. Muslims. *Analyses of Social Issues and Public Policy* 13(1): 70–76.

McCauley, C., & Moskalenko, S. (2015). Western Muslims volunteering to fight in Syria and Iraq: Why do they go, and what should we do? *Freedom from Fear Magazine* (issue 11). Available at http://f3magazine.unicri.it/?p=1073.

McCauley, C., & Scheckter, S. (2011). Reactions to the war on terrorism: Origin-group differences in the 2007 Pew poll of U.S. Muslims. *Perspectives on Terrorism* 5(1): 38–54.

McCauley, C., & Stellar, J. (2009). U.S. Muslims after 9/11: Poll trends 2001–2007. *Perspectives on Terrorism* 3(3): 35–47.

Munson, Z. (2008). *The making of pro-life activists: How social movement mobilization works*. Chicago: University of Chicago Press.

---

16 Khouri, R. G. (2015). Beware the hoax of countering violent extremism. Al Jazeera America, September 29. Available at http://america.aljazeera.com/opinions/2015/9/beware-the-hoax-of-countering-violent-extremism.html. Accessed December 13, 2015.

CHAPTER SEVENTEEN

Them and Us

A FTER SIXTEEN CHAPTERS, with many people and ideas introduced along the way, this concluding chapter looks forward in
three directions. First we look at issues raised by considering
together all the mechanisms of radicalization identified in earlier chapters. How do mechanisms combine? Is ideology a mechanism? Can
these mechanisms be a force for good? Where does emotion appear
in the mechanisms? Then we turn to a closer look at the mechanism
of jujitsu politics, beginning from the Paris attacks of November 2015.
We argue that the power of jujitsu politics depends on anger more
than fear. Finally, we emphasize that most mechanisms of radicalization are reactive and interactive: terrorism is a form of political conflict
in which both terrorists and their targets are radicalized.

Taken Together, What Do We See?

We have identified thirteen mechanisms of political radicalization. At
the individual level, these included *personal grievance*, *group grievance*,
slippery slope, *love*, *risk and status seeking*, *unfreezing/disconnection*, and—
from consideration of lone-wolf terrorists in chapter 15—*escape*. At the
group level are *polarization*, *competition*, and *isolation*. And at the mass
level are *jujitsu politics*, *hatred*, and *martyrdom*. Taken together, the thirteen mechanisms raise several questions that we consider in this section.

Osama bin Laden's trajectory to terrorism, as described in chapter 14, shows many mechanisms at work. His life gives evidence of group grievance, slippery slope, love, group polarization, group conflict, and group isolation—most of the mechanisms of individual-level and group-level radicalization—at work in one individual. This concatenation of multiple mechanisms is more the rule than the exception. Although we introduced the mechanisms of radicalization one by one, we do not expect that any one mechanism is necessary for radicalization to occur, and only in rare cases—perhaps group grievance for some lone-wolf terrorists—is one mechanism sufficient for radicalization. Bin Laden's trajectory suggests instead the importance of thinking about how mechanisms may combine.

The first thing to note about the thirteen mechanisms is that they are not *separated* by levels—they are *nested* by levels. Individual mechanisms do not disappear when an individual joins a group, and group mechanisms do not disappear when a group participates in some larger organization or mass public. All of the mass-level mechanisms—jujitsu, hate, martyrdom—can operate at the group and individual levels, and individual-level mechanisms—especially grievance, slippery slope, love, risk and status seeking—can operate within a cohesive group. The levels are interactive in ways that need elucidating in future research.

In the simplest case of combination, for instance, two mechanisms may combine either additively or multiplicatively. One possibility is that each mechanism adds its independent contribution to radicalization. The second possibility is that the power of multiple mechanisms is more like a multiplication than an addition. There could be synergisms such that particular combinations of mechanisms are particularly potent.

The possibility of this kind of synergism was raised at the end of chapter 2. Our cases of individual radicalization by personal grievance showed considerable overlap in experience with cases of individual radicalization by group grievance. We were led to recognize that these two kinds of grievance are often found together. Indeed either kind of grievance is likely to produce the other. Personal grievance can lead an individual to seek out and cooperate with others feeling anger toward the same perpetrator: the personal then becomes political. Group grievance can lead to involvement in conflicts with the government and police that are experienced as unjustified repression: the political then becomes personal. The mutual reinforcement of personal and group grievance may be only one example of how particular combinations of mechanisms can be more potent than the simple sum of their separate effects.

Is Ideology a Mechanism of Radicalization?

We have not identified ideology as a mechanism of radicalization because, as described in chapter 16, belief is cheap and action is expensive. There is a long history of research in social psychology that shows that beliefs alone are a weak predictor of action (see Abelson as quoted in chapter 8), but the separation of belief and action is particularly notable in the realm of politics.

Of the millions of Americans who believe that abortion is murder, how many have acted to protest or change U.S. laws that legalize abortion? Of the millions of Muslims who believe that the war on terrorism is a war on Islam, how many have acted to protest or attack Americans? Self-justification may lead us to beliefs consistent with our actions (chapter 4), but acting in accord with our beliefs is much more difficult.

As already described, there are many paths to radicalization that do not involve ideology. Some may join a radical group for risk and status, some for love, some for connection and belonging. Personal and group grievance can move individuals toward violence, with ideology serving only to rationalize the violence. Indeed videos of Muslims killed or maimed in "crusader" attacks are often cited as motivation for jihadi attacks.

Hussain Osman, arrested in connection with the attempted bombings in London on July 21, 2005, reportedly told his Italian interrogators that "Religion had nothing to do with this. We watched films. We were shown videos with images of the war in Iraq. We were told we must do something big. That's why we met."[1]

Osama bin Laden's speeches point in the same direction. He emphasized Muslim grievances against the United States—support for authoritarian Muslim leaders, support for Israel, U.S. troops in Muslim countries—but spent little time selling the global caliphate that he asserted to be the answer to these grievances. As was the case with the Weather Underground, ideology for jihadist groups may be more a product of contention than a cause of contention.

---

1. Leppard, D., & Follain, J. (2005). Third terror cell on loose: Intelligence warns of new wave against soft targets. *Sunday Times* July 20, p. 31.

As explanation of action, ideology is too general and too indefinite; it cannot prescribe action under changing circumstances. Ideology requires interpretation in order to connect with current action. But every major ideology, from Christianity to Marxism, offers some textual foundation for use of violence. When we move to violence, we seek out the interpretations of our ideology that can support use of violence. There is always such an interpretation available, always someone who can claim authenticity for the interpretation.

The key part of the required interpretation is a moral frame. Humans do not attack and kill others without talking about it, without having a framing and interpretation that make violence not only acceptable but necessary. The Weather Underground framed its situation as a choice between complicity with U.S. killing in Vietnam and "bringing the war home" (chapter 9). This is a moral frame only loosely related to the Marxist jargon of its political statements about a people's war against global capitalism.

In chapter 16 we laid out the four parts of the jihadist frame: Western powers make war on Islam, jihadists take up arms in defense of Islam, the violence they use is justified, good Muslims are obliged to join in the jihad. This frame does not refer to the Koran or the Hadith and offers no textual analysis; notably it does not deal with Koranic strictures against attacking civilians. This is not an ideological frame. Rather it is a moral frame that claims injustice, identifies the perpetrators, and justifies violence by those who fight back.

Case materials suggest to us that, for many terrorists, the moral frame is no deeper than retribution: they did it to us, now we do it to them. Why does Islamic State dress its Western prisoners in orange jumpsuits? Because the U.S. dresses Muslim prisoners at Guantánamo in orange jumpsuits. Why does Islamic State execute a caged Jordanian pilot by fire? Because pilots bombing Islamic State, including the captured Jordanian pilot, bring death by fire to those trapped in bombed buildings.

This is not ideology; this is reciprocity: return favor for favor, return injury for injury. The reciprocity rule is the closest thing to a cultural universal that social scientists have uncovered. Requiting injury—retribution—is such a powerful impulse in human affairs that more complex ideology, though sometimes reassuring, is seldom necessary.

In sum, if ideology means anything more complex and text-based than the reciprocity rule, then we judge that ideology is not required for terrorist violence.

Are the Thirteen Mechanisms at Work in Other Forms of Collective Action?

We have focused in this book on extreme examples of radicalization, where the trajectory progressed all the way to terrorism. Extreme examples are useful in showing the power of the mechanisms identified, but less extreme examples of radicalization appear to depend on the same mechanisms.

The case of Fadela Amara (chapter 2) shows that radicalization can move from legal activism to lawbreaking without reaching violence; indeed Amara moved on to government office. Similarly, George Plechanov (chapter 8) was radicalized to activism and even some violence but stopped short of terrorism when he broke with the faction of the Land and Freedom movement that became People's Will. Even those cases in which the trajectory of radicalization went all the way to terrorism—most of the cases we describe—show the same mechanisms at work early in the trajectory when radicalization had not yet reached the extreme of terrorism.

It seems likely, then, that the same mechanisms that move a few to terrorism move many to lower levels of commitment and risk taking for a political cause. Lower levels can include legal political action (activism) as well as illegal political action short of terrorism (radicalism) such as taking over buildings, illegal marches, and violence against property. These levels are represented in the second and third levels of the action pyramid advanced in chapter 16.

Furthermore, we suspect that at least some of the mechanisms of radicalization identified in relation to political action are also at work in other kinds and directions of collective action.

The importance of unfreezing in relation to cult recruiting was noted in chapter 7. Like cult recruiting, military training also prepares young people for self-sacrifice. Reviewing basic training procedures in the U.S. Army, Moskalenko finds mechanisms of slippery slope, love, unfreezing/disconnection, group polarization, group competition, group isolation, and perhaps martyrdom.[2]

These mechanisms, which are not tied to politics in the way that individual and group grievance are, may be important in understanding recruitment to many different kinds of group and organization, including labor unions, street gangs, missionary organizations, and

---

2. Moskalenko, S. (2012). Civilians into warriors: Mechanisms of mobilization in US Army recruitment and training. *Dynamics of Asymmetric Conflict* 3(3): 248–268.

nongovernmental organizations (NGOs) such as Doctors without Borders. Indeed mobilization of individuals, groups, and mass publics for beneficent purposes may depend on many of the same mechanisms as mobilization for political conflict and intergroup violence (our thanks to Michael Schwerin, RTI International, for this observation).

As an example, consider the 2010 earthquake in Haiti that brought an outpouring of concern and support from the United States. Mobilization of support likely included the following elements. Some individuals had personal connections with family or friends threatened and suffering in Haiti (personal grievance). Some identified with Haitians and felt their suffering despite the absence of any personal connection (group grievance). Some individuals were moved to help by affection and connection with others already engaged in helping (love), and many increased their helping in small steps (slippery slope). Individuals with fewer responsibilities, such as students and retired people, were able to do more (unfreezing/disconnection); group members within churches and NGOs began to compete to help more (status seeking, group polarization by social comparison); mass-media attention to the disaster multiplied giving (mass mobilization); and individuals giving their all by traveling to live and work among the victims in Haiti inspired others to give more (martyrdom).

Thus, it seems possible that the mechanisms of political radicalization identified in this book are general mechanisms of collective action, operating in mobilizing not just for political conflict but for any group or cause in which self-interest is compromised in communal purpose.

How Is Emotion Implicated in Mechanisms of Radicalization?

Our account of mechanisms of radicalization in chapters 2 through 13 is incomplete. We did not give sufficient attention to the emotional components of these mechanisms. But chapter 15, in which we examined the challenge of lone-wolf terrorists, forced us to attend to emotions in a new way as the disconnected-disorder profile and the caring-compelled profile represent two kinds of emotional experience. It is time to make this attention more explicit.

Nearly all the mechanisms of radicalization described in this book involve significant emotions. Personal and group grievance are associated with experience of anger or outrage. Slippery slope desensitizes an individual to the fear or disgust associated with committing violence. Risk and status seeking succeeds when an individual feels pride.

Unfreezing/disconnection, when social ties are lost or chronically weak, is associated with feelings of loneliness and fear. Escape is a push factor for individuals suffering from depression, loneliness, fear, or the absence of emotion that is boredom. Martyrdom can elicit an emotion of awe or elevation from a sympathetic audience and possibly shame for not doing more when the martyr has done so much.

Love and hate are not themselves emotions but give rise to emotions. Love of individual or group is a strong form of positive identification that can be the occasion of many emotions. Depending on what is happening to the loved one, the lover can feel joy, sadness, pride, humiliation, anger, fear, or relief. Hate, which we have interpreted as an extreme form of negative identification that includes perception of a bad essence, likewise can be the occasion of many emotions. The hater feels joy, relief, or pride when those hated are suffering or diminished but feels sadness, humiliation, or fear when the hated is prospering. Jujitsu politics depends on the angry reaction of those targeted by terrorists, and this mechanism requires separate attention.

Another Look at Jujitsu Politics

In this section we use the Paris attacks of November 2015 to ask why jujitsu politics is so easy, yet so hard to see.

Jujitsu Politics in the Paris Attacks

We are revising this chapter in the shadow of the attacks in Paris on November 13, 2015. Seven attackers killed 130 and wounded 358. The attacks were organized and claimed by Islamic State (IS, aka Islamic State of Iraq and al-Sham [ISIS] and Islamic State of Iraq and the Levant [ISIL]). Why would a group aiming for a Sunni state in Syria and Iraq—a group already under attack by the armed forces of Syria, the United States, the United Kingdom, France, and Russia—commit resources for a terrorist attack in Paris?

Every terrorist attack and every counterterrorist response is a communication to multiple audiences. We need to look at these audiences separately to see what IS is up to.

For Sunni Muslims chafing under Shi'a domination in Iraq and Syria, the message is power. IS can best defend Sunnis because it has power that can reach even to Paris. For young Sunni men in the Middle East, the message is "Don't think about joining 'moderate'

Sunni rebels, don't think about joining a local tribal militia, don't think about joining al Qaeda. Join the winning team—IS." This is the form of intergroup competition called *outbidding* in chapter 9.

For Muslims in Europe there is also a message of power, but more important there is jujitsu politics—IS trying to use Western strength against the West. With jujitsu politics terrorists aim to elicit an over-reaction that mobilizes new sympathy and support for their cause. A response to terrorism that creates collateral damage, that harms individuals previously unsympathetic to the terrorists, can bring new status and new volunteers for the terrorists.

This is the result IS seeks in France and in Europe more generally. It hopes for government reaction that will target Muslims with new restrictions and new surveillance. It hopes also for a public reaction against Muslims, including increased discrimination and hostility targeting Muslims. It would like to see a strengthening of anti-immigrant political parties not only in France but in other European countries. In short, IS looks for European reactions to push European Muslims toward giving up on Europe and joining in the construction of a new caliphate.

Is it working?

Responding to the attacks, the French parliament decreed a state of emergency: "All over France, from Toulouse in the south to Paris and beyond, the police have been breaking down doors, conducting searches without warrants, aggressively questioning residents, hauling suspects to police stations and putting others under house arrest."[3] The targets of this escalated policing are predominantly Muslims, giving IS the jujitsu politics it hopes will convince Muslims all over Europe—19 million Muslims in the European Union—that they have no future in Europe.

Perhaps the most dangerous force for hostility and discrimination against Muslims is the definition of the enemy as "fundamentalist Muslims." Marine Le Pen, leader of an anti-immigrant party in France, offered this target in an interview with NPR's Robert Siegel: "We must eradicate Islamic fundamentalism from our soil."[4] Siegel did not challenge Le Pen's definition of the problem. But the fact is that the great majority of Islamic fundamentalists are devout rather than political.

---

3. Nossiter, A. (2015). Paris attacks spur emergency edict and intense policing in France. *New York Times*, November 23.

4. National Public Radio. (2015). France's National Front leader criticizes Hollande's response to Paris attacks. November 16. Available at http://www.npr.org/2015/11/16/456254001/frances-national-front- leader-criticizes-hollandes-response-to-paris-attacks.

Defining religious ideas and religious practice as the enemy will target ninety-nine peaceful Muslims for every jihadist reached. Jujitsu politics will be winning.

Why Is Government Overreaction so Easy to Elicit?

France watched as the U.S. response to the 9/11 attacks took the United States into Afghanistan and Iraq. It is fair to ask, why does France fall so easily to a new round of jujitsu politics?

We asked this question in chapter 9 as we first described jujitsu politics as a mechanism of radicalization. We offered a few possible answers, one of which invoked the power of anger. We suggested that eliciting fear may not be the most important goal of terrorism and that, although often suppressed and little studied, emotional reactions to terrorism include anger, outrage, and humiliation.

There is now evidence that anger is indeed the dominant reaction to terrorist attack. An innovative study by Back, Kufner, and Eglof examined emotion words in millions of words of texts sent in the United States on September 11, 2001. Anger-related words increased throughout the day, ending six times higher than fear- and sadness-related words.[5]

In addition, experiments have found that U.S. students responding to images of the 9/11 attacks with anger are more likely to favor aggressive reactions to terrorism, whereas reactions of fear and sadness are related to support for more defensive reactions.[6] Across several experiments, anger reactions were related to support for attacking terrorist leaders in foreign countries, support for war against countries harboring terrorists, and out-group derogation of Arab Americans and Palestinians. In other studies fear reactions were associated with increased support for government surveillance and restriction of civil liberties.[7]

5. Back, M. D., Kufner, A. C. P., & Egloff, B. (2010). The emotional timeline of September 11, 2001. *Psychological Science* 21(10): 1417–1419.
6. Wetherell, G., Weisz, B. M., Stolier, R. M., Beavers, A. J., & Sadler, M. S. (2013). Policy preference in response to terrorism: The role of emotions, attributions, and appraisals. In S. J. Sinclair & D. Antonius (Eds.), *The political psychology of terrorism fears*. New York: Oxford University Press, pp. 125–138.
7. Pemberton, A. (2011). Al Qaeda and vicarious victims: Victimological insights into globalized terrorism. In R. Letschert & J. van Dijk (Eds.), *The new faces of victimhood: Globalization, transnational crimes and victim rights*. New York: Springer, pp. 233–252.

In short, the predominant U.S. reaction to the 9/11 attacks was not fear but anger. The action tendency associated with anger is retribution; thus, anger in response to a terrorist attack is associated with aggression and out-group derogation. Fear is associated with defensive strategies of surveillance and curtailed civil rights. Fear brings costly defensive tactics, but anger is the emotion sought by terrorists aiming for jujitsu politics.

The power of this strategy and the importance of anger reactions in making the strategy successful are hidden in definitions of terrorism that focus only on fear and coercion.

Why Is Jujitsu Politics so Hard to See?

Most government definitions of terrorism include three elements: a nonstate group aims to coerce a state by terrorizing its citizens. The U.S. Department of Defense, the FBI, and a the United Nations Security all define *terrorism* by specifying an intent to provoke fear in order to coerce a government or population.[8]

As states through history have used terror to coerce, compel, and intimidate, states facing nonstate violence find it obvious that coercion based on fear is what the terrorist threat is about. This easy projection of state motives to terrorist motives must be resisted, however, because it has several unhelpful consequences.

The first consequence is to make terrorist motivations difficult to analyze. When one among many possible motives for a terrorist attack is enshrined in the very definition of terrorism, all other possibilities tend to disappear. For this reason, no social scientist would put a hypothetical explanation of a phenomenon in the definition of the phenomenon of interest. It is perhaps an indicator of the status of social science in government offices that so many government definitions of terrorism make this move.

The second consequence of identifying terrorism with coercion is to focus on fear as the key emotion for understanding and resisting terrorism. Terrorists want to terrorize! If the target of terrorist attacks,

---

8. Department of Defense. Terrorism. Available at http://www.dtic.mil/doc-trine/dod_dictionary/data/t/7591.html. United Nations. (2004). *A more secure world: Our shared responsibility*, p.52. Available at http://www.un.org/en/peace-building/pdf/historical/hlp_more_secure_world.pdf. FBI. Definitions of terrorism in the U.S. Code. Available at https://www.fbi.gov/about-us/investigate/terrorism/terrorism- definition.

both the government and its citizens, can resist being intimidated, then the terrorists cannot succeed. And how better to demonstrate the conquest of fear than to strike back against the terrorists, to mobilize new resources to fight terrorism, to strengthen government power to fight terrorism—in short, to declare war on terrorism. Unfortunately, as just described, terrorists count on anger and outrage at least as much as they count on fear.

A third and related consequence of including fear and coercion in government definitions of terrorism is that citizens are blinded to the dangers of jujitsu politics. This is a mass psychology problem, not a specialist problem. Many who study terrorism, inside government as well as outside, understand that fear and coercion are not the only goals of terrorist attacks. But the citizens who read and hear government definitions of terrorism, especially as these are embodied in the opinions of politicians and pundits, believe that as long as they do not give in to fear and as long as they support war against terrorists, they have done their best. The easy success of jujitsu politics is the price of focusing on fear and ignoring anger as the predominant reaction to terrorist attack.

Happily there is one U.S. government definition, in the U.S. Code of Federal Regulation, that does not refer to intimidation and coercion: "premeditated, politically motivated violence perpetrated against noncombatant targets by subnational groups or clandestine agents, usually intended to influence an audience."[9] If the U.S. Code definition were to replace other government definitions, then citizens, policy makers, and security officials might more easily see the power of jujitsu politics.

Greater recognition of this power would have at least one important consequence: it would make clear that terrorism is a problem of intergroup conflict in which what government does is as important as what the terrorists do. The last section of this chapter expands this perspective.

Them and Us

A strong commonality of the mechanisms identified is their reactive quality. Of the thirteen mechanisms, only three are more autonomous than reactive. Slippery slope is a mechanism of self-radicalization via

9. National Institute of Justice. (2011) Terrorism. September 13. Available at http://www.nij.gov/topics/crime/terrorism/pages/welcome.aspx.

self-justification, in which new beliefs and values are adopted in order to make sense of past behaviors. These new reasons then support more extreme behavior in the same direction. Group polarization is also more an autonomous than a reactive mechanism: the events pushing the group toward increased extremity are within the group, including a biased array of arguments and competition for status among group members. Escape is a push away from an unsatisfactory life and does not depend on political events.

The other ten mechanisms are more clearly reactive and interactive. They begin from and respond to a perception of conflict and a dynamic of opposition in which the significant events are the actions of others. Individuals react to personal and group grievance, including government action against comrades. Groups challenging a government react to threats from the state, threats from other groups competing for the same base of sympathizers (outbidding), and threats from internal dissension (fission). Group reactions to threat are multiplied by group isolation. Finally, individuals, groups, and mass publics react to government actions that injure the innocent (jujitsu politics), to the example of martyrs, and, in long conflicts, to a perception of the enemy as less than human (hate).

The reactive character of these mechanisms is important because, as noted in chapter 1, efforts to understand radicalization usually focus on the radicals. Terrorism research, in particular, tends to focus on *them*—the terrorists. But mechanisms of radicalization do not work only on the radicals and the terrorists. The same mechanisms work as well on those who react to radicals and terrorists—on *us*. The friction of conflict heats both sides.

Even a cursory look at the experience of the United States since the attacks of September 11, 2001, can suggest that those attacked have not escaped a radicalization of their own. Without 9/11 it is difficult to imagine U.S. troops in Afghanistan and Iraq, difficult to imagine the expansion of government powers in the Patriot Act, and difficult to imagine government lawyers and eminent academics laboring to define torture so as to permit sleep deprivation, stress positions, hypothermia, and the near-drowning that is called "waterboarding."

Examination of two other conflicts tells the same story: we found radicalization of both sides in the conflict between the czar and Russian student radicals and in the conflict between U.S. security forces and 1970s student radicals.

To see how radicalization develops out of political conflict is the starting point for understanding both terrorist groups and government response to these groups. Political radicalization of individuals, groups, and mass publics occurs in a trajectory of action and reaction, and the course and end of the trajectory can seldom be controlled by either side alone. Radicalization emerges in a relationship, in the friction of intergroup competition and conflict that heats both sides. It is this relationship that must be understood if radicalization is to be kept short of terrorism.

Focusing on *them* is not enough. Focusing on *us* is not enough. Focusing on the dynamics of conflict over time is essential. A leading indicator of this dynamic perspective will emerge when there are as many databases of government reactions to terrorism as there are databases of terrorist groups and terrorist actions. Currently no government maintains an inventory of its own reactions to terrorism, which would need to include not just military and security measures but changes in law, court procedures, banking, investment, insurance, taxes, communication networks, social safety nets, mass-media regulation, diplomacy, and international agreements. This kind of database could be useful for evaluating government reactions to terrorism: it is difficult to determine what works if we don't know what we've been doing.

Our perspective is hopeful. The competition between government and groups that challenge the government is none other than politics. Western countries, including the United States, have experience and expertise in political competition. The usual tools are survey research and focus groups to track perceptions of current policies and, especially, to test new policies. These tools determine political positions and political advertisements that will satisfy old supporters and develop new sympathizers. No candidate for U.S. president would mount a campaign without research to test issues, slogans, and promises. No counterterrorism campaign should be mounted without research to determine how multiple audiences are likely to see and respond to the government's actions. The relevant audiences include not only citizens at risk but terrorist sympathizers and important government allies and potential allies.

Most of all, we hope that attention to mechanisms of radicalization will support a new culture of political resilience in Western countries. Political resilience is the capacity of citizens to suffer terrorist attack without demanding 100 percent security, a level impossible even for the president of the United States. Political resilience is the capacity of citizens to suffer terrorist attack without turning against the entire group that the terrorists claim to represent, that is, the capacity to resist jujitsu politics. Political resilience, weak or strong, sets the boundary conditions for government policies in response to radicals and terrorists. Political resilience will be stronger, and counterterrorism policies can be more effective, when citizens see that the same mechanisms of radicalization move both them and us.

Looking Further

Back, M. D., Kufner, A. C. P., & Egloff, B. (2010). The emotional timeline of September 11, 2001. *Psychological Science* 21(10): 1417–1419.

Crenshaw, M. (1995). Thoughts on relating terrorism to historical contexts. In M. Crenshaw (Ed.), *Terrorism in context*. University Park, PA: Pennsylvania State University Press, pp. 3–26.

Karagiannis, M., & McCauley, C. (2006). Hizb ut-Tahrir al-Islami: Evaluating the threat posed by a radical Islamic group that remains nonviolent. *Terrorism and Political Violence* 18(2): 315–334.

McCauley, C. (2012). Discussion point: Introducing "political resilience." START, August 31. Available at http://www.start.umd.edu/news/discussion-point-introducing-political-resilience.

Pemberton, A. (2011). Al Qaeda and vicarious victims: Victimological insights into globalized terrorism. In R. Letschert & J. van Dijk (Eds.), *The new faces of victimhood: Globalization, transnational crimes and victim rights*. New York: Springer, pp. 233–252.

Wetherell, G., Weisz, B. M., Stolier, R. M., Beavers, A. J., & Sadler, M. S. (2013). Policy preference in response to terrorism: The role of emotions, attributions, and appraisals. In S. J. Sinclair & D. Antonius (Eds.), *The political psychology of terrorism fears*. New York: Oxford University Press, pp. 125–138.

Index

Zhelyabov involvement in, 58, 116
see also People's Will
language, power of, 191–92, 210
leaderless resistance, 244
Lenin, Vladimir, 25, 203. *See also* Ulianov, Vladimir
Lewin, Kurt, 91
liberalization, Alexander II, 8–10
Liberation Tigers of Tamil Eelam (LTTE), 16, 145, 208, 211
Libya, 32, 181–82
Lincoln, Abraham, 11, 208–11
Lin Piao, 141
Lipetsk, Land and Freedom assembly in, 16, 58, 115–17, 118
Lofland, John, 92, 93
lone-actor terrorism, 244
lone wolf, 244
lone-wolf terrorism, 28, 36, 256–57, 274
lone-wolf terrorists, 243–57
case studies of, 243–48, 252–55
family pair, 253–55
possible profiles of, 248–52
power of emotion, 245–46
radicalization mechanisms, 245–46
self-radicalization, 252–53
Long Kesh Prison, 122
The Looming Tower (Wright), 238
"Lost Territories" of French Muslims, 18
love, 122, 206, 269, 277
case studies of, 55–60, 61–64, 234–35
emotion in radicalization, 282–83
radicalization for, 60–61, 234–35
lovebombing, 93
Luqmanul Hakiem boarding school, 63

Maldonado, Daniel, 52
Malik, Tashfeen, 253–54, 255
The Maltese Falcon (film), 211
Malvo, Lee Boyd, 26
Manson, Charles, 191
Mao Tse-tung, 141, 163
al-Maqdisi, Abu Mohammed, 79–80
Marighella, Carlos, 182
Marquez, Enrique, 254
martyrdom, 99, 197–215, 277
case studies of, 199–205, 213–15
celebrations of, 208, 211

emotional power, 212–13
making of, 206–8
meaning in, 197–98
mobilizing power of, 208–11
outbidding power of, 212
psychology of, 205–6
in Russia, 199–205
saints of, 198
student activist, 203–4
suicide bombing, 145, 183, 208, 212, 232–33, 267–68, 271–72, 275
terrorist, 211–15
in United States, 208–11
Marx, Karl, 25, 163, 173
Marxism, 122, 280
Marxist-Leninist vocabulary, Weatherman, 141, 143
Masadah (Lion's Lair), 226
Massoud, Ahmed Shah, 180, 233
mass radicalization
hatred, 185–96
jujitsu politics and, 171–83
martyrdom and, 197–215
mechanisms overview of, 167–70
psychology of, 167–70, 259
McAdam, D., 114
McCain, John, 167
Meinhof, Ulrike, 163, 193
Melkonian, Monte, 146
Members of People's Will of the '80s and '90s, 89
men, psychology of, 69–78, 138–39, 169
meta-opinion, 168–69
Mezentsev, Nikolai, 39, 40, 44, 67–68, 114, 186, 192
Michailov, Adrian, 39–46
Land and Freedom involvement, 42–45, 58
Mezentsev's assassination and, 39
Michailov, Alexander
Barannikov and, 65–66, 68, 151, 204
death of, 157, 204
Land and Freedom involvement, 116, 151–53
People's Will and, 65–66, 68, 152–55, 161–62, 204
Milestones (Qutb), 33, 215
Milgram, Stanley, 46, 47, 48–49, 137

risky shift, 118. *See also* group polarization

Riyadh bombing of 2003, 233–34

Rudd, Mark, 142

Rummel, Rudolph, 178

Russia

    Afghanistan *vs.*, 63, 79, 82, 226–27, 234

    age of idealism in, 109–12

    Alexander II's reforms of, 8–10, 13, 58, 110–11, 125–26, 136

    Bloody Sunday of 1905 in, 177–78

    Chechen Black Widows, 16

    Decembrists of, 199

    educational reform, 110–11

    emancipation reforms of, 14

    golden age of literature, 111–12

    Ivan the Terrible's rule of, 197

    jujitsu politics in, 171–78

    land reform, 126

    Lenin's rule of, 25, 203

    martyrdom in, 199–205

    Nicholas I rule of, 199

    Peter the Great's rule of, 197–98

    Stalin's rule in, 150, 158, 177, 191

    student activism in, 23, 45, 57–58, 67, 91–92, 98, 113–14, 120, 126–29, 140, 161, 203–4

Russian Orthodox Church, 13, 198

al-Sadat, Anwar, 33–34, 215

Sageman, Marc, 95–96

St. Boris, 198

St. Gleb, 198

St. Petersburg, 16, 23, 35, 41–42, 44–45, 55–58, 60, 67, 89, 113, 127, 131, 151–52, 171, 175, 177, 186–87, 199–200, 202

St. Thomas More, 207

Salafism, 5, 50–53

San Bernadino attack of 2015, 238

    family pair terrorists, 253–54

Sapolsky, R., 76

Sarkozy, Nicholas, 19

Saudi Arabia, 5, 215, 219–21, 228–32, 235, 238–39

Scheuer, Michael, 220

Schwerin, Michael, 282

SDS. *See* Students for a Democratic Society (SDS)

self-justification, 279, 288

self-radicalization, 287–88

serfs, Russian population, 7, 9

sexual attraction psychology, 72–75

al Shabab, 50, 52–53

Sharp, Gene, 177

Sherif, Muzafer, 138–39

shock studies, 47, 48–49

Siegel, Robert, 284

Sinn Fein, 61

60 Minutes, 122

slippery slope progression, 39–53, 277

    case studies of, 39–46, 50–53, 235

    to jihadism, 50–53

    Milgram's obedience studies and, 47

    no-authority condition for, 48–50

    psychology of, 46–50

    radicalization mechanism, 235

"The Smiling Terrorist," 61–64

social comparison, 119

social ladder, status of climbing, 68–69

social movement theory, 91–92, 114, 271–72

socioeconomic class, 68–69, 70, 75–76

solitary confinement, 114, 130–32, 150

Somalia, 50–53, 90, 97, 167, 230

Spain, penal policy in, 123

Spears, Britney, 31, 167

splitting group competition, 146–47

Sprinzak, E., 191

Stack, Joseph, 20

Stalin, Joseph, 150, 158, 177, 191

Stark, R., 92, 93

starvation, 73, 114, 123, 208

status. *See* risk-taking and status

stereotyping, 139, 182, 188, 214

    racism and, 190–92

strong reciprocity, 28–30

student activism

    communal living, 109, 128

    educational reform's influence on, 110–11, 126

    group competition case study of, 126–29

    group polarization in, 117–21

    martyrdom, 203–4

    propaganda by fact, 113–14

    in Russia, 23, 45, 57–58, 67, 91–92, 98, 113–14, 120, 126–29, 140, 161, 203–4

    in United States, 120, 140–44